Nigeria Since Independence

Nigeria Since Independence

Forever Fragile?

J.N.C. Hill
Senior Lecturer in Defence Studies, King's College London, UK

© J.N.C. Hill 2012
Foreword © Dr Kwasi Kwarteng 2012
Softcover reprint of the hardcover 1st edition 2012 978-0-230-29852-1

All rights reserved. No reproduction, copy or transmission of this publication may be made without written permission.

No portion of this publication may be reproduced, copied or transmitted save with written permission or in accordance with the provisions of the Copyright, Designs and Patents Act 1988, or under the terms of any licence permitting limited copying issued by the Copyright Licensing Agency, Saffron House, 6–10 Kirby Street, London EC1N 8TS.

Any person who does any unauthorized act in relation to this publication may be liable to criminal prosecution and civil claims for damages.

The author has asserted his right to be identified as the author of this work in accordance with the Copyright, Designs and Patents Act 1988.

First published 2012 by
PALGRAVE MACMILLAN

Palgrave Macmillan in the UK is an imprint of Macmillan Publishers Limited, registered in England, company number 785998, of Houndmills, Basingstoke, Hampshire RG21 6XS.

Palgrave Macmillan in the US is a division of St Martin's Press LLC, 175 Fifth Avenue, New York, NY 10010.

Palgrave Macmillan is the global academic imprint of the above companies and has companies and representatives throughout the world.

Palgrave® and Macmillan® are registered trademarks in the United States, the United Kingdom, Europe and other countries

ISBN 978-1-349-33471-1   ISBN 978-1-137-29204-9 (eBook)
DOI 10.1057/9781137292049

A catalogue record for this book is available from the British Library.

A catalog record for this book is available from the Library of Congress.

10 9 8 7 6 5 4 3 2 1
21 20 19 18 17 16 15 14 13 12

To my parents, Clement and Enid, and my wife, Sophie,
with love and gratitude

Contents

Foreword	ix
Acknowledgements	xi
List of Abbreviations	xii

Introduction		1
1	**Fear of Failure: Negative Sovereignty and the Birth of State Failure**	**8**
	The causes and consequences of state failure	10
	Identifying failed states	10
	Failure to promote human flourishing	16
	The spread and spread of the concept of state failure	17
	Conclusions	19
2	**The Enemy Within: Insurgency and the Failure of the Nigerian State**	**22**
	The ways and extent of Nigeria's failure	25
	Boko Haram	26
	The MEND	29
	Failure to control	32
	Failure to promote human flourishing	34
	Failure to provide security	34
	Failure to provide healthcare and education	38
	The dangers of disintegration	39
	Conclusions	41
3	**The Emperor's New Clothes? Federalism, the Decline of Old Loyalties and the Rise of New Jealousies**	**44**
	The post-independence background to federalism	46
	The function of federalism	53
	'Not a nation': federalism and the preservation of difference	54
	A spur to ethnic tensions	55
	Damage to national unity	56

viii *Contents*

Damage to political rights	58
Corruption	59
Out of many came forth one: federalism and the quest for unity	62
Conclusions	66

4 Fuel to the Flames: Oil and Political Violence in Contemporary Nigeria — **70**

A brief history of the Nigerian oil industry	73
Oil and its lubrication of Nigeria's failure	80
Damage to the economy	80
Damage to the environment	82
Damage to democracy	85
Corruption	87
Failure to promote human flourishing and the spread of armed violence	88
Secessionism	89
On troubled waters: oil and its contribution to Nigeria's unity	91
Conclusions	92

5 Of the People but for the People? Nigeria and Its Armed Forces — **95**

The legacy and reputation of Nigeria's armed forces	99
The armed forces' contribution to Nigeria's failure	104
A failure to defend	105
The abuse of human rights	108
The armed forces' efforts to prevent Nigeria's failure and disintegration	109
Maintaining and preserving security	110
Strengthening public participation and trust in the political process	112
Promoting social integration and harmony	115
Conclusions	118

Conclusions — **122**

Notes	128
Select Bibliography	151
Index	169

Foreword

The modern history of Nigeria is a story of conflict, corruption and simmering ethnic tensions. Added to this combustible mix are religious differences which, in recent times, have led to sporadic outbursts of violence.

Yet, despite these immense strains, modern Nigeria remains a united country. It has a distinctive character, and it is often described as a nascent superpower. Jon Hill's book is a much needed and subtle appraisal of the manner in which modern Nigeria has avoided fracture.

After independence in 1960, Nigeria's federal constitution almost immediately succumbed to secessionism. The Biafra war, which started in 1967, is perhaps the defining event of modern Nigerian history. In many ways, it was the first war of the modern media era. International pop stars, Swedish students, international aid agencies all made their contribution in different ways to the conflict. The civil war has also been represented in literature and film. Today, the tensions which gave rise to the civil war have been superseded by other controversies.

The continued existence of Nigeria as a unified state is a frequent matter of debate and speculation. In his penetrating book, Hill identifies three principal causes which have ensured the unity of this diverse state. The three causes in general terms can be characterised as federalism, oil and the armed forces. Federalism is perhaps the most difficult of these notions to grasp, given its ambivalent nature. It is often remarked that the diversity of Nigeria is, in itself, a source of both weakness and strength.

The very term 'Nigeria' first appeared in print in an editorial written for *The Times* in London in April 1897. This fact alone showed the extent to which Nigeria itself was an artificial construct. It had only been in 1892 that Lord Salisbury, the British prime minister, had observed that 'we have been engaged in drawing lines upon maps where no white man's foot has ever trod; we have been giving away mountains and rivers and lakes to each other, only hindered by the small impediment that we never knew exactly where the mountains and rivers and lakes were.'

Despite this artificiality, federalism does still have a resonance among the political elite. Many Nigerians feel a particular affinity to their region or ethnic group, while maintaining a significant sense of nationhood. This sense has been deepened by the enormous oil wealth which Nigeria commands. Oil damages the environment and encourages insurgency. Yet oil contributes to the nation's unity as non-oil producing regions remain fully committed to preserving Nigeria on account of its oil wealth.

Above this simmering cauldron, so to speak, sit the armed forces, which remain the most visible symbol of national unity. The contribution of the Army, in particular, to Nigeria's political life since 1960 has been enormous. The number of coups which have occurred since independence, as well as the civil war itself, is proof of this.

There remains a question about how the Army will accommodate itself to civilian rule in the future, although recent developments, particularly the presidency of Goodluck Jonathan, show that some form of directly elected leadership can be sustained.

The future of Nigeria is of enormous consequence to the stability of Africa and to international politics generally. The economic development of Africa has been one of the most conspicuous features of the international scene in the past ten years. As developed economies struggled in the aftermath of the financial crisis of 2008, political commentators, economic and financial analysts have become aware of markets outside Europe and North America, notably in the Middle East, Asia and, most recently, in sub-Saharan Africa.

If it remains a united country, Nigeria's position and role in this new world will be significant. If the country falls apart, however, it is difficult to see how this chaotic situation would resolve itself. In either case, the future of Nigeria is one in which politicians, academics, commentators and analysts all over the world should maintain a considerable interest. Jon Hill's book is an important contribution for all those wishing to develop that interest.

Dr Kwasi Kwarteng
MP for Spelthorne, Surrey, UK and author of Ghosts of Empire:
Britain's Legacies in the Modern World (2012)

Acknowledgements

'There are three secrets', declared Somerset Maugham, 'to writing a novel. Unfortunately nobody knows what they are.' No such mysteries, however, surround the production of academic texts. And just as crucial to this bitter–sweet process as thinking, reading, research and writing is the help and support provided by friends and well-wishers, colleagues and peers. It is with profound sincerity, therefore, that I would like to thank all those who have assisted me in writing this book. For individually and collectively they have improved it beyond measure and deserve nothing but credit. Whatever mistakes remain or shortcomings the book still has are due to me and me alone.

In particular, I would like to thank Ashley Jackson, Ioannis Mantzikos, Ken Payne and Andrew Stewart for patiently reading various chapters; Matt Uttley and the Defence Studies Department at King's College London for giving me time to write; Dr Kwasi Kwarteng for taking an interest in the book and kindly writing the foreword; John Campbell, Ricardo Soares de Oliveira, John D. Paden and Paul D. Williams for answering my questions and offering their opinions; Sheikh Nasir Kabara, Sheikh Ismail Ibrahim Khalifa, Abba Kyari, Ahmed Nuhu and Sanusi Lamido Sanusi for their wise and helpful advice; Harriet Barker, Christina Brian, Ellie Shillto, Renee Takken and the rest of the team at Palgrave Macmillan for making the publication process so painless; and Kate Airey, Reid Cooper, Duncan Low, Mike Osman, Sheena Zain, and the Hagues and the Hills for taking an interest. Finally I would like to offer special thanks to Sophie. Not only has she read every word (several times over) and provided unstinting encouragement, but she has also helped to bear the burden of writing and done so without complaint. But for her support, the book would never have been finished.

Abbreviations

AG	Action Group
ANPP	All Nigeria People's Party
AQILBS	Al Qaeda in the Islamic Lands beyond the Sahel
ASUU	Academic Staff Union of Universities
AU	African Union
CPS	Crown Prosecution Service
DOE	Department of Energy
DP	Dynamic Party
DPR	Department of Petroleum Resources
EFCC	Economic and Financial Crimes Commission
FCB	Fourth Commando Brigade
FCO	Foreign and Commonwealth Office
FCT	Federal Capital Territory
FEPA	Federal Environmental Protection Agency
FG	Federal Government
GIA	Armed Islamic Group
GDP	Gross Domestic Product
HRW	Human Rights Watch
IBB	Ibrahim Badamasi Babangida
ICG	International Crisis Group
ICISS	International Commission on Intervention and State Sovereignty
IMN	Islamic Movement in Nigeria
IRIN	Integrated Regional Information Networks
JTF	Joint Task Force
KPP	Kano People's Party
LSUF	Lagos State United Front
MASSOB	Movement for the Actualisation of the Sovereign State of Biafra
MDF	Mid-West Democratic Front
MEND	Movement for the Emancipation of the Niger Delta
MIR	Movement for the Islamic Revival
MOPOL	Mobile Police

List of Abbreviations   xiii

MOSOP	Movement for the Survival of the Ogoni People
NBA	Nigerian Bar Association
NACOD	Nigerian Army Central Ordinance Depot
NCNC	National Council of Nigerian Citizens/National Council of Nigeria and the Cameroons
NCS	National Council of State
NDC	Niger Delta Congress
NDPVF	Niger Delta Peoples Volunteer Force
NDVF	Niger Delta Vigilante Force
NEPU	Northern Elements Progressive Union
NNA	Nigerian National Alliance
NNDP	Nigerian National Democratic Party
NNPC	Nigerian National Petroleum Corporation
NPC	Northern People's Congress
NPF	Northern Progressive Front
NYSC	National Youth Service Corps
OAS	Organisation Armée Secrète [Secret Army Organisation]
OAU	Organisation of African Unity
OPEC	Organization of the Petroleum Exporting Countries
PDP	People's Democratic Party
RP	Republic Party
SSI	Strategic Studies Institute
SSS	State Security Service
UMBC	United Middle Belt Congress
UN	United Nations
UPGA	United Progressive Grand Alliance
ZCP	Zamfara Commoners Party

Introduction

Nigeria has long been stalked by failure. From the moment it achieved independence its demise was predicted. Its name was not coined until the late nineteenth century and was not some ancient title brought back to life by either a colonial officer with an eye to the past or an enthusiastic nationalist eager to reassert an ancient heritage. Rather it was the invention of a journalist who went on to marry the man who became its first Governor-General.[1] Even then, it originally did not apply to all the lands it was eventually to cover.[2] From the beginning it was a partial name imposed from without on just some of the fragmented territories over which the British held sway.[3]

Nigeria did not become a single political entity until 1 January 1914.[4] The disparate terrains it came to include were home to a bewildering array of ethnic groups. Never before had they all shared one government.[5] And colonial rule did much to perpetuate and extend the divisions between them. The flimsiness of the cultural, linguistic and religious links between these communities stood in stark contrast to the strength of those they shared with the inhabitants of neighbouring countries. Hausa in the north were bound far more tightly to their kin in Niger and Cameroon than they were to the Ijaw in the south–south.[6] And Yoruba in the south-west looked to Benin and Ghana before Kano and Sokoto.

That Nigeria is a failed state is now beyond doubt – present tense not future. It is a failed state for two main reasons. First, the writ of its government does not run the length and breadth of its territory. There are places in the Niger Delta and in and around the north-eastern city of Maiduguri that lie beyond the direct and continuous control

2 *Nigeria Since Independence*

of the federal, state and local governments. These areas are controlled instead by a range of insurgent groups such as the Movement for the Emancipation of the Niger Delta (MEND), the Niger Delta Vigilante Force (NDVF) and the Niger Delta Peoples Volunteer Force (NDPVF) in the Niger Delta, and Boko Haram in the north-east.

Nigeria is also a failed state because its government does not promote the flourishing of all its citizens. It does not provide all Nigerians with the public goods or social services they have a reasonable right to expect to receive including law and order, basic health care, primary education and impartial justice. By failing to provide these services the government is not only compromising the quality of life of millions of Nigerians today but it is also denying them crucial opportunities to improve their lot and that of their families tomorrow. It is undermining their standards of living and damaging their potential to improve them.

Despite being a failed state, Nigeria has avoided breaking up. It has, of course, come close to doing so on a number of occasions most notably during the civil war when the south-eastern province of Biafra seceded from the federation for around two-and-a-half years before its eventual, forcible readmission. Yet, in this instance, as on all other occasions, enough people had sufficient resolve to see off the threat and prevent the country's disintegration. The determination to ensure Nigeria's survival was greater than that seeking its demise. But is this still the case today? Are the forces keeping the country together stronger than those tearing it apart? How long can this struggle continue for? How long will Nigeria remain a unified failed state?

There is, of course, a close relationship between state failure and secessionism. Secessionism – the desire of a particular province or region to either establish itself as an independent state or to become part of another state – can be either a cause or an effect of failure. Somalia has experienced both types of secession over the past two decades. Its failure was first triggered in 1991 by the unilateral declaration of independence made by the leaders of, what had been, British Somaliland. And its failure and break up was compounded when Puntland's leaders declared that it too was an independent state in 1998. British Somaliland's secession helped cause Somalia's failure while Puntland's secession was made possible and desirable by it.

Introduction 3

Scarcely has the need for answers to these questions been so great, as Nigeria is becoming more, not less, failed. This much is confirmed by its steady rise up the Fund for Peace's Failed State Index rankings. In the 2011 and 2010 indexes,[7] Nigeria was identified as the fourteenth most failed state in the world. In 2009, however, it was considered the fifteenth most failed state,[8] in 2008 the nineteenth,[9] in 2007 the seventeenth,[10] in 2006 the twenty-second,[11] and in 2005 the fifty-fourth.[12] In just six years, therefore, the country has climbed 40 places in the Fund's index and is now grouped with such acknowledged basket cases as Somalia, Sudan, the Democratic Republic of the Congo and Afghanistan.

The Fund for Peace's findings are contributing to the urgent debates currently taking place in Abuja, Washington, London and Brussels over Nigeria's short-term future. Can the country remain united despite its growing failure? Is the popular and political resolve to keep it together as strong today as it was in the past? And is the state still able to resist and defeat those forces which are threatening to tear it asunder?

Nigeria's failure is already a major cause for concern. The country's National Bureau of Statistics recently announced that, as of 2010, 60.9 per cent of all Nigerians were living in absolute poverty compared to 54.7 per cent in 2004.[13] This increase represents a near doubling of the total number of people living in poverty from 68.7 million in 2004 to 112.47 million in 2010.[14] The mass human suffering denoted by these figures is both a cause and an effect of Nigeria's failure. For it not only highlights the state's failure to promote the flourishing of all its citizens, but it also helps explain the origins of the anger and desperation fuelling the insurgencies in the Niger Delta and north-east. Nigeria's failure is of grave concern, therefore, for both humanitarian and security reasons.

Yet it is feared that even these immense problems would be dwarfed by those which could be generated by the country's break up. First, there would be the disruption to whatever few public goods and services the state currently provides. Second, there would likely be inter-communal violence and the accompanying mass migration of people around the country and away from it. Third, there would be the exposure of the nearby failing states of Chad, Côte d'Ivoire, Niger and Sierra Leone to the highly destructive political, economic and humanitarian shockwaves released.[15] Fourth, there would be the

4   *Nigeria Since Independence*

loss of Nigeria's contributions to the African Union/United Nations sponsored peacekeeping forces currently operating around Africa. And fifth, there would be the disruption of the flow of Niger Delta oil onto the international market and the concomitant spike in global energy prices. Nigeria's disintegration would be a local, regional and global disaster.

The aim of this book, therefore, is to offer some answers to these most urgent questions. More specifically, the book focuses on both the factors fuelling the insurgencies in the Niger Delta and the north-east and the main mechanisms helping to keep the country together. It does so for two reasons. First, the existence and activities of these factions are the main cause of Nigeria's failure as a state. Through the force of their arms and the appeal of their political messages, these groups have created spaces, places on the map, in which the writ of the Federal Government does not run. Only by better understanding the insurgencies can we better understand the causes, extent and complexion of Nigeria's failure.

This examination has two additional benefits. The first is that it highlights many of the ways in which the Federal Government is failing to promote the flourishing of all its citizens. For the growth of these insurgency groups is intimately bound to the state's prolonged failure to provide its people with the basic public goods they can reasonably expect to receive. Put another way, these factions were founded in anger and frustration at the state's inability to do what it ought to. Moreover, at least some of the support they command is the result of the promises their leaders have made to improve this provision once they are in power. They have sworn to do what the state cannot.

The second benefit of this examination is that it identifies the origins and maps the extent of the secessionist pressures currently being exerted on Nigeria. The MEND, the NDVF and the NDPVF are all fighting to win independence for some or all of the various ethnic groups who inhabit the six states that make up the Niger Delta sub-region.[16] They are waging their armed campaigns to break up Nigeria. Indeed, their campaigns not only highlight the intimate relationship between state failure and territorial integrity but also confirm the seriousness of the threat to the country's continued unity. And there are other organisations seeking to win autonomy for this or that community by peaceful means.

The second reason the book focuses on the factors fuelling the insurgencies and the main mechanisms helping to keep the country together is to cast some much needed light on the likelihood of Nigeria breaking up. Certainly the book makes no predictions as to what the future will look like or claims as to its ability to do so. But by identifying and analysing these mechanisms, what they are and how they work, the book draws attention to what currently matters and helps highlight those critical agencies and institutions which hold the key to whether Nigeria stays together or not.

The picture of Nigeria's failure painted by this examination is full of paradoxes. For some of the main factors fuelling the insurgencies in the Niger Delta and north-east also double as vital mechanisms for keeping the country together. The book concentrates on three of the most important factors/mechanisms, namely, federalism (the process of building and developing Nigeria's state structures and political practices), oil and its associated revenue (generated by the rents the Federal Government charges oil companies and its sale on the international market) and the armed forces (its operations and activities, and as a major institution of the Nigerian state).

The contributions made by federalism, oil and the armed forces to the country's failure fall into two broad categories. The first comprises of those actions which inspire an insurgent group directly. These contributions either give succour to a faction (persuade them that their cause is just and that victory is possible), or antagonise them sufficiently to reaffirm their commitment to their campaign (fortify their resolve and determination to act). The second category includes those contributions which undermine the state's ability to promote the flourishing of its citizens. These contributions strike at the government's provision of public goods, at its ability to maintain law and order, to offer basic health care and primary education and to provide fair and impartial justice to all Nigerians.

There are four main ways in which federalism, oil and the armed forces are resisting Nigeria's failure and also helping it to preserve its integrity. First, they are countering the insurgents. In different ways and to varying degrees these mechanisms are resisting and combating the groups which are driving the country's failure. Second, they are strengthening the state. They are buttressing and rehabilitating its institutions and agencies and improving its operation thereby enhancing its ability to provide Nigerians with the public goods

6   *Nigeria Since Independence*

they are due. Third, they are helping to build a nation. They are promoting ideas of nationhood and inculcating in the population a loyalty to the nation above and beyond those to kith, kin, locale and religion and which are the mainstay of secessionism.[17] Fourth, they are facilitating the pursuit of self-interest. They are helping select groups within society to advance their interests and, in so doing, persuade them that they have more to gain from Nigeria remaining intact than they do from it breaking up.

Some of the ways in which these mechanisms are combating failure and preserving Nigeria's unity are self-defeating. The corrupt practices engaged in by many politicians, state functionaries and military personnel are a major reason why Boko Haram is waging its armed campaign, commands the support that it does, and the government is unable to promote the flourishing of all its citizens. Encouraging certain groups to exploit Nigeria's unity so that they might advance their interests at the expense of everyone else may be helping to keep the country together, but it is also contributing to Nigeria's failure. Even so, at certain times and in certain ways these mechanisms help preserve Nigeria's unity in all these fashions. That their roles can be contradictory emphasises the paradoxical nature of Nigeria's failure.

The book is divided into five chapters. The first outlines the understanding of state failure it adopts. The chapter explains how changes to the international moral environment ushered in by the Second World War led to the establishment of a new sovereignty regime. This new regime resulted in the creation of many states in Africa, including Nigeria, which did not have the necessary capabilities to exercise *de facto* sovereignty but which, nevertheless, continued to be recognised by the international community. The second chapter then maps the contours of Nigeria's failure specifically. It pays particular attention to the activities of the various insurgent groups currently operating there and the ways in which the Federal Government is failing to promote the flourishing of all its citizens. Finally the chapter looks at the scale of the threat to Nigeria's unity posed by secessionist movements.

After explaining what state failure is and why Nigeria is a failed state, the next three chapters each examine a core cause of the country's failure and important mechanism for its continued unity. Chapter 3 focuses on federalism and the ways in which it has simultaneously encouraged political corruption, which is helping to drive the insurgencies, and diluted the regional loyalties which posed such a danger to the country's integrity. Chapter 4 then looks at oil and the revenues generated by its sale to show how it is fuelling the insurgencies in the Niger Delta and the secessionist demands made by these factions as well as fortifying the determination of the rest of the country to stop the Delta from breaking away. Finally Chapter 5 examines the armed forces and how they are fighting to keep Nigeria whole but are doing so in ways that are driving the insurgencies.

This analysis leads the book to arrive at three main conclusions. The first is that, despite decades of failure, Nigeria continues to avoid disintegration. Second, that Nigeria is likely to remain failed for the foreseeable future. And third, that much greater precision is needed when applying terms like failed and failing. In this way, Nigeria informs the book's analysis of state failure, just as the debate on state failure informs the book's examination of Nigeria.

1
Fear of Failure: Negative Sovereignty and the Birth of State Failure

Two thousand and ten was a momentous year for Africa. During its course Benin, Burkina Faso, Cameroon, the Central African Republic, Chad, Côte d'Ivoire, the Democratic Republic of the Congo, Gabon, Madagascar, Mali, Mauritania, Niger, Nigeria, the Republic of the Congo, Senegal, Somalia and Togo all celebrated their half centenaries. Nearly 400 million men, women and children,[1] or around two-fifths of all Africans, in seventeen countries spread across four of the continent's five main sub-regions, marked 50 years of independence and self-rule.[2] Seldom have so many people in so many places been brought together in remembrance of an historical moment that is at once both common and unique. All continue to live with colonialism's legacies. All continue to experience them in different ways.

In many places the celebrations were muted if, indeed, they took place at all. The ongoing violence in Somalia helped ensure that both its independence days passed with barely a murmur,[3] while the bomb attacks in Abuja cast a long and frightening shadow over the festivities in Nigeria.[4] More widely felt though was the disappointment that came as a result of the introspection this milestone inevitably invited. For the end of colonial rule had not brought with it the prosperity, freedoms and opportunities that many had hoped it would, or which had been promised to them by the nationalists who had demanded independence on their behalf and the politicians who assumed power once it had been won.

Fear of Failure 9

The grandiloquent speeches that rang out in the Freedom Squares and the Independence Avenues, in front of the national assemblies and the parliaments and the presidential palaces, served, quite unintentionally, to emphasise the promises still to be honoured, the potential yet to be fulfilled and the hopes waiting to be realised. Only the most Panglossian Burkinabés and Ivoirians, Congolese and Madagascans, Malians and Mauritanians, Nigerians and Somalis were willing to claim that the last half-century had unfolded exactly how their early leaders and, more crucially, their compatriots had hoped it would. For the political instability, economic stagnation and social strife that so mark these places tell a very different tale: one of waste and of want and of squandered opportunity.

Today many of these states are described as failed.[5] They exist on maps. They belong to international organisations. They have governments and armed forces, flags and coats of arms, national anthems and airlines, Olympic committees and football teams, monuments to their glorious dead and statues of living legends. They possess many of the trappings of statehood. Yet to a goodly number of their citizens, they have little meaningful existence. Their ministries, departments, institutions and agencies tend to be clustered in capital cities, far removed from the rural masses. Their agents have only infrequent contact with discrete parts of the population. And what limited services they provide benefit often only a minority of people for just some of the time. These states are more legal entities than material realities.

The concept of state failure has undertaken a profound intellectual and political journey over the past 30 years. From its early origins in the academy, it is now embraced by policy makers, security providers, aid and development workers, journalists and ordinary people the world over. Terms such as weak state, failing state, failed state and collapsed state are today used and applied in a myriad of ways, to the extent that state failure is simultaneously an academic thesis and mainstream label. It is a process and a description, an explanation of what has happened and a prediction of what is to come, a lament and a warning, a reprimand and a cry for help.

State failure is a modern phenomenon. It is unique to the post-Second World War period. It has only been made possible because of changes in global attitudes towards colonialism. This shift in moral reasoning was orchestrated by the United Nations and

10 *Nigeria Since Independence*

Organisation of African Unity (OAU), and it led to the establishment of a new sovereignty regime. Under its rules, self-determination became an unequivocal right for everyone. No longer could Europe's imperial powers argue that their colonial subjects were unsuited to or unready for independence. This led to decolonisation being carried out at breakneck speed and the establishment of states which did not possess the political, economic and social wherewithal to survive. And some have not.

This chapter has two main aims. The first is to explain why state failure occurs. And the second is to specify what makes a state failed rather than quasi or weak or failing or collapsed. In pursuit of these goals, the chapter is divided into three main sections. It begins by detailing the shift in normative attitudes towards colonialism and empire, examining the rules of the new sovereignty game, considering the differences between *de facto* and *de jure* statehood and also failure to control and failure to promote human flourishing. It then moves on to look at the concept's embrace by non-academics, to examine the international events that propelled state failure into the mainstream, before offering some conclusions.

The causes and consequences of state failure

The concept of state failure has two distinct yet interconnected dimensions which can be usefully separated out under Paul D. Williams's headings of 'failure to control' and 'failure to promote' human flourishing. The main distinction between these is their respective points of focus. Failure to control concentrates mainly on capabilities, on the capacity of states 'to penetrate society, regulate social relationships, extract resources, and appropriate or use...[them] in determined ways.'[6] Failure to promote human flourishing, on the other hand, focuses on responsibilities, on what states should be doing for their citizens, on their obligations to deliver public goods, on their duties to nurture and on their requirements to protect.

Identifying failed states

The process of identifying failed states is, at root, comparative. Failed states are distinguished not by what they are, but by what they are not. Failed states are those that 'can no longer perform the functions required for them to pass as states.'[7] They are states that 'cannot or will not safeguard minimal civil conditions for their populations.'[8] They are states that are 'consumed by internal violence and cease delivering positive public goods to their inhabitants.'[9] They are states in which 'the public authorities are either unable or unwilling to carry out their end of what Hobbes...called the social contract.'[10] Failed states do not do what they should. Failed states do not provide their citizens with good governance, welfare services and, above all, security.

Underpinning these descriptions are assumptions of what states should be doing, of what a successful state is, of what it is failed states are failing to be. The determining criterion of success is the possession of positive sovereignty. Robert Jackson draws on Max Weber's concept of the 'ideal state',[11] to argue that positive sovereignty 'presupposes capabilities which enable governments to be their own masters: it is a substantive rather than a formal condition.'[12] Indeed, a positively sovereign state 'not only enjoys rights of non-intervention and other international immunities but also possesses the wherewithal to provide political goods for its citizens.'[13] Its leaders are able to 'collaborate with other governments in defence alliances and similar international arrangements and reciprocate in international commerce and finance.'[14]

Successful states, therefore, possess positive sovereignty. They enjoy international legal recognition (their statehood is formally acknowledged by a majority of other states and international organisations), are able to project and protect their authority throughout their entire territories (not just part of them) and can enter into collaborative arrangements with other states (voluntarily and as partners of worth). Negative sovereignty, on the other hand, 'can be defined as freedom from outside interference: a formal-legal condition but nothing else.'[15] Negatively sovereign states also enjoy international legal recognition. But, unlike positively sovereign states, they are unable to project and protect their authority throughout their entire territories or enter into collaborative arrangements with other states. Positive sovereignty has *de facto* and *de jure* dimensions, negative sovereignty *de jure* alone.[16]

Negative sovereignty has only existed since the end of the Second World War, and it came about as a result of the profound changes the United Nations and the OAU made to key international normative regulations.[17] The driving force behind these changes was the

12 *Nigeria Since Independence*

governments of the states that replaced the colonial territories in Africa, Asia and elsewhere. As decolonisation gathered pace their number and influence in the United Nations' General Assembly grew, to the extent that, with a little coordination, they were able to make recommendations and pass resolutions which challenged established shibboleths and long-standing truths about colonial rule. Indeed, Europe's imperial powers found it increasingly difficult to control the debate about empire as they once had.

The governments of these new states were aided and abetted, in different ways and to varying degrees, by both the Soviet Union and the United States. Moscow was keen to weaken Europe's empires in whatever ways it could and to draw the states that emerged out of them into its sphere of influence. And Washington was just as eager to prevent that from happening. Yet whereas the USSR could be open and vehement in its condemnation of the evils of colonialism, the United States had to be cautious and considered. It was forced to walk a fine line between supporting its European friends and appeasing the African and Asian nationalist movements clamouring for self-determination and their newly independent allies. Often its approach was to change its policy as the situation demanded. And this usually meant switching its support from the coloniser to the colonised.[18]

The post-World War II shift in moral reasoning led to the emergence and consolidation of a 'new sovereignty game.'[19] Under its rapidly petrifying rules, Europe's imperial powers found that the old paternalist arguments of duty and civilisation no longer carried the weight they once did. No longer could they describe their colonial subjects as culturally and intellectually unsuited to self-government. No longer could they claim an overriding moral responsibility to govern. No longer could they offer only vague promises to relinquish power someday, in the future, when the time was right, eventually. No longer could they claim to be protecting their colonial subjects from themselves.[20] Bit by bit, they were forced to accept the rules of this new game and to prepare to surrender power sooner rather than later.

This shift in reasoning was both confirmed and consolidated by United Nations' General Assembly Resolution 1514. It was passed on 14 December 1960 and gave 'all peoples...the right to...freely determine their political status and...pursue their economic, social and cultural development.'[21] Its promulgation gave official weight and

Fear of Failure   13

mainstream respectability to groups and causes which had hitherto been labelled criminal and illegitimate by Europe's imperial powers. Indeed, it gave additional voice to these organisations and movements, making them better able to drown out those defending colonial rule and cautioning against rapid decolonisation. Some of the arguments made by the defenders of empire were undoubtedly racist, self-serving and unworthy as they sought to preserve the imperial powers' preferential relationships with their respective colonies and deny the people who lived there the rights and liberties enjoyed by many European citizens. But others had merit. They raised valid and pressing concerns about the readiness of certain colonies to assume independence in the near future.

Territories like the Belgian Congo, French Equatorial Africa and parts of French and British West Africa were woefully ill-prepared for independence when it arrived. They suffered from a severe shortage of experienced political leaders, trained civil servants, qualified technocrats, university graduates, school-leavers and even people who could read and write. The offices of government and organs of state they inherited were often created in haste and were poorly designed as a result. Their economies were illogically structured and remained heavily dependent on the former Metropole for their markets and much of their investment. Their societies were deeply fragmented, divided into dozens, sometimes hundreds, of querulous ethnic groups. The problems confronting many post-independence governments were often as vast as the means they had at their disposal to deal with them were limited.

In most instances, these difficulties were either created or exacerbated by colonial rule. Indeed it was the abusive and self-serving aspects of imperialism that inspired both local nationalists and the global anti-colonial movement. Yet decolonisation did not bring with it any easy solutions to these problems. They did not simply melt away in the sunlight of independence. Their endurance ensured that many of the states and governments that emerged out of the wreckage of empire were inherently weak. The continent's new leaders did not have the means to adequately deal with the fundamental flaws that blighted the states they took charge of.

Under the rules of the old sovereignty game, these failings might have been enough to kill off at least some of these states. In the very least, they would have been left vulnerable to aggressive

14 *Nigeria Since Independence*

neighbours and predatory empires. But under the rules of the new game these threats were lessened significantly. For just as General Assembly Resolution 1514 asserted that everyone had a right to self-determination, the 1963 OAU Charter committed Africa's new leaders to 'respect...the sovereignty and territorial integrity of each State and...inalienable right to independent existence.'[22] Together, they proclaimed Africans' right to self-government but only within the borders of the states that were granted independence. These boundaries were declared sacrosanct regardless of how nonsensical they might be or the ability of the governments of the states that lay within to defend them.

Almost at a stroke, capability and functionality were eliminated as essential pre-requisites for the survival of Africa's states. The international community deemed its recognition of them sufficient to ensure their continued existence. And just as Resolution 1514 and the OAU Charter protected them from international challenges and threats, General Assembly Resolution 1541 secured them from internal ones.[23] It was passed on 15 December 1960 and specified that a population only had the right to self-determination if it was both 'geographically separate...and distinct ethnically and/or culturally from the country administering it.'[24] Together, these criteria worked to prevent the break-up of Africa's states by denying any legitimacy to demands for self-determination made by sub-national groups.

Even today, the international community is deeply reluctant to recognise any new states in the continent. It still refuses to officially acknowledge the independence of provinces like Somaliland and Puntland which have been governing themselves for years. It chooses, instead, to believe in Mogadishu's almost entirely nominal claim to sovereignty over them. In these instances, *de facto* authority seems to carry little weight, certainly far less than the paper rights of the Somali government. And only recently has the international community formally recognised the independence of South Sudan which has had its own government, armed forces and even passports for decades.[25] In fact, it remains one of only two breakaway regions to be granted *de jure* statehood in the continent since the end of empire.[26]

Yet the positive sovereignty – negative sovereignty binary does not precisely mirror its successful state – failed state equivalent. For while all successful states have positive sovereignty and all failed ones negative, not all negatively sovereign states are failed. Indeed, a significant number are simply weak. Together, they make up the thick band of grey that lies between the two poles. But not all weak states are the same. Some are weaker than others. Attempts to capture the many shades of grey that exist have resulted in a profusion of names and labels. Among those currently in use are welfare state, infected state, never-do-well state, bedridden state, comatose state, expired state, anarchic state, phantom state, mirage state, anaemic state, captured state and aborted state.

Some of these titles refer to discreet steps between success and failure. The six coined by John Ayoade (welfare, infected, never-do-well, bedridden, comatose and expired) together form a 'continuum of function.'[27] They represent fixed points in a graded scale which states move along as their capabilities wax and wane. Passage between them is sequential. States cannot jump from one end to the other without first passing through the intervening stations no matter how quickly. Others though, such as the five invented by Jean-Germain Gros (anarchic, phantom/mirage, anaemic, captured and aborted), are non-linear categories. They are not '"stages" through which nations must go before descending into the abyss.'[28] Nor do they have to be occupied in isolation, states can 'straddle [several of] them at particular points in their history.'[29]

Others still refer to neither stages nor related categories of weakness but simply describe different varieties of weak state. Robert Rotberg's three classes of weak state consist of those held together entirely by repression, those which have serious yet manageable 'inter-communal antagonisms' and those which have always existed on 'the edge of failure' but do not suffer from 'ethnic, religious, or other communal' strife.[30] Each class is discrete. They do not overlap or merge into one another, and states are unlikely to move between them or occupy more than one at any given time. It is doubtful, for example, that a perennially weak state with a harmonious society will either experience serious inter-communal hostilities or develop the capabilities it needs to manage them effectively even if it did. These are essentially different breeds of weak state. The only thing they have in common is their weakness.

Yet, despite their differences, these explanations mostly agree on where the thresholds between weakness and failure, and failure and collapse lie. Failure is caused by the persistence of intra-societal violence. This conflict need not be intense, just long lasting.[31]

16 *Nigeria Since Independence*

And collapsed states are 'rare' or 'extreme' versions of failed states.[32] For even though the governments of failed states are unable to project and protect their authority throughout the whole of their sovereign territories, they still exist. Collapsed states, on the other hand, have absolutely no central government at all. In states like these 'security is equated with the rule of the strong.'[33] Its provision, therefore, is often as unpredictable as it is arbitrary.

Failure to promote human flourishing

Failure to promote human flourishing, on the other hand, refers chiefly to individuals, communities and specific sections of society, and it is used by academics and others alike with two objectives in mind. First, to give a human face to some of the consequences of failure to control, to show what impact it can have on the unfortunate people who live in a failed state. In this instance, failure to promote human flourishing is both an effect and a metric by which failure to control can be measured. The less able a state is to provide its people with public goods, the more failed it is. Secondly, the term is used to indicate a government's intent. This, then, is a quite different explanation of failure. For it is failure through neglect, failure through negligence, failure through disregard rather than of an inability to control.

This second use of failure to promote human flourishing is far broader and more widely applicable than either the first iteration or failure to control. And it has very little to do with the post-Second World War changes to the international normative environment. For it is really referring to a failure of governance, the unwillingness of political leaders and regimes to provide all of their citizens, rather than a fortunate few, with the public goods they have a reasonable right to expect. This duty of care has, since the publication of the International Commission on Intervention and State Sovereignty's (ICISS) 2001 report,[34] ossified into the responsibility to protect.[35]

The responsibility to protect was formally adopted by the members of the United Nations General Assembly in 2005. The World Summit Outcome resolution for that year clearly set out what the responsibility to protect entailed and the obligations its signatories were taking on by agreeing to it.[36] Under its terms, each state promised 'to protect [their] population from genocide, war crimes, ethnic cleansing and crimes against humanity' and to work to prevent 'such crimes, including their incitement, through [the] appropriate

Fear of Failure   17

and necessary means.' In addition, the signatories also promised to 'encourage and help States to exercise this responsibility and support the United Nations in establishing an early warning capability.'[37]

The responsibility to protect, therefore, has both individual and collective dimensions. By embracing it, each state has signed up to a code of behaviour as to how they will treat their citizens, what they will and will not do for them. And this includes working with other states to enforce the code across the world. The mechanisms for such cooperation already exist in Chapters VI, VII and VIII of the United Nations Charter.[38] Even though, as Williams observes, states routinely ignore these commitments, providing for the safety and security of their citizens remains their most important obligation. For without this security, individuals and communities are unable to fully exploit any other opportunities that might exist and, indeed, are unable to flourish.

The spread and spread of the concept of state failure

State failure has ceased to be a solely academic topic of discussion. The terms weak state, quasi state, failed state and collapsed state are no longer confined to scholarly debate or the pages of learned books and journals alone. Both the concept and its associated vocabulary have escaped the academy's cloisters to enter mainstream discourse. Today political figures, military leaders, economists, aid providers, development workers and journalists all use the concept and employ its descriptions. They do so for a variety of reasons. To explain what has happened to a particular state or group of states; to highlight or draw attention to an ongoing process of failure; to warn of what is to come if remedial action is not swiftly taken; and to admonish governments, international organisations and citizenries for not doing enough to help those in need.

The concept of state failure, then, has both explanatory and emotive powers. It is used to help explicate what has happened, what is going on and what is likely to occur. Yet it has also acquired significant emotional and rhetorical currency. It has become a catch-all concept for a host of miseries and a range of dangers. State failure is frequently cited as the principal cause of all manner of political abuses, economic hardships, social ills and cultural injustices suffered by peoples and communities throughout Africa and beyond. And

18   Nigeria Since Independence

just as often, it is identified as the unpalatable, yet likely, outcome of the numerous tragic dramas unfolding around the world at any one time. State failure has become a monster which needs either to be kept in check or slain at the earliest opportunity.

The concept's rise to prominence is a result of its securitisation. The terror attacks on the World Trade Centre and Pentagon on 11 September 2001 marked the start of the transformation of failed states into vectors of global danger. Or rather, they triggered a rapid and decisive shift in perception. After the attacks of 2001, North American and European governments looked upon such states with renewed suspicion. They quickly determined that they were not as safe from the consequences of failure, even when it occurred far from their shores, as they had thought they were. At least some of the dangers that confronted the citizens, political leaders and nearest neighbours of failed states threatened them also.

The main cause of concern for Washington, London, Paris and Brussels was the breakdown in law and order. Or more specifically, the inability of official police forces and militaries in failed states to exercise effective control over the entire areas under their jurisdiction. For their failure to do so helped to create both security blind spots – places where the true extent of what was happening there was not known – and no-go zones – towns and regions where the police and armed forces rarely ventured or were unable to hold for long periods of time. These spaces were dangerous because they provided malevolent groups – organisations and factions which wanted to cause North American and European countries harm – with the perfect environments to operate in.[39]

As a result of the attacks on the World Trade Centre and Pentagon, failed states came to be seen as safe havens for criminal gangs, pirate crews, terrorist cells and armed militias.[40] It became an article of faith in Washington, London, Paris and Brussels that such factions were busily setting up training bases and operational headquarters within the dangerous spaces that existed within failed states to plan and organise attacks against North American and European interests. And that they were exploiting the suffering of the local populations to generate support for their causes and find new recruits for their ranks. Failed states were giving these groups a home and often providing them with the members they needed to perpetuate themselves and their campaigns.

Fear of Failure 19

That was not the sum of the dangers that were thought to emanate from these places. They were also seen as hotbeds of communicable disease and political instability. The breakdown in health and education services meant that their unfortunate citizens were more likely to contract HIV/AIDS, malaria, typhoid, sleeping sickness and other serious maladies for which they would probably receive inadequate treatment. While the decline in living standards and simultaneous rise in personal insecurity endured by many of these people prompted some to seek sanctuary and opportunity abroad. In so doing, they exposed the populations and communities they came into contact with to the illnesses and diseases they were carrying.[41]

Political leaders and policy makers in Western capitals also feared that those fleeing failed states might destabilise the countries they were travelling to and through. The sudden arrival of significant numbers of destitute men, women and children would place an additional burden on the, often already overstretched, welfare infrastructures of the recipient states. The likely tensions this would give rise to between migrants and local inhabitants would only add to the host government's problems as it struggled to cope with the political and economic shockwaves generated by the failure of one of its near neighbours. Instability would beget instability, fragility would beget fragility and failure would beget failure.

Little wonder then that in the wake of the 2001 attacks on the World Trade Centre and Pentagon, North American and European governments quickly identified the prevention of state failure and resuscitation of failed states as key strategic objectives.[42] Stopping failure from happening and reversing it when it did occur was seen as vital to improving their security and that of their citizens and other states and societies around the world. By securitising failed states in this way, these governments helped propel the concept of state failure into mainstream discourse.

Conclusions

Africa is bound to state failure and it has been for many years now. To begin with, a majority of the states identified as failed by bodies like the Fund for Peace are found there. In fact, Africa has a higher concentration of failed states than any other continent. This will continue to be the case for the foreseeable future. For a great many of

20 *Nigeria Since Independence*

its states remain extremely vulnerable to the political, economic and social problems that are habitually identified as key contributing causes of failure. They do not have caring and accountable governments. They do not have effective and responsible militaries. They do not have dynamic and growing economics. They do not have stable and integrated populations.

Yet this is not the sum of Africa's links to state failure. Its ties go beyond instances of occurrence, the predominance of so many of the world's failed states there. For state failure was born out of the same changes in global politics and the same shifts in the international normative environment that led to the end of colonial rule and the establishment of the independent states that replaced the imperial territories. Indeed, Africa's political development since the end of the Second World War has occurred in tandem with that of state failure. Both the states that now make up the continent and state failure are the outcome of the same historical seizures.

Of course, Africa's imperial territories were not the only ones to receive their independence once the Second World War was over. But at the time the fighting stopped, no other continent was so heavily colonised. So much so, that the UN's General Assembly clearly had Africa in its collective mind when it passed resolutions 1514 and 1541. And the OAU quickly came to play a pivotal role in discrediting the institution of empire and harrying the colonial powers that remained in the continent into giving up their territories and, in the process, creating the new international normative environment that made state failure possible.

State failure, as it is widely understood today, is a modern phenomenon. Prior to the emergence of the new international normative environment, states either existed or they did not. *De facto* and *de jure* existence went hand in hand in an age when invasion, occupation, conquest and annexation were frequent and more acceptable. State failure is only possible because of the separation of *de facto* from *de jure* statehood. Today, there are states that exist as legal entities, but which lack the governments and state institutions to have any day-to-day reality for portions of the populations that live within their borders. Such states are shells. There is little inside the outer international legal coating.

There are now two main understandings of state failure – failure to control and failure to promote human flourishing. Failure to control

Fear of Failure 21

is the main understanding and refers to the disjuncture between *de facto* and *de jure* statehood. Failure to promote human flourishing is far more prevalent and is less tied to the shifts in the international normative environment. Instead it speaks of a failure of governance, of the inability or unwillingness of regimes and political leaders to provide their citizens with the public goods that they can reasonably expect to receive. Yet there is still a broad overlap in the causes of these two types of failure. Certainly the specific and dynamic causes are largely the same. As social instability and domestic violence, political incompetence and neglect, economic stagnation and decline, social tensions and ethnic competition help drive both.

The concept of state failure has now entered mainstream use. It has broken through the relative confines of the academy and been embraced by politicians, military leaders, economists, aid providers, development workers, journalists and private citizens alike. This spread in usage has been driven by its securitisation which came about mostly as a result of the terror attacks on the World Trade Centre and Pentagon on 11 September 2001. These outrages prompted North American and European governments to look at failed states with renewed fear. No longer, it seemed, were the consequences of failure confined to the states that had failed or their nearest neighbours. These governments now believed that the dangerous spaces that existed within failed states were being exploited by malevolent groups and organisations which threatened the whole world.

The concept's entry into mainstream discourse has led to a proliferation in the use of its associated terms. The descriptions weak state, quasi state, failing state, failed state and collapsed state are habitually used by a range of people in a variety of contexts. Indeed, their growing use has resulted in a broadening of their application.[43] Not only are these different labels applied to the same state at the same time, but they are also used in ways far removed from what was originally intended. In fact, more often than not these innovations are inappropriate. Not least because they heighten the risk of the concept and its terms being devalued by over use. The more they are applied the less they mean. The more they describe the less they explain.

2
The Enemy Within: Insurgency and the Failure of the Nigerian State

There are two parts to Nigeria's failure. First, the Federal Government does not exercise total control over the whole of the country's sovereign territory. There are places in the Niger Delta and the north-eastern state of Borno in which Abuja's writ does not run. Second, the Federal Government does not provide all of its citizens with the security, basic health care, primary education and other public goods that it should. It is failing to protect and promote the flourishing of all Nigerians.

The Federal Government is unable to fully control its sovereign territory for two main reasons. First, the activities of various insurgent groups, and in particular those of Boko Haram and the MEND, prevent it from doing so. By force of arms these factions have created spaces in the country beyond the Federal Government's direct and continuous control. The political and symbolic importance of these redoubts is greater than their size. For they have not been abandoned freely by the Federal Government. On the contrary, it wants to control these areas. It is actively attempting to bring them under its authority. It is using all the means at its disposal to extend its writ over them. Yet it is unable to do so. These places deny the Federal Government's authority, and in so doing, damage its reputation and diminish its sovereignty.

Second, there are limits to the Federal Government's power over the country's armed forces. That its control over them is stronger

The Enemy Within 23

than before is beyond question. The years of military rule during which senior officers answered to no one but each other are over. And the longer they remain out of power the stronger the current civil–military order grows. Yet few Nigerians are truly convinced that the army has renounced politics for good. This attitude is understandable given that only 15 years had passed since the military last held power. And many of the factors which prompted it to intervene before can be found today. The limits of the Federal Government's control over the armed forces matter because where they lie mark the extent of Abuja's authority. As in most other states, the military is the most powerful tool the government has for enforcing its will.

The Federal Government is failing to promote the flourishing of all its citizens in three main ways. First, and most crucially, it is not providing adequate security in many parts of the country. Over the past two years thousands of men, women and children have been killed and injured in attacks carried out by either Boko Haram or the MEND. The brunt of this violence has been borne by the inhabitants of the Niger Delta and the north-east. Though residents in other parts of the country have not been spared entirely. Indeed, since the start of 2012, Boko Haram has bombed dozens of civilian targets right across the north and central belt region. Few states or communities have escaped the bloodshed completely.

In addition to its failure to stem the rising tide of violence, the Federal Government has, on occasion, made it worse. Indeed, the armed forces and police have killed and wounded nearly as many civilians as the insurgents. Time and again, they have responded to an attack carried out by either Boko Haram or the MEND with disproportionate and indiscriminate force. And they have used similar levels of violence when quelling riots and suppressing demonstrations. Not only have suspects had their civil and human rights abused, but so too have innocent bystanders.

Second, the federal, state and local authorities are not providing adequate health care to hundreds of thousands of Nigerians. Right across the country, but especially in remote and rural areas, there is a chronic shortage of doctors and nurses, hospitals and clinics, modern equipment and in-date medicines. As a result, thousands of men, women and children die each year of preventable diseases and treatable conditions. The pitiable state of Nigeria's health service

24 *Nigeria Since Independence*

is most clearly emphasised by the mundane and the rare. Medical procedures like childbirth which are routine in many parts of the world continue to claim the lives of an inordinate number of people in Nigeria. Conversely, so too do diseases like polio which are now unknown nearly everywhere else.

Third, the federal, state and local authorities are not providing adequate primary, secondary or tertiary education to hundreds of thousands of young Nigerians. The exponential growth in the size of the country's population over the past 20 years has created a huge number of children and adolescents in need of schooling. Yet, over the same period, government spending on education has fallen steadily. As a result, there simply are not enough schools, colleges, universities, laboratories, libraries, teachers, computers and learning materials to meet demand. And what there are require urgent upgrade. Buildings are in disrepair, campuses are dilapidated, books are falling apart, teachers are not properly trained and lecturers are not regularly paid.

These two expressions of Nigeria's failure are mutually reinforcing. First, the Federal Government is unable to fully control its territory because of the activities of groups like Boko Haram and the MEND. And, quite clearly, it will struggle to provide public goods to the inhabitants of those areas over which it has little meaningful authority. Moreover, its efforts to combat these factions are exacerbating the insecurity endured by millions of Nigerians. Their safety is threatened by the attacks carried out by these groups and the counter insurgency operations mounted by the security forces. Indeed, Boko Haram and the MEND are a major cause of the Federal Government's failure to both control its territory and secure its citizens.

The Federal Government's failure to take adequate care of its citizens is driving some to support one or other of the insurgent or separatist groups operating in the country today. Organisations such as the Movement for the Survival of the Ogoni People (MOSOP) and the Movement for the Actualisation of the Sovereign State of Biafra (MASSOB) argue that the interests of the communities they claim to represent would be better served by breaking away from Nigeria. Only by establishing themselves as independent states will they win the rights and opportunities they deserve. Both the insurgents and the separatists offer visions of alternate and, so they argue, better futures for some or all of Nigeria's citizens. By exploiting the Federal Government's failings they are able to gain sufficient support to either limit its authority or challenge the country's continued existence.

The chapter is divided into three sections. The first focuses on the Federal Government's inability to exercise total, continuous control over the whole of Nigeria's sovereign territory. It does so by focusing on the activities and strength of both Boko Haram and the MEND, and the limits of the Federal Government's authority over the country's armed forces. The second section then charts the extent of the Federal Government's failure to take care of all its citizens and provide them with the security, health care and education that it should. Finally, the third section considers the strength of the various secessionist movements operating in Nigeria today and the extent of the threat they individually and collectively pose to the country's continued unity.

The ways and extent of Nigeria's failure

Nigeria's failure has been a cause of considerable disquiet for a number of years now. Some of the earliest concerns about it were raised by the National Secretary of the ruling People's Democratic Party (PDP) of the time, Ojo Maduekwe, in 2004. He warned that 'unless crucial strategic moves both within the polity and economy are undertaken in the months ahead, the nation is at risk of slipping back ... to a failing state or even a failed state status with severe consequences, not only for all our people, but ... the whole sub-region.'[1] His anxieties have been echoed by a host of other prominent public figures both at home and abroad.

In August 2009 the head of the Nigerian Bar Association (NBA), Oluwarotimi Akerdolu, lamented the country's slide 'toward being a failed state.'[2] In March 2010 Nobel Prize winning author, Wole Soyinka, struck an even more pessimistic note by admitting that he did not 'rule out Nigeria breaking up' as that is 'what can happen to a failed state.'[3] His sentiments were echoed by the Academic Staff Union of Universities (ASUU) which, in an open letter to President Jonathan sent in February 2011, warned that 'unless ... sufficient resolve in ... terminating the ... abduction business' is shown 'this country may become a failed state like Somalia.'[4] And, in July 2011,

26 Nigeria Since Independence

prominent civil rights activist, Dr Joe Okei-Odumakin, cautioned that living standards had fallen so low 'that we are beginning to see the symptoms of a failed state in all that we do.'[5]

Nigeria's failure is intimately bound to the existence and activities of Boko Haram and the MEND. First, it is they, rather than the government, who exercise day-to-day authority over parts of the north-east and Niger Delta. Second, their armed campaigns are undermining the safety and security of Nigerians all over the country. Third, they are driving the police and military into launching countermeasures which often heighten the insecurity endured by ordinary people. Fourth, they are recruiting those individuals left angry and disillusioned by the state's behaviour. Boko Haram and the MEND have helped create the vicious cycle whereby the Federal Government's failure to control begets its failure to protect which begets its failure to control.

Boko Haram

Over the past decade, Boko Haram has undergone five important transformations. The first is the development of its goals. When the group initially emerged in 2002 it mostly resembled a religious commune. It had around 3,000 members many of whom were women and children. It was not an armed faction made up solely of fighters. And their shared ambition was not to impose their politico-religious views on everyone else, but to live quietly and piously as the earliest Muslims had done, removed from the rest of society. To that end, they recreated the Prophet's *hijara*, or flight from Mecca to Medina, and withdrew to a remote corner of Niger State in the north-west of the country.

The insular and largely peaceable goals Boko Haram had at that time distinguished it from the other main Islamist groups from which it evolved. Its founder and original leader, Mohammed Yusuf, had belonged to both Ibrahim Zakzaky's Islamic Movement in Nigeria (IMN) and Abubakar Mujahid's *Ahl al-Sunnah wal-Jama'ah*, *Ja'amutu Tajidmul Islami* (Movement for the Islamic Revival, MIR). Its main financial backer, Alhaji Buji Foi, had close ties with Sheikh Abubakar Gummi's and Dr Ahmed Gummi's *Jama'atul Izalatul Bid'ah Wa'ikhamatul Sunnah* (*Izala*). The IMN was *Shiite*, pro-Iranian and committed to fomenting revolution. The MIR was willing to use violence to turn Nigeria into an Islamic state. And the *Izala* had direct links to the Saudi Arabian government.[6] Boko Haram had no such ambitions, intentions or connections.

Yet, over the next few years, its objectives changed. Today it too wants to turn Nigeria into an Islamic state. This much was confirmed by its spokesman, Abu Qaqa, who declared that 'we will consider negotiation only when we have brought the government to their knees. Once we see that things are being done in accordance to the dictates of Allah, and our members are released [from prison], we will put aside our arms – but we will not lay them down. You don't put down your arms in Islam, you only put them aside.'[7]

The second transformation Boko Haram has undergone since its establishment is its use of violence in pursuit of its developing goals. The group launched its armed campaign in late December 2003 when around 200 of its members attacked police stations in the towns of Kanamma and Geidam in Yobe State close to the group's new base. Several police officers and 18 militants were killed. On 23 September 2004 Boko Haram militants attacked police stations in Gwoza and Barma in neighbouring Borno State killing four policemen and two civilians. Then on 10 October 2004 gunmen ambushed a police convoy close to the town of Kala-Balge near the border with Chad. A dozen police officers were abducted and later murdered.

The attack on the police convoy was one of the last the group carried out for nearly five years. Indeed, it was not until the summer of 2009 that its militants again clashed with the security services. Between 26 and 30 July, hundreds of armed Boko Haram members fought running gun battles with police officers and troops throughout the north-east of the country. Much of the heaviest fighting took place in Maiduguri. But there were further outbursts of deadly violence in the nearby city of Bauchi, and towns of Potiskum and Wudil. As a result of the fighting, more than 700 people lost their lives,[8] including Yusuf, who was shot and killed while in police custody.[9]

The third transformation undergone by Boko Haram is the expansion of its list of targets. Nearly all of the attacks it carried out in 2004 and the summer of 2009 were against the security forces. Indeed its return to arms was a direct response to the operation launched against it by the police and army in June 2009 which resulted in the deaths of 17 of its members. Since then it has attacked scores of police stations and military outposts across the north and central belt region. Yet over the past two years it has steadily increased its

28 Nigeria Since Independence

range of targets to the extent that today there is virtually no group or individual it would not attack.

The first new group added to Boko Haram's list of possible targets was civilian politicians. Its addition was first confirmed by the murder of the All Nigeria Peoples Party's (ANPP) candidate for the forthcoming election for the governorship of Borno State, Alhaji Awana Ali Ngala, on 29 December 2010.[10] The second group added was community and religious leaders. Its addition was first confirmed by the assassination of prominent Muslim cleric, Ibrahim Birkuti, on 6 June 2011.[11] The third group added was Christians living in the north and central belt region. Its addition was confirmed by the bombing of a church in Maiduguri on 16 June 2011. Three children died in the attack.[12] The fourth group added was civilians engaged in, what Boko Haram considered, irreligious activities. Its addition was first confirmed by the bomb attack on a Maiduguri beer garden on 27 June 2011 that left 25 people dead and a dozen more injured.[13] And the fifth group added was international organisations and foreign governments and citizens working and living in Nigeria. Its addition was first confirmed by the bombing of the United Nations' headquarters in Abuja on 26 August 2011.[14]

The fourth transformation undergone by Boko Haram is the steady expansion of its area of operations. Most of the attacks it carries out take place either in or around the city of Maiduguri. Those it launched in 2004 and 2009 all took place in this area. But over the last couple of years, it has carried out an increasing number of bombings and shootings in towns and cities right across the north and central belt region. To date, it has carried out attacks in Adamawa, Bauchi, Borno, Gombe, Jigawa, Kaduna, Katsina and Yobe States as well as the Federal Capital Territory. This amounts to nine out of thirty-seven, or one in three, of the country's states.[15]

Finally the fifth transformation undergone by Boko Haram is the development of its operational capabilities. Since 2009 it has steadily increased the range of attacks it can carry out. It has now proven its ability to mount ambushes and frontal assaults,[16] lightening raids and prison breakouts,[17] mass casualty strikes,[18] including suicide bombings,[19] and targeted assassinations.[20] This development has been driven by both the group's extension of its target range and determination to avoid becoming predictable. It has changed its tactics to better suit the effect it is trying to achieve and to prevent the security forces from easily anticipating what it will do next. This development highlights the group's growing confidence, expertise and capabilities. It is prepared to launch new types of operation and has the ability to do so.

The changes undergone by Boko Haram are fuelling speculation that it is not one group but several. Both the breadth and speed of its transformation speak of an organisation moving in multiple directions all at once. Indeed, it appears so dynamic that it is hard to imagine all these changes being instigated and directed by a small group of clearly defined leaders. It seems far more likely that it is a confederacy made up of broadly likeminded factions each with their own fighters, leaders, agendas and capabilities. Certainly this would explain the speed and unpredictability of the changes to its operational direction; why one day (25 August 2011) it is attacking police stations and banks in Adamawa State and the next (26 August 2011) launching suicide bombers against the United Nations in Abuja.

The MEND

The MEND is the largest and best known of the insurgent groups currently operating in the Niger Delta. It was established in response to the arrest of Alhaji Dokubo-Asari, the founder and leader of the NDPVF, in September 2005.[21] It is part of a much older protest movement which first emerged in organised form in 1990 following the creation of the Movement for the Survival of the Ogoni People. The MEND is both similar and different from these earlier groups. Like the MOSOP it wants environmental and economic justice for its constituents, and like the NDPVF most of its members are Ijaw. Unlike the MOSOP it is committed to using violence, and unlike the NDPVF it has a less hierarchical, more diffuse organisational structure.[22]

The MEND's evolution has been both slower and less dramatic than that of Boko Haram. First, the MEND has always been a fighting force. It was established to ensure that there would be no let-up in the armed campaign waged by the NDPVF against the Federal Government following the arrest of its leader. Indeed, the MEND carried out its first attack, against the Opobo pipeline in Delta State, on 20 December 2005 mere days after its foundation. And despite the various ceasefires it has called, only some of which it has observed, it has yet to renounce its struggle or lay down its arms entirely.

30   *Nigeria Since Independence*

While there is no doubt that Boko Haram is now also an insurgent group, it did not begin life as one.

Second, the MEND's core goals have not changed nearly as much as Boko Haram's have over the years. It issued its first set of demands on 11 January 2006. In them it called for the immediate release of Dokubo-Asari and disgraced former Bayelsa State governor, Diepreye Alamieyeseigha, from prison;[23] the oil companies operating in Nigeria to pay $1.5 billion in compensation to the inhabitants of the Niger Delta for the damage they had caused to the region's environment and economy; and the Federal Government to return half of all the revenue it earned from oil to the people most affected by its extraction. Since then it has issued numerous other demands calling for, amongst other things, 'Henry Okah to be held in good condition,' and for the Federal Government to 'begin a staged military withdrawal from the Niger Delta,' increase its spending on 'the poor and disadvantaged,' and 'propose a time table for the practice of true federalism.'[24]

Despite the seeming range of demands made by the MEND, most of them are variations of the same desires and determinations. More often than not, the MEND has called for the release of key individuals from custody; control of the Niger Delta's resources to be handed to its inhabitants; more of the revenue accrued from oil to be returned to the region's residents; an end to corruption; and the oil companies to pay vast sums in compensation. Indeed, whatever evolution its objectives have undergone has been relatively superficial; it still mostly wants to achieve the same things that it did in 2006. The development of Boko Haram's goals, in contrast, has been far more substantial as evidenced by its rejection of isolation in favour of turning Nigeria into an Islamic state.

Third, the MEND has a shorter and less-diverse list of targets than Boko Haram. Its potential victims can be grouped into five distinct categories. The first comprises of police officers and service personnel, the second of politicians and state functionaries, the third of wealthy private citizens, the fourth of foreign nationals living and working in the Niger Delta and the fifth of oil companies and their employees. It largely tries to avoid attacking ordinary Nigerians. Indeed, it expressed deep regret at the civilians who were killed when it bombed the Ministry of Justice headquarters in Abuja on 1 October 2010.[25] This was one of the few mass casualty attacks mounted by the group. Moreover there is considerable overlap between these categories. Most of the Niger Delta's wealthiest residents work in the oil industry. As do nearly all of the foreign nationals found there. Unlike Boko Haram, which is prepared to attack pretty much anyone, the MEND still observes certain boundaries.

But the MEND is not only targeting key individuals and groups. It is also attacking the country's oil infrastructure (pipelines, pumping stations, wells, platforms and vessels) and steals (or bunkers) significant amounts of oil. These attacks are intended to increase both the economic and international political pressure on the Federal Government. By disrupting the extraction, transportation and storage of oil, the MEND is seeking to reduce the Federal Government's income while simultaneously increasing its own by selling the oil it bunkers on the global black market. By reducing the amount of oil Nigeria exports, it is hoping to increase the pressure placed on Abuja by foreign governments anxious to stabilise and lower the price of oil to reach a settlement with it. This resource campaign, with its economic and international political dimensions, further distinguishes the MEND from Boko Haram.

Fourth, the MEND has not extended its area of operations nearly as far as Boko Haram has. Almost all of the attacks it has carried out since its establishment have taken place in the Niger Delta and its coastal waters. The one notable exception to this was the group's bombing of the Ministry of Justice in Abuja. Yet, despite frequently threatening to carry out similar strikes, both before and after this attack, it has not done so. Moreover, certain types of operation are mounted almost exclusively in certain parts of the Niger Delta. Nearly all of those abducted by the group are snatched from either Port Harcourt or vessels in the Gulf of Guinea. Boko Haram, in contrast, has carried out attacks right across the north and centre of the country.

Fifth, the MEND has not developed its operational capabilities to the same extent that Boko Haram has. In the months immediately following its establishment the MEND quickly expanded the range of attacks it could carry out. It has now proven its ability to bomb oil installations,[26] intercept and board vessels at sea,[27] ambush Joint Task Force units,[28] abduct wealthy Nigerians and foreign oil workers,[29] and assassinate prominent and well-protected individuals.[30] Yet it has not sought to expand its operational repertoire to the same extent that Boko Haram has. Rather it carries out the same

32 *Nigeria Since Independence*

types of attack time and again as it has done for the past six years. That it does so reflects both its more limited goals and targets. Unlike Boko Haram, it has not declared war on vast swathes of the population. Neither is it seeking to seize control of Nigeria.

Failure to control

There are two possible dimensions to the Federal Government's failure to control. First, that it does not have total control over the official agencies of violence. Second, that it has this control but the agencies do not have an overwhelming presence in all parts of the country because they are evenly or overmatched by groups like Boko Haram and the MEND.

Concerns that the military might once again march on the capital escalate whenever there is a political crisis, and Nigeria is no stranger to political crises. Speculation that the army was readying itself to seize power last peaked in the spring and early summer of 2010 when confusion over President Yar'Adua's whereabouts and health was at its height. He had left Nigeria the previous November to receive medical treatment in Saudi Arabia for his various ailments. During that time he was seen by only a handful of medical staff, immediate family members and close advisers, giving rise to rumours that he was either in a coma or dead. And even when he finally did return to Nigeria on 24 February 2010, his condition remained shrouded in mystery. Indeed, the public neither saw him nor was officially informed of his illness prior to his death on 5 May 2010.

Remarkably though, his wife, Tuari, and other close associates such as his Deputy Chief of Staff, Tanimu Yakubu, and the Governor of Kwara State, Bukola Saraki, insisted throughout this period that he was fully able to discharge his duties as president. Their statements contributed greatly to the uncertainty and confusion that reigned, especially when compared to the little news on the state of his health that did filter out and the length of time he remained in hospital in both Saudi Arabia and Nigeria. With each day that passed popular expectations that the military might soon intervene to resolve the situation grew.[31] In fact, it was seen by many as the only institution capable of bringing the crisis to an end.

Such faith highlights the complex relationship the Nigerian public has with its military. On the one hand, it is a source of considerable pride and an object of significant affection. General Yakubu Gowon has long been venerated for first saving Nigeria from disintegration and then treating the defeated Biafrans with respect and sensitivity.[32] Similarly Generals Murtala Mohammed and Muhammadu Buhari are remembered with a great deal of fondness for establishing the least corrupt and most effective regimes the country has ever had. Under these leaders, the military seemed to work far more for the people even if it did suspend their political rights and civil liberties. There were undoubted costs to having it hold power, but there were tangible benefits too.

Yet, on the other hand, the armed forces are rightly blamed for reinforcing many of the nefarious political and economic practices which continue to degrade Nigerians' democratic rights and standards of living. Certainly Generals Ibrahim Badamasi Babangida (or IBB as he is better known) and Sani Abacha proved themselves to be every bit as corrupt and mendacious as the civilian leaders they claimed to be protecting the country from.[33] Not only did they help institutionalise the bad governance that now blights Nigeria, they also permitted and ordered some of the most offensive abuses of human rights ever perpetrated in the country. Under these leaders, the people seemed to exist to serve the military. Their political rights were suspended and their civil liberties were infringed but with few tangible benefits in return.

The complexity that lies at the heart of the Nigerian public's relationship with its armed forces is both a cause and an effect of the insurgencies in the north-east and Niger Delta. For a start, the military's response to these rebellions generates almost as much approbation as it does opprobrium. The praise its actions garner from some sections of society is balanced against the anger they induce in others. This, in part, accounts for the mixed success of its campaigns to date. For any degradation they cause to the fighting capabilities of the MEND and Boko Haram is offset by the recruits and sympathisers they drive into the rebels' arms and the demand they help maintain for black market military weapons. In fact a goodly number of the insurgents operating in the Delta and the north today are armed with weapons sold to them by serving soldiers and sailors.[34]

The endurance shown and victories won by the MEND and Boko Haram have led to parts of the country being placed beyond the military's direct control. The military no longer has exclusive authority

34 *Nigeria Since Independence*

over the whole of Nigeria's sovereign territory but is instead forced to share it with these groups in some areas and even surrender it to them in others. Just as crucially, it lacks the wherewithal to dislodge them, either the force of arms or the willpower or the strategic acumen it needs to drive them once and for all from their respective strongholds. It is compelled, therefore, to accept both their presence and their authority.

The total area that lies beyond Abuja's day-to-day control is neither fixed nor, when compared to the size of the territory over which it retains authority, that large. It comprises of pockets of terrain scattered across both the Niger Delta and the north-eastern state of Borno. The size of each of these no-go zones and the position of their respective borders are in constant fluctuation. They change according to the rise and fall in the fortunes of the various belligerents, how well Boko Haram, the MEND, the NDVF and the NDPVF are doing against the army, MOPOL and the Joint Task Force. For theirs are zero-sum contests: what is beneficial to Boko Haram's campaign is harmful to the military's. A victory for the MEND is a defeat for the Joint Task Force.

Failure to promote human flourishing

Nigeria's failure is not confined to Abuja's inability to exercise direct and continuous control over the whole of its territory. Nigeria is also failed because the Federal Government does not take adequate care of all of its citizens. More specifically, it does not provide significant numbers of them with the public goods that it should, including security, health care and education. Its failure to do so is not only undermining the quality of life of tens of thousands of Nigerians but also depriving them of vital opportunities for self-betterment. The anger and frustration this failure gives rise to helps account for some of the support shown to Boko Haram and the MEND. The Federal Government's failure to promote the flourishing of its people is exacerbating its failure to control Nigeria's territory.

Failure to provide security

The most important public good any government can provide its citizens is security. First, security permits assumptions. It allows ordinary people (individuals with neither the means nor the know-how to make their own, private security arrangements) to go about their daily lives with some degree of confidence that their persons, their loved ones and their property will be fairly safe. Second, security permits planning. For with this confidence ordinary people can look to the future and lay plans as to what they will do and hope to achieve in the short, medium and long terms. And third, security enables engagement. It allows and encourages ordinary people to take part in public life. That is, they can do things outside of the home such as work, go to school, take part in political life and, more broadly, make a contribution to society and its development.

Ordinary people can, of course, enhance their security by reducing the risks that they take. First, they can avoid engaging in certain types of behaviour, activities which, either by custom or by design, have greater dangers to life, limb and property associated with them. Second, they can avoid going to places of heightened risk, areas and locations where threats are more abundant and harder to evade. And third, they can limit their activity, or certain types of activity, to particular times of the day. But this risk management is only possible if a certain level of security is already in place. Indeed, the management of risk presupposes that certain behaviours, places, and hours of the day are more secure than others.

Yet, at present, tens of thousands of Nigerians are living in a state of considerable insecurity. That they are doing so is due in no small measure to the ineffectiveness of the country's main security agencies – the police, the armed forces and the intelligence services. Their limitations are the result of four main factors. First, all three agencies are under-resourced. They simply do not have the personnel or the equipment, the training or the technical expertise to be much more effective than they are at present. The police, in particular, are overstretched and have only a partial presence in many states.[35] To the extent that troops are performing many police duties either alongside or in place of civilian forces in 20 of the country's 36 states.[36]

Second, there is no real culture of public service. None of these agencies is very interested in making ordinary people and their property more secure. This neglect is the result of a toxic cocktail of causes which includes corruption and the pervasive *Oga* mentality.[37] Many police officers now view their duties as a means of making money. That they do so is due to both their avarice and their straitened circumstances. The *Oga* mentality, which runs the length and breadth of Nigerian society, links power and wealth to importance. Without either an individual can be either ignored or treated with surly contempt by officialdom.[38]

Third, these agencies do not work well together. In fact, communication between them is at best limited and strained, and at worst non-existent or openly hostile. The recent operation to locate and liberate the British and Italian citizens abducted in the north of the country on 12 May 2011 was led,[39] at the Nigerian end, by the State Security Service (SSS). But its directors completely excluded their military counterparts from the planning and organisation process and only allowed the army to become involved towards the end. And relations between the military and the police are no better. This much is clear from the frequent armed clashes which take place between soldiers and police officers.[40]

Fourth, the security agencies are, at times, the main cause of insecurity.[41] Such accusations have long been levelled against the Federal Government and its agents. Time and again the police and the military are accused of not doing enough to minimise civilian casualties when using lethal force,[42] deliberately firing upon unarmed protestors and demonstrators,[43] and summarily executing suspects and prisoners.[44] And such abuses do not always occur at moments of crisis or heightened insecurity. They do not always happen during or immediately after a riot or a gun battle or a counter-insurgency operation. They cannot always be attributed, therefore, to heightened emotions brought on by the heat of the moment. Some are premeditated and are carried out during the course of routine activities and duties.[45] They happen with such frequency that they have become part of the security forces' *modus operandi*.

The high level of insecurity endured by many Nigerians can be measured by the number of insurgent attacks carried out since December 2011. Most of these assaults have been mounted by Boko Haram, which increased the intensity of its campaign, although a few have been launched by the MEND and various other groups. This new, even more deadly, phase of Boko Haram's armed struggle began on Christmas Day 2011 when it carried out coordinated attacks against targets spread right across northern and central Nigeria. It began by bombing a Catholic Church in the town of Madala on the outskirts of Abuja before bombing other churches in the city of Jos in Plateau State and towns of Damaturu and Gadaka in Yobe State.

Two other bombs were discovered in Jos but were diffused before they could explode. More than 35 people died and dozens more were injured in these attacks.[46]

Then on 5 January 2012 Boko Haram militants shot and killed six people and wounded a further ten when they opened fire on the congregation of the Deeper Life Church in Gombe, Gombe State.[47] Two days later, its gunmen murdered at least 17 people and wounded many more when they attacked a meeting of Igbo Christians held at the town in Mubi in Adamawa State.[48] Then on 20 January 2012 fighters belonging to the group attacked four police stations and the SSS headquarters in Kano, Kano State. At least 185 people were killed and dozens more were wounded.[49] And six days later Boko Haram gunmen abducted a German engineer from close to his home in Kano.[50]

The following month began in the same bloody fashion that the old one had finished. On 7 February 2012 a Boko Haram suicide bomber, dressed in military uniform, blew himself up outside the army barracks in Kaduna, Kaduna State. At least five people died in the attack.[51] Less than a week later, on 13 February 2012, armed men thought to belong to the MEND attacked a cargo ship sailing around 125 miles south of Lagos. The vessel's captain and chief engineer were shot and killed in the assault.[52] Then, on 16 February 2012, Boko Haram fighters bombed their way into the federal prison at Koto-Karifi in Kogi State and freed 118 inmates. One guard was killed in the attack.[53] Finally, on 26 February 2012, the group bombed a church in Jos killing three people and injuring a further 40.[54]

Since then the frequency of attacks has decreased slightly. But they have not ended altogether. Indeed, there were further deaths on 8 March 2012 when British Special Forces stormed a compound in the city of Sokoto, Sokoto State, to free the British and Italian hostages being held there by members of a new insurgent group called Al Qaeda in the Islamic Lands beyond the Sahel. Both captives and several of the kidnappers died in the raid. Then, on 11 March 2012, a Boko Haram suicide bomber attacked St Finbar's Catholic Church in Jos killing himself and at least three other people.[55] And, on 29 April 2012, Boko Haram bombed a lecture theatre at the University of Bayero in Kano where Christian students were holding a service. At least 16 people died in the attack, killed either by the blast or by the waiting gunmen who opened fire on the victims as they tried to flee.[56]

38 *Nigeria Since Independence*

Thousands of people have died since Boko Haram took up arms again in the summer of 2009. It has killed indiscriminately; men, women and children, security forces personnel and civilians alike. There are few parts of the country which have not been touched by the violence. Indeed, so wide is its area of operation that when it is added to those of the MEND and the other insurgent factions there is nowhere that is safe from attack. This reality alone highlights the level of insecurity that many Nigerians must live with. That the police, armed forces and intelligence services cannot protect them shows just how much pressure the Federal Government is under and the extent of Nigeria's failure.

Failure to provide healthcare and education

The Federal Government is not only failing in its duty to protect many ordinary Nigerians. It is also failing to provide them with adequate health care. Of course, this accusation is not unusual and is frequently levelled against service providers the world over. Yet it is the degree of shortfall between what those in Nigeria offer and what is actually needed which makes this criticism both legitimate and so concerning. Indeed, the latest data on the state of the Nigerian nation's health and education is extremely worrying. First and foremost, the average life expectancy of its members currently stands at just 48.3 years for women and 47.3 years for men,[57] only slightly higher than what it was in 1970 after three years of brutal civil war.[58] This average continues to be dragged down by the high rates of infant and maternal mortality. Out of every 1,000 children born in the country, 186 will not live to see their fifth birthday, and out of every 100,000 expectant mothers, 1,100 will die giving birth.[59]

More broadly, tens of millions of Nigerians continue to endure general ill health brought on by a lack of access to clean drinking water, adequate medical care and food that is sufficiently nutritious. Indeed, less than one-in-two (45 per cent) have access to drinking water that is safe,[60] while one-in-three (34 per cent) cannot attain sufficient calories each day even if they spend all their income on food alone.[61] There are just four doctors for every 10,000 people,[62] most of whom are clustered in the major towns and cities far removed from the rural population. Indeed, in the remoter districts of the Niger Delta and the far north, health care provision is virtually non-existent.

The federal, state and local authorities are also failing to maintain Nigeria's education system. As of 2009, only 60.8 per cent of the adult population was literate placing the country squarely in the low human development bracket.[63] Its position is hardly surprising given how few Nigerians go to school, and the quality of the education they receive while there. As of 2007, only 62.1 per cent of children who were eligible to attend primary school and 25.8 per cent of those who could go to secondary school did so. Of those who attended primary school a full fifth (20.1 per cent) dropped out early. They joined the 37.1 per cent, or 8,653,439 children, who never went.[64]

If the federal, state and local authorities are only partially to blame for this low attendance record, then they are entirely responsible for the poor quality of the teachers. Only 36 per cent of those teaching at primary level and 33.1 per cent of those teaching at secondary level were properly trained.[65]

The dangers of disintegration

The Federal Government's failure to take adequate care of its citizens is leading some of them to ask whether there is any point to Nigeria. Certainly it offers them little hope or pride or opportunity. Indeed, it is all but absent from their everyday lives. And when it can be found, it is often an unhelpful or even malignant presence, threatening and intimidating rather than encouraging and uplifting. Being Nigerian brings with it few benefits. Being Nigerian does not make one the envy of the world.

Nigerians' loyalty to their country is not unconditional. As for everyone else, it needs to be won and maintained, and is the outcome of a transaction. Most Nigerians have little say on their nationality, on whether they wish to be a Nigerian or not. Yet being Nigerian does not automatically stimulate loyalty to Nigeria. Nigerians still get to 'choose their allegiances' just 'not under circumstances of their own choice.'[66] To make itself a focus of their loyalty, Nigeria must provide its people with rights, goods and services of political, economic or symbolic value.[67] Its prolonged failure to do so is leading some to ask whether their interests might be better served elsewhere, by forsaking Nigeria for some other state.

It is this impulse which drives tens of thousands of Nigerians to seek new lives abroad each year.[68] Yet some, because they lack either

40 *Nigeria Since Independence*

the means or the desire to leave, dream of becoming citizens of new states carved out of Nigeria's current territory. Such aspirations take a range of forms. Some are amorphous and organisationally incoherent. They are shared by individuals and groups who have no clear leadership or goals, and pursue whatever objectives they do have erratically and with little coordination. This is certainly true of northern secessionism at present. It is virtually indistinguishable from Hausa-Fulani nationalism and, like all nationalisms, is built on a veneration of the past. At its heart is a glorification of the Sokoto Caliphate during its pomp and prime in the late nineteenth century. Its victories on the battlefield and traditional power structures remain a great source of pride to many northerners leading some to harbour hopes of its return.

Other separatist aspirations take more coherent forms usually because they are stimulated and led by specific organisations. One of the most significant secessionist group in Nigeria today, aside from the MEND, is the Movement for the Actualisation of the Sovereign State of Biafra. It was established by Ralph Uwazurike on 22 May 2000 and fits squarely within the post-independence tradition of Igbo agitation. Indeed, as its name suggests, it is keen to claim political and intellectual descent from earlier groups and movements. Its main goal, like that of its forebears and expressed in the so-called Aba Declaration which marked the group's creation, is to establish the 'necessary structures that may sustain the sovereignty of the new Biafra State.'

Yet, unlike its predecessors, it forswears violence and is instead committed to winning a negotiated settlement. It wants to achieve by peaceful means what General Chukwuemeka Odumegwu Ojukwu failed to accomplish by violent ones. To that end, the Aba Declaration asserts that 'no single life is expected to be lost in the realization of our new Biafra State.' But it also makes clear that the process of creating this state 'admits ... [both] negotiations, dialogue and consultation ... and ... non-co-operation and passive resistance.' While the MASSOB might eschew taking up arms, it is quite prepared to confront the Federal Government in order to assert what it calls 'Biafrans ... fundamental right ... to choose ... [their] nationality.'[69]

At an electoral level the MASSOB appears to pose little threat to Nigeria. It is not registered as a political party and none of the country's main parties share or support its objectives. But it does command the support of a significant number of Igbo. This much was demonstrated by the community's general observation of the one-day strike it called on 26 August 2004. Its growing importance and influence can be measured, in part, by the reaction of the federal authorities. For over the past few years they have steadily cracked down on the group and its members. This persecution has been sufficiently serious to prick the concern of international human rights observers.[70]

Conclusions

Early in the afternoon of 8 March 2012 news broke that an attempt to rescue two European hostages being held captive by Islamist terrorists had ended in failure. The Briton and the Italian had been snatched ten months earlier by fighters belonging to the hitherto unknown group, Al Qaeda in the Islamic Lands beyond the Sahel.[71] Their precise location had remained a mystery until it was revealed by a member of the group after he was apprehended by Nigerian soldiers. A few hours later, marines of the UK's Special Boat Service and Nigerian troops stormed the compound on the outskirts of the city of Sokoto where they were being held. But they were shot and killed before their rescuers could reach them.[72]

The high level of international interest generated by this failed rescue attempt can be attributed to three main factors. The first was the nationality of the captives. Abductions are common in Nigeria especially in the Niger Delta as the MEND and other insurgent factions see them as an important means of both making money and raising their respective profiles. But most of the victims are Nigerian and, therefore, considered scarcely newsworthy by the international media. Only those cases involving someone of particular importance or foreign oil workers receive any attention. The kidnappers knew this; that was why they snatched a Briton and an Italian.

The second factor was the direct involvement of British Special Forces. For a start, their deployment was unprecedented. Never before had they, or any British military units for that matter, been sent to Nigeria to rescue an abducted UK national even though several had been snatched over the previous few years and some held captive for prolonged periods of time.[73] Their involvement on this occasion immediately marked the episode out as extraordinary. This was in addition to the dangerous glamour usually associated with their

42 *Nigeria Since Independence*

missions. Indeed, the deployment of this elite unit on such a daring, and initially covert, operation was sure to excite international attention as soon as it became known.

Then there were the questions which the Special Boat Service's involvement inevitably invited. Why was it there? Why was the rescue bid not led by the Nigerians? Why had it intervened when it did? What did the British, Italian and Nigerian governments think was about to happen? Who was this group and what did it want? What links did it have to Al Qaeda? What was its relationship to Boko Haram? How had its members evaded capture for so long? How many more of them were there? Did it have much popular support? Was it planning any further attacks? What dangers did it pose to Nigeria? Was it a serious threat to the rest of the world? And what could be done to help the Federal Government and its security forces?

The third factor, therefore, was the alarm and uncertainty the abduction and rescue attempt both gave rise to. For they only added to the international community's growing sense of unease over Nigeria's stability and long-term future. First, the emergence of yet another insurgent group could not be interpreted as anything but an ill omen. Second, the links it claimed to Al Qaeda merely confirmed fears that Nigeria was being drawn inexorably into the global war on terror. Third, the group's willingness to hold its captives for so long and finally to execute them highlighted its resolve. Fourth, the involvement of the Special Boat Service gave some indication of just how seriously London took this threat. And fifth, the deployment of British Special Forces raised fresh concerns over the ability of Nigeria's own security forces to meet the multiple challenges confronting them.

Indeed, this entire episode seemed only to confirm the international community's fears that Nigeria was both a failed state and close to breaking up. Its failure is bound to the existence and activities of the various insurgent groups currently operating within its borders. Both individually and collectively, these factions, of which Boko Haram and the MEND are the largest and most important, are preventing the Federal Government from exercising total, continuous control over the whole of the country's territory. Such is their grip on parts of the north-west and Niger Delta that they – not the federal, state or local governments – exercise all meaningful authority.

These groups are also eroding the Federal Government's ability to take adequate care of all its citizens. More specifically, by waging their armed campaigns they are undermining the security of tens of thousands of Nigerians right across the country. Security is the most important public good a government can provide its constituents with. If it does not do so then it is failing to promote their flourishing. But these groups are, in addition, leading the police and armed forces to abuse the civil and human rights of many ordinary people. In so doing, they are not only further undermining the security of the Nigerian public but are also leading some members of it into the arms of the insurgents. The Federal Government's failure to control is exacerbating its failure to promote human flourishing which is exacerbating its failure to control.

Abuja is failing to look after its citizens in other ways too. Most notably, it does not provide enough of them with basic health care or primary education. Today, Nigeria has some of the highest rates of infant and maternal mortality anywhere in the world, and even those citizens who make it past their fifth birthdays or who survive childbirth are unlikely to live much beyond the age of 45. Diseases like malaria, cholera, tuberculosis and typhoid continue to kill tens of thousands of people every year. While millions more die prematurely of manageable illnesses because they do not get the help and treatment they need.

The anger and frustration this neglect gives rise to is helping to sustain the secessionist campaigns mounted by groups like the MEND and the MASSOB. For the longer the Nigerian state fails to take care of its citizens the more some of them look to these organisations to deliver the rights and improvements in living standards they so desire. Perhaps inevitably, support for secession is strongest among those who feel the most neglected, within those sections of society who believe they suffer the worst discrimination because of their race or ethnicity or religion. To them, secession offers the best, if not only, hope of fairer treatment. Only by becoming citizens of new, less prejudiced states will they cease to be so ill-used and granted the opportunities they deserve.

3
The Emperor's New Clothes? Federalism, the Decline of Old Loyalties and the Rise of New Jealousies

Federalism is contributing to Nigeria's failure in four main ways. First, it is fuelling the ethnic tensions and religious hatreds that are undermining the quality of life of tens of thousands of Nigerians. The cities of Kano, Kaduna, Maiduguri and Jos are regularly plunged into sectarian violence resulting in considerable loss of life and damage to property. At least some of this death and destruction is caused by the federal and state authorities who permit and instruct the police and army to respond with extreme force. The widespread anger and resentment this causes continue to drive some Nigerians into the arms of insurgent groups and others to support secession. By fuelling these tensions the Federal Government is not only failing to promote the flourishing of all its citizens, but it is also assisting groups and organisations which are either preventing it from exercising total control over its territory or seeking to break Nigeria up.

Second, federalism has disempowered and disadvantaged tens of thousands of Nigerians right across the country. One of the central laws of the federalism process dictates that certain public goods are only available to those people living in their state of origin. This is not necessarily the state in which they live or were even born, but that to which they formally belong. A significant portion of the millions of Nigerians who have moved from one part of the country to another, either to find work or to flee violence, are denied access

The Emperor's New Clothes? 45

to certain services and opportunities. By permitting this, federalism is not only compromising the standards of living and life opportunities of many Nigerians, it is also encouraging sectarianism and undermining the country's unity.

Third, federalism is damaging Nigerians' political rights and, in particular, their freedom to choose their president. For federalism sustains the practice of rotating senior positions in the government, federal bureaucracy, armed forces, and other national institutions and agencies between the main ethnic groups. Not only does ethnicity hold the key to high office, but democracy is subverted as only those individuals from the right ethnic group are allowed to assume certain posts.

And fourth, federalism has greatly increased the cost of government and created many new opportunities for corruption and graft. Over the past half century, the number of states has grown exponentially. In 1960 the country was divided into three regions and a capital territory. Today it is split into 36 states and the Federal Capital Territory. Every state is endowed with its own governor, deputy governor, state house, bureaucracy and judiciary. Each of these offices commands its own budget. So with every new state that is established, the federal authorities must find additional money to finance the range of institutions and organs that are created along with it. And each new organ provides an opportunity for corruption, another chance for those who staff it to access and misappropriate state funds.

Despite its contributions to Nigeria's failure, federalism is helping to keep the country together in three important ways. First, it is weakening the ethnic and regional loyalties which have long threatened the country's unity. By endowing new states, federalism has broken up the old regions which were critical points of focus for much of the separatist agitation of the past. In their place, it has created an ever-increasing number of new political units which, by virtue of their existence and the resources allocated to them, demand the attention and invite the loyalty of those who live within them. State creation has had the additional benefit of giving the members of the many smaller ethnic groups' greater visibility, voice and stake in Nigeria.

Second, federalism is strengthening the country's unity by building and promoting a sense of nationhood. Federalism was initially adopted by the central government in order to counteract the chronic political instability which gripped the country in the

46 *Nigeria Since Independence*

years immediately following independence. In particular, it set about replacing the institutions and practices of government left by the British with new ones which nullified sectarianism and promoted harmony. Its architects, of course, drew inspiration from elsewhere. But they adapted and developed what they saw to Nigeria's circumstances to create a system of government that was resolutely Nigerian. Indeed, these new institutions and practices were Nigerian in both purpose and design and as such helped make real in word and deed the Nigerian nation.

Third, federalism is helping to banish sectarianism from political life in two important ways. First, under the rules which were established as a part of it, presidential candidates must win a minimum number of votes in a majority of states in order to get elected. It is not enough for them to win an overall majority based on the overwhelming support of a minority of states, or one or two ethnic groups. They must command strong support throughout the country, and from a range of communities. Second, political parties cannot represent any one ethnic group or religious community. They have to be open to all and maintain offices and field candidates in a certain number of states or enter into coalition with other parties to win national office.

The first section of this chapter provides an overview of the political and social circumstances in which federalism was adopted, and which continue to determine what it seeks to achieve and why. The second section then sets out what federalism is. The third section then looks at how federalism is contributing to Nigeria's failure. The section identifies and examines the main ways in which it has undermined the Federal Government's provision of public goods and ability to control Nigeria's territory, and the country's unity by encouraging sectarianism and eroding public faith in Nigeria. And finally the fourth section examines the ways in which federalism has improved the Federal Government's provision of social services and exercise of authority, and helped bind the country more tightly together.

The post-independence background to federalism

To understand fully what federalism is, it is first necessary to consider why it was introduced. For federalism remains a product of the

The Emperor's New Clothes? 47

circumstances which led Nigeria's leaders to adopt it. Indeed it was adopted as a late, if not last, resort to the profound social and political upheaval which was threatening to overwhelm the entire country. From the very beginning, therefore, it had two distinct dimensions. The first was as a process, as a means of pursing a political settlement. The second was as an end, as a form of political settlement. These dimensions are of course complementary. Federalism the settlement can only be achieved by engaging in federalism the process.

A significant cause of this upheaval was the structures of government put in place by the colonial authorities shortly before Nigeria gained its independence. The country was divided into three regions – the north, the west and the east – which each broadly corresponded with one of the main ethnic groups – the Hausa/Fulani, the Yoruba and the Igbo respectively. Each region was largely self-governing with its own constitution, government, legislature, civil service and judiciary.[1] Relations between them, along with those parts of public policy which were deemed to be of national importance, such as defence, were managed from the centre by the federal government and the Nigerian parliament.

By allowing each major ethnic group to manage its own affairs, the architects of the post-independence political settlement had hoped to minimise the frictions between them. The Hausa and Fulani in the north, Yoruba in the west and Igbo in the east were to be governed, for the most part, by their own kind, by individuals who shared the same values, prayed to the same gods, ate the same food and spoke the same language as a majority of their constituents. Nigeria was to achieve unity by catering for diversity, to be a nation of different yet equal communities. No one ethnic group would dominate so that all could have a stake in the country and its future.

This ambition, however, was fundamentally compromised from the outset. For a start, the settlement all but ignored the smaller ethnic groups whose combined members numbered many millions. Not everyone who lived in the east was an Igbo. Not every citizen of western Nigeria wanted to be represented by Yoruba politicians. Even more damaging was the constitution's unequal distribution of the country's population between the three regions. With slightly over half of all Nigerians living within its borders, the north received the greatest share of the national revenue and elected more representatives to the federal parliament than both the west and east

48 Nigeria Since Independence

combined. This gave rise to widespread fears in both regions that the north would use its advantage to force through federal legislation which would harm their interests and lead to the inexorable spread of northern values, attitudes and culture across the rest of the country.[2]

This intense competition was played out, among other ways, through party politics. Four of the largest parties, until they were finally ousted from power by the military in January 1966, were the Northern People's Congress (NPC), the Northern Elements Progressive Union (NEPU), the National Council of Nigerian Citizens (NCNC), formerly the National Council of Nigeria and the Cameroons, and the Action Group (AG).[3] The NPC and the NEPU were the two largest parties in the north and were led by Ahmadu Bello and Tafawa Balewa, and Amino Kano respectively. The NCNC was the dominant party in the east and was headed by Nnamdi Azikiwe. And the AG was the biggest party in the west and was led by Obafemi Awolowo.

Each party relied heavily on the support it received from the voters of one particular region for its electoral success and broader political influence. None had truly national appeal. None could claim to represent the interests of all Nigerians. And none could dare to do so for fear of alienating the voters of the region on whom they so depended. In the 1959 parliamentary election the AG won 33 (or slightly under half) of its 73 seats in the west while the NPC won all of its 134 seats in the north. The closest Nigeria got to a cross-regional party was the NCNC/NEPU alliance which won 83 seats. Yet even then, the appeal of each member party barely reached beyond its core region. The eight seats the alliance won in the north were all taken by the NEPU while the 58 it gained in the east were won by the NCNC.[4]

The size of the NCNC's haul was crucial as it not only confirmed the party's position as the alliance's dominant partner but also emphasised how much weaker the NEPU was than the NPC. And just as important was the combined success of all four parties as together they won 296 of the 312 seats available in the federal parliament. The outcome of the 1959 election along with the stipulations of the 1960 constitution established a pattern of party politics which reinforced, rather than eroded, the ethnic divisions and regional divides in Nigeria. Each of the three major communities, separated into their respective strongholds, now had its own political party. Far from

The Emperor's New Clothes? 49

rendering issues of race and ethnicity irrelevant, the 1960 constitution helped perpetuate their urgency.

Little wonder then that the 1962 census assumed such importance and became a major cause of social instability and political violence. For, in identifying the size of each region's population, it directly affected the number of seats they were awarded in the federal parliament, the amount of revenue they received from central government and, because of the intimate relationship they each enjoyed with a particular party, the number of parliamentarians the NPC, the NEPU, the NCNC and the AG were likely to win. The importance of the census accounts for the extensive fraud that was perpetrated by each region. Since the last count in 1952, the north's leaders claimed that the region's population had grown by 30 per cent, the west's by 70 per cent and the east's by 71 per cent.[5] The sheer implausibility of these figures and shrill accusations of dishonesty levelled by each region's leader at one another prompted Prime Minister Balewa to dismiss the results and order a recount. But the 1963 census proved to be no more accurate or reliable. This time the east's population was reported to have grown by 65 per cent, the north's by 67 per cent and the west's by a staggering 100 per cent.[6]

Yet between the 1962 and 1963 counts, Nigeria's political plates had moved just enough to persuade Prime Minister Balewa that a further re-run of the exercise was unnecessary. With the backing of the western faction of the NCNC, he accepted the outcome. And, in so doing, confirmed the north's numerical and political supremacy. Of Nigeria's 55.6 million inhabitants, 30 million were alleged to live in the north.[7] Yet, he also confirmed the south's worst fears; that it was losing the struggle for power, influence and resources. So the violence and instability which had been plaguing the country since independence continued as political leaders in the west and, in particular, the east called on their followers to take to the streets to voice their anger and frustration. Between 1960 and 1963 Nigeria was gripped by a succession of bloody riots as the populations of each region fell on the inhabitants from others living in their midst with murderous intent thereby triggering reprisals elsewhere in the country.

Paradoxically though, the outcome of the 1963 census, which was widely interpreted as a victory for the north, helped to resolve the dilemma that had been plaguing the leaders of the NCNC and AG

50 *Nigeria Since Independence*

since independence as to how they could best compete with the NPC in the forthcoming 1964 election. The AG in particular had struggled to decide whether to ally itself with the NPC or with some other party.[8] Its predicament had been complicated further by the various lawsuits filed against its leaders and, more importantly, the creation of the mid-western region on 9 August 1963. For this new province was carved from the territory of western Nigeria which had been the party's main stronghold in the 1959 election.

The Federal Government's endorsement of the 1963 census result brought an immediate end to Azikiwe's and Awolowo's shared hope that the number of seats allocated to the north in parliament might be significantly reduced. The only option now left open to them for containing northern power was to defeat the NPC in the 1964 election. Yet, to do this, the NCNC and AG would have to work together as neither of them could hope to win enough seats in parliament to take on the NPC by itself. In late 1963, therefore, the two parties joined forces with the NEPU, the United Middle Belt Congress (UMBC), the Northern Progressive Front (NPF), the Kano People's Party (KPP), and the Zamfara Commoners Party (ZCP) to form the United Progressive Grand Alliance (UPGA).

To maximise the alliance's chances of victory, its various members agreed not to field candidates in the same constituencies as each other but rather to help and support whichever one among them was most likely to win in any given borough. In this way, they strove to avoid wasting their time and energy fighting among themselves to be better able to concentrate their fire on the NPC. By extension, they also hoped that the northern members of the alliance – the NEPU, the NPF, the KPP and the ZCP – might be better placed to compete with the NCP in its northern heartland than the outsider parties of the NCNC and AG. In the very least, the alliance hoped that these groups might be able split the vote in the region and weaken the NCP's stranglehold on it.

To prevent this from happening and in turn strike a blow against the NCNC's and AG's electoral campaigns, the NPC created its own coalition; the Nigerian National Alliance (NNA). Its members were drawn from the four southern regions in which the NPC was largely anonymous as a political force, including the Nigerian National Democratic Party (NNDP), the Mid-West Democratic Front (MDF), the Dynamic Party (DP), the Niger Delta Congress (NDC), the Lagos

The Emperor's New Clothes? 51

State United Front (LSUF) and the Republic Party (RP). Like their rivals in the UPGA, the NNA's members agreed not to challenge one another in their respective strongholds but to concentrate their efforts on trying to take votes and seats from parties outside of the alliance, which they did with notable success.

In the end, it was the NNA which won picking up 198 seats to the UPGA's 109.[9] Unsurprisingly, most of these were taken by the NPC which, in increasing its tally, strengthened its grip on parliament.[10] The defeat was a major blow to both the UPGA and the south. Yet their shared hope of containing northern power and influence was not wholly at an end. One opportunity still remained in the western regional election of November 1965. The UPGA hoped that a good victory in it would force the NNA, and in particular the NPC, to pay greater consideration to the south's concerns and agendas. The NNA similarly recognised the importance of the opportunity. For victory in it would turn the NNA's strong political position into a dominant one. Both 'literally as well as metaphorically' this was 'to be an election to end all elections.'[11]

Given the importance of what rested on the election's outcome, neither side was prepared to leave it to chance. The fraud and corruption which had so marked the 1964 election were even more widespread as the leaders of both coalitions spent fortunes bribing public officials, community leaders, indeed, anyone who might be able to help them to achieve victory. When the NNA eventually did win, the result was immediately decried by the UPGA. Yet it was scarcely in any position to claim the moral high ground. The disgraceful behaviour of the country's civilian politicians helped drive the First Republic's reputation to a new low. With little considered worth saving and the north's political primacy now confirmed, a group of mid-ranking Igbo army officers launched a *coup d'état* on 15 January 1966.

The coup was bloody, badly organised and poorly executed. The conspirators' attempt to decapitate the state by liquidating its most senior politicians only partially succeeded. The prime minister, leaders of the northern and western regions, many members of their respective governments, and several high-ranking military officers were all assassinated. But the president and premiers of the east and mid-west were all spared. In light of the deaths and the chaos, the remainder of the Federal Government handed power to the army's most senior officer General Johnson Aguiyi-Ironsi.

52 *Nigeria Since Independence*

Initially the coup received widespread backing. Most ordinary Nigerians, it seemed, were similarly disillusioned with the First Republic and its leaders. But, very quickly, this support turned into suspicion in many areas as the coup took on a decidedly Igbo hue. The core group of army officers who had launched it had all been Igbo. Many of the politicians who had been spared were Igbo. And the man to whom power was given was also Igbo. So just six months later, on 29 July 1966, a second *coup d'état* was launched, this time by a group of northern army officers. General Aguiyi-Ironsi was killed and replaced by the army's most senior northerner, General Yakubu Gowon.

Yet the military governor of the eastern region, Colonel Odumegwu Ojukwu, refused to accept General Gowon's accession to power. To calm the situation, General Gowon called an *ad hoc* constitutional conference in September 1966 to come up with a political framework that was acceptable to all parties and would prevent the country from breaking apart. The conference was attended by delegates from each region, including the east, constitutional experts and lawyers. By the time it broke up in early October 1966, it had made some important progress. The protracted argument over whether the country should be a federation or a confederacy was settled in favour of the former. And all the delegates agreed that it should remain intact.

Away from the conference hall, however, events in the country only strengthened the eastern government's intransigence. The disappearance of General Aguiyi-Ironsi remained a major point of contention.[12] Yet more serious were the pogroms being carried out against Igbos in the north. Between May and September 1966 between 80,000 and 100,000 easterners were killed and many more thousands injured in attacks carried out all over the north.[13] In late September, Colonel Ojukwu urged Igbos living in the north, west, mid-west and Lagos to return to the eastern region. A final attempt to resolve the situation peacefully was made in January 1967 when the ruling Supreme Military Council met in Aburi in Ghana to thrash out a solution.

But, in March 1967 Colonel Ojukwu announced that, from 1 April, his government would take over all federal departments, institutions and services in the east. General Gowon's government responded by declaring the move illegal and unconstitutional. On 27 May 1967, the government of the eastern region declared its independence as the Republic of Biafra. Fighting between federal and Biafran forces

The Emperor's New Clothes? 53

broke out six weeks later on 6 July 1967. These clashes marked the start of the Nigerian civil war.

The function of federalism

Federalism was introduced in response to the growing unrest and spiralling violence. And official commitment to it only increased the more unstable Nigeria became. Federalism's early influence on Nigerian politics can be seen in the 1963 constitution and its establishment of the presidency. The creation of the office of the president was the first vital step along the path towards recasting the federal government's relationship with the regional authorities, and the Nigerian public's role within the political process. It was a bold and ambitious measure that delivered a break with the past while making a firm nod to the future. Never before had Nigeria been a republic and parts of the country, most notably Lagos,[14] had been subject to the British crown for over a century.

Yet the 1963 constitution's greatest accomplishment was also its most dangerous blunder. The mistake did not lie in the idea of a presidential system. Indeed, the reasons for its creation were sound, just as the examples of such systems working fairly and effectively elsewhere in the world were plentiful. Rather, the fault lay in its execution, in the type of presidency created by the 1963 constitution. Paradoxically the new office was simultaneously endowed with too many powers and too few. It was accorded sufficient rights and authority to confirm its importance but not so many as to enable whoever occupied it to really stamp their mark on political life in the country.

For even though the powers conferred on the president were not nearly as great as they were to become under later constitutions, they were sufficient to arouse the jealousy and chauvinism of the members of the various communities. Especially since whoever held the office was considered to be the first citizen, the epitome of Nigeria and its people. The Hausa/Fulani and Igbo, northern Muslims and southern Christians were anxious that this paragon of the nation be one of their own. They did not want to be represented either at home or abroad by someone they considered a cultural and religious rival.

Yet, at the same time, these authorities were not so great as to enable the president to achieve and maintain true ascendency over the

54 *Nigeria Since Independence*

regional leaders and political institutions. As well as being contested, the president's supremacy over the armed forces was nominal and unproven. Indeed, as events of the next few years demonstrated, civilian heads of state were commander-in-chief in name alone. True power over the military remained concentrated in the hands of its officer corps. Just as true power over vast swathes of the country and those who lived there was exercised by local *Ogas* who owed their positions to either the traditional titles of authority they held or the elected offices they had won, by fair means or foul, in the new state.

Yet Nigeria's descent into civil war did not sound the death knell for federalism. On the contrary, General Gowon was, from the very start of his time as the country's head of state, convinced that there had been too little federalism rather than too much. His response, even as Nigeria hurtled towards war and possible disintegration, was to pursue a far more ambitious programme of federalism than any of his predecessors had. Timidity, of course, was not really an option for him as Nigeria's fate hung in the balance. In fact, the onset of civil war and the urgent political imperatives it presented imbued federalism with the impetus that has sustained its centrality to the Nigerian state and nation building processes until the present day.

Federalism sets out to organise the state and regulate political life in order to achieve balance and promote compromise, to establish a fair and mutually profitable equilibrium between different sections of society, the sub-national political units into which the country is divided, and these units and the central government so as to build popular faith in the state, create a common belief among the individuals and communities who live within it that they will all have the same rights and access to whatever political, economic and social opportunities are on offer. Through the institutional and political mechanisms it puts in place, federalism looks to eliminate the worst manifestations of sectarian jealousy and hostility, and to peacefully manage any mistrust which might remain.[15]

'Not a nation': federalism and the preservation of difference

Nigeria is a failed state in two main ways. First, the writ of the Federal Government does not run the length and breadth of the country. There are areas in both the Niger Delta and in and around the north-eastern city of Maiduguri which lie beyond its direct and continuous control. Second, the federal, state and local authorities do not provide their citizens with all of the basic public goods and social services that they should. The anger and frustration this gives rise to is helping to sustain the insurgencies in the north and south which are undermining the Federal Government's authority. Abuja's failure to promote human flourishing is causing its failure to control its sovereign territory.

Federalism is contributing to both parts of Nigeria's failure in four main ways. First, it is fuelling the ethnic tensions which are undermining the safety and security, and standards of living of tens of thousands of people in towns and cities right across the northern and central parts of the country. Second, it permits and, indeed, requires the denial of a range of basic services to thousands more and is undermining national unity. Third, it is weakening democracy by insisting on the rotation of power between the country's main ethnic groups. Fourth, it has created numerous more opportunities for corruption which erodes the effectiveness of the state and reduces the number and degrades the quality of the public services it provides.

A spur to ethnic tensions

Federalism is fuelling the ethnic tensions which are undermining the quality of life of many thousands of Nigerians, driving some to join the insurgencies. Federalism has been embraced by successive governments for two main reasons. First, to counteract the sectarian rivalries and prejudices which have long threatened Nigeria's continued existence. Second, to strengthen the country's unity by fortifying Nigerians' sense of nationhood. A vital part of federalism's approach to achieving these objectives has been the process of state creation. By establishing new states, Nigeria's political leaders aimed to break up ethnic enclaves and force the country's various communities to interact with each other more.

> State creation is a multifaceted process and requires 'a request, supported by at least a two-thirds majority of members (representing the area demanding the creation of the new State) in ... the Senate and the Housse of Representatives, the House of Assembly

56 *Nigeria Since Independence*

in...the area, and the local government councils in...the area, is received by the National Assembly; a proposal for the creation of the State is thereafter approved in a referendum by at least two-thirds...of the people of the area...; the result of the referendum is...approved by a simple majority of all the States of the Federation supported by a simple majority of members of the Houses of Assembly; and the proposal is approved by a resolution passed by two-thirds majority of members of each House of the National Assembly.'[16]

Yet some of the states which federalism has encouraged the creation of can be volatile and dangerous places. For the interaction it has forced between the communities who live there has not always led to greater understanding or harmony. On the contrary, it has often resulted in bouts of devastating violence and sickening bloodletting. Plateau State, in particular, has suffered greatly. Sitting astride the country's main religious fault line separating the mainly Muslim north from the predominantly Christian south, it has endured numerous sectarian clashes which have left its principal city, Jos, and some of the towns and villages surrounding it looking like battlefields. The distrust and antipathy that have long existed between these communities have been given an extra deadly twist as they compete for access to the same state-provided resources and opportunities.

In these instances, federalism's desire to engender greater understanding and cooperation between communities by making them constituents of the same state seems dangerously utopian. For the loss of life, destruction of homes, damage to commercial properties and fall in trade that seem inevitably to follow are undermining the quality of life and standards of living those who reside there.

Damage to national unity

Federalism is being used to discriminate against thousands of Nigerians and deny them access to certain public goods. State governments all over the country are exploiting the definition of indigene set out in successive constitutions to channel jobs and opportunities to some groups and away from others. Articles 277, 329 and 318 of the 1979, 1989 and 1999 constitutions respectively, all declare that '"belong to" or its grammatical expression when used with reference to a person in a State refers to a person either of whose parents or any of whose grandparents was a member of a community indigenous to that State.'[17] State membership is determined not by where someone lives or even where they were born, but where their parents and grandparents came from.

Over the past three decades, some state governments have used this definition to deny non-indigenes access to certain education, health and housing schemes, and employment opportunities.[18] Such discrimination has undermined the standards of living and life opportunities of thousands of Nigerian citizens. Moreover, it directly violates the 1999 constitution's requirement that the state 'provide adequate facilities for and encourage free mobility of people, goods and services throughout the Federation; secure full residence rights for every citizen in all parts of the Federation; encourage inter-marriage among persons from different places of origin, or of different religious, ethnic or linguistic association or ties; and promote or encourage the formation of associations that cut across ethnic, linguistic, religious and or other sectional barriers.'[19]

On the one hand, federalism is encouraging Nigerians to move around the country and to have as much contact and interaction with compatriots of different ethnic backgrounds as possible. It is also urging the federal and state authorities to do what they can to help those who do and facilitate their integration into the local communities. On the other, it still permits the preferential treatment of indigenes and defines who they are in such a way as to discourage intra-Nigeria migration. The existence of this loophole raises questions as to the commitment of the country's political leaders to combatting sectarianism. Especially since, it has been included in each of the last three constitutions.

Yet the damage this definition inflicts on both the cause of Nigerian unity and the sense of nationhood federalism is trying to promote, is more serious than that. For by placing such emphasis on where everyone's parents and grandparents come from, it privileges the past over the present and the future. Regardless of what anyone does or where they choose to live in Nigeria, they will always be defined by the ethnic group to which their forebears belonged and where they came from. There is little scope in this understanding of identity to build a sense of Nigerian-ness let alone engender loyalty to it above all sectarian allegiances. For every Nigerian's identity is already set by their parents. And central to that identity is locale and ethnic group, not nation.

58 *Nigeria Since Independence*

Damage to political rights

Federalism is also compromising Nigerians' political rights. Since the restoration of civilian rule in May 1999, it has been the agreed practice of senior politicians and other public figures to rotate the country's top jobs between the main ethnic groups. Hausa will follow Yoruba who will follow Fulani who will follow Igbo. Today, the main distinction is not drawn between ethnic groups but regions, between the north and the south, between northerners and southerners.[20] It was partly in accordance with this practice that President Olusegun Obasanjo's efforts to extend his time in office by a third term failed.[21] For it was felt by many that it was now another ethnic group's turn to occupy Aso Rock.[22] And it was wholly in accordance with this practice that Obasanjo, a southerner, was succeeded by Umaru Yar'Adua, a northerner.

In truth, this practice has been pursued on and off since the earliest years of independence. Indeed, when Obasanjo stood down as head of state after his first spell in office in the late 1970s, he handed the reins of power to Shehu Shagari, an aristocratic Fulani from Sokoto.[23] But since the recent restoration of civilian rule it has been followed more rigorously, mainly because power is ceded rather seized as it was under the military. And a great deal of importance is attached to maintaining the cycle by both public figures and ordinary Nigerians. This much was made clear by the uncertainty that greeted news of President Yar'Adua's death on 5 May 2010, and the anger that followed in the north when he was replaced by Goodluck Jonathan. For Yar'Adua died midway through his first term, and many northerners believed that the north should retain control of Aso Rock for both the remainder of that term and the second that would have inevitably followed had Yar'Adua lived.

Indeed, the furore over Yar'Adua's death and Jonathan's subsequent promotion exposed the profoundly undemocratic character of this practice. For Article 146 of the 1999 constitution clearly states that 'the Vice-President shall hold the office of President if the office of President becomes vacant by reason of death or resignation, impeachment, permanent incapacity or the removal of the President from office for any other reason.'[24] Legally it was absolutely right and proper that Jonathan replaced Yar'Adua. In fact, given Yar'Adua's prolonged incapacity, Jonathan should have taken over the presidency much sooner than he did. Yet such constitutional arguments carried little weight with many in the north. It was their turn and they wanted Aso Rock back.

Their unease turned to outrage when Jonathan won the People's Democratic Party's nomination to stand as its candidate in the presidential election of May 2010. With the PDP's support, Jonathan's victory was virtually assured and he was duly elected president. His triumph and impending occupation of Aso Rock for at least four years, and possibly eight, convinced many northerners that they had been cheated out of, what convention dictated, was rightfully theirs.[25] Yet nowhere in the constitution does it say that a northerner must become president after a southerner or vice versa. And nowhere does it say that every president is entitled to two terms in office.

Yet these are the norms which have been established and maintained by federalism. And they make a mockery of democracy. For it is not the country's voters who decide who will be the next president of Nigeria. It is senior public figures and party bigwigs. The electorate do not have total freedom of choice. For barring acts of god, like Yar'Adua's premature death, they will have as their next head of state whichever northerner or southerner has been chosen to take on the role. They will not get a southerner when it should be a northerner, and they will not get a northerner when it should be a southerner. The unofficial rotation cycle dictates this and denies them real choice.

There are, of course, some important benefits to this cycle. In a fractious and sectarian society like Nigeria's, mechanisms are needed to maintain the peace between the various ethnic groups and religious communities. Rotating the presidency and other senior public posts between them is one way of doing this. Yet it undermines Nigerians' democratic rights and deepens the divide between the governors and the governed. Moreover, it perpetuates the political importance of ethnicity and region. As presidents and other senior public figures are not chosen solely on the basis of their ideas, experience, personal qualities or track records, but where in the country they come from.

Corruption

Federalism is helping to fuel corruption. Nigeria's reputation as one of the most corrupt countries in the world is fully deserved. Year after year it appears near the bottom of Transparency International's

60 *Nigeria Since Independence*

Corruption Perceptions Index. The index 'ranks countries and territories according to their perceived levels of public sector corruption' from least to most corrupt.[26] In the 2011 index, Nigeria was identified as the 143rd most corrupt country out of the 182 that were included. In 2010 it was 134th out of 178, in 2009 130th out of 180, in 2008 121st out of 180, in 2007 147th out of 179, in 2006 142nd out of 163, in 2005 152nd out of 158, in 2004 144th out of 145, in 2003 132nd out of 133, in 2002 101st out of 102, and in 2001 90th out of 91.

Corruption undermines the standards of living of tens of millions of Nigerians in three main ways. First, right at the start of the funding chain, high-level politicians and officials siphon off huge sums of money to line their own pockets and maintain the clientelist networks on which they depend. From the outset, the health, education, infrastructure and other budgets are deprived of funds to the detriment of those who rely on the services they pay for. Of the money that is spent on the public's behalf much is poorly invested. Contracts are routinely awarded to companies that are owned and managed by the friends and relations of senior public figures. As a result, they are often overinflated and poorly executed. Rarely do the public get good value for money.

Second, at the other end of the funding chain, low-level officials and state employees habitually demand additional payments from those requesting their help. On occasion these demands are motivated by greed. Some doctors, nurses, police officers and petty bureaucrats exploit their positions of authority to make ordinary people pay for services which should be provided either free of charge or more cheaply. But, at other times, these state employees are forced to make these requests either because their salaries are too small to cover their cost of living, or because they have not been paid at all. The frequent misappropriation of public funds by high-level officials, therefore, not only normalises and legitimises corruption but also forces lower-level state employees to act corruptly.

Third, many ordinary Nigerians are left feeling angry and disillusioned by the failure of the federal, state and local authorities to deliver the public services that they should, and at having to bribe officials to do their jobs. Some are outraged by the government's disinterested incompetence – its almost total inability to make anything work properly. Others are infuriated by the constant demands made on their purses, at having to bribe public workers into doing what they are supposed to. And others have simply renounced all hope of receiving the services they are due, so long has it been since they were last provided if, indeed, they were ever provided at all.

Corruption is greatly impairing the state's ability to promote the flourishing of all its citizens. By engaging in it, officials at all levels are depriving the public sector of much-needed funds and eroding its ability to provide Nigerians with the services that it should. The state's failure to deliver basic health care, primary education, law and order, and impartial justice is undermining the quality of life of millions of people and downgrading their opportunities for self-betterment. Moreover, it is also contributing to the Federal Government's failure to control. For the feelings of anger and resignation it gives rise to are fuelling the insurgencies which are preventing the government from exerting its authority throughout the whole of Nigeria's sovereign territory.

In accordance with the 1999 constitution, each state is endowed with a range of public institutions, offices and positions. Every state has its own governor, deputy governor, house of assembly, speaker, deputy speaker, clerk, auditor general, civil service commission, independent electoral commission and judicial service commission. Each house of assembly must have no fewer than 24 representatives and no more than 40. Each commission has a chairperson and members. Each civil service has a staff. And each judiciary has judges and court officials. With every state that is established a whole new layer of government is conjured into being: dozens of new offices, organs and bodies employing thousands of new public sector workers.[27]

The establishment of a state represents a significant financial commitment for both the Federal Government and the state's new taxpayers. First, the federal authorities have to meet many of the start-up costs associated with creating these new offices, organs and posts. Second, they must expand federal institutions and bodies, such as the National Assembly, to accommodate the new state's senators, representatives and other functionaries. Third, they must redivide the revenue they receive from oil to ensure that the new state receives its share. Yet once the state has been created, much of the financial burden for its day-to-day running falls on its new taxpayers. They, of course, are used to maintaining a state government. But now there will be fewer of them to do so.

62 *Nigeria Since Independence*

Just as the financial burden increases with each new state that is established, so do the number of opportunities for corruption and graft. Every house of assembly and civil service, judiciary and commission, agency and organ commands its own budget and resources. Every governor and representative, civil servant and judge, chairperson and commissionaire has access to these resources. Moreover, they all occupy posts which allow them to extort money out of those seeking access to the public services they provide. Federalism, then, has extended the apparatus of a state left pre-disposed to corruption by its embrace of rentierism.

Out of many came forth one: federalism and the quest for unity

While the establishment of new states as part of the process of federalism has undoubtedly contributed to Nigeria's failure to promote the flourishing of all its citizens, it has helped preserve the country's unity. More specifically, it has diluted the sectarian tensions which so destabilised the country during the early years of independence. The political settlement left by the departing British had three major flaws. First, the broad alignment of each major ethnic group with a different region created competing ethnic enclaves. Second, the far greater size of the north was a cause of constant anguish to the Yoruba and Igbo. Third, the frailty of the federal government meant that there was no central authority capable of imposing order or forcing cooperation.

The distrust between the main ethnic groups, which the settlement encouraged, soon threatened to tear Nigeria apart. The country suffered its first *coup d'état* in January 1966, its second six months later and finally sank into civil war in July 1967. Federalism was pursued by successive governments in order to manage and reduce these tensions. One of the main ways it attempted to do so was by dismembering the old regions. This led to a fourth region being added to the original three in June 1963 and then their replacement with first 12 states (1967–1976); then 19 (1976–1987); then 21 and a Federal Capital Territory (FCT) (1987–1991); then 30 and a FCT (1991–1996); and finally 36 and a FCT (1996-present).

But, the federal authorities have not restricted their assault on the regions to solely creating an ever-increasing number of new states.

The Emperor's New Clothes? 63

Later governments have also established states, like Kogi, which cut right across the old regional boundaries. During this final phase of the destruction of the regions, Abuja has set about wiping the last few remaining traces of the regions from the political map. Destruction has turned into eradication.

Of course, the systematic demolition of the regions has not brought an end to the sectarian violence which has plagued Nigeria for so long. The country's various ethnic groups and religious communities continue to eye one another with considerable distrust and ill-concealed hostility. Over the past five years there have been numerous deadly clashes between Muslims and Christians, Hausa/Fulani and Igbo, and Hausa/Fulani and Yoruba in Bauchi, Jos, Kaduna, Kano, Maiduguri, Sokoto and Zaria. Many thousands have died in Jos alone in a series of three-way skirmishes fought between the city's Muslim and Christian inhabitants and the security forces.

While sectarianism may persist, it does so in an altered form. For federalism has changed it in two important ways. First, it no longer poses the same danger to Nigeria's unity that it once did. Unlike the Biafrans in the late 1960s, the secessionists of the MEND and the MASSOB must orchestrate their respective campaigns across numerous states and negotiate with the other ethnic groups living there. Many members of them would rather be part of Nigeria, in which they are one community among many, than join a new country that will be dominated by just one other ethnic group. Especially since the creation of ever more states has given the smaller groups greater visibility and voice. Indeed, as an Ijaw, Goodluck Jonathan provides testament to this.

Second, federalism has changed popular views of where the north, south-west and south-east begin and end. This is not, of course, due to any significant alteration to the position of the country's international borders. Nigeria has not, like Poland, moved markedly westwards, eastwards or in any other direction. Rather federalism has changed where most Nigerians now think these areas are. Today, the north is understood as the 12 states which adopted *sharia* law in the first months of the new millennium. The southern border of this area consists of the southern boundaries of Niger, Kaduna, Bauchi, Gombe and Borno States. Yet, crucially, it falls hundreds of miles to the north of the southernmost border of where the northern region used to run.

64 *Nigeria Since Independence*

By dismantling the regions, federalism eliminated the political units which had been the focus of much separatist agitation. Crucially, it has broken the link between place and ethnicity. And to the extent that concepts like the north, the south-west and the south-east still exist, they do not exactly correlate with the regions of the past. Indeed, the task of the secessionist today is much harder than what it was. Messages have to be disseminated and campaigns managed across a range of states. But federalism's contribution to Nigeria's unity has not been one just of disruption. It has done more than simply thwart the country's enemies. It has also strengthened Nigeria's nationhood.

It has done so in two main ways. First, it has put in place political structures designed to bind the country's various ethnic groups and religious communities more tightly together. These structures are designed not only to prevent sectarianism but also to promote belief in and loyalty to Nigeria. Second, the structures themselves have become part of Nigeria's national narrative. They were introduced to rescue the country from the chronic disunity of the 1960s. They replaced the system of government put in place by the colonial powers which was modelled on what existed in Britain. These structures were a Nigerian response to Nigerian problems caused, to a considerable degree, by the inappropriate system imposed by an alien and domineering power.

Finally, federalism is helping to eliminate sectarianism from politics in two important ways. First, it is forcing the country's most senior politicians to look beyond their own ethnic groups and religious communities for political support, and to develop truly national reputations and appeal. For victory in a presidential election depends on much more than simply winning the most votes. Success is also contingent on receiving the support of Nigerians from all over the country. Indeed, having the overwhelming backing of voters in a handful of states is not enough to get a candidate elected even if their combined ballots give them the greatest number of votes. They must receive national backing.

This much is made clear by Articles 133 and 134 of the 1999 constitution which state that 'a candidate for an election to the office of President shall be deemed to have been duly elected to such office where…he has the highest number of votes cast at the election; and…not less than one-quarter of the votes cast at the election in

The Emperor's New Clothes? 65

each of at least two-thirds of all the States in the Federation and the Federal Capital Territory, Abuja.'[28] These requirements help counter sectarianism by lessening its utility. Any candidate with realistic hopes of being elected president must appeal to voters in states and of ethnic and religious groups not their own. Any immediate or local benefits they might derive from pandering to one community at the expense of another, playing on the prejudices of a particular section of society, or from pitting one group against another will have to be balanced against the damage done to their reputation and support elsewhere.

Second, federalism has imposed similar obligations on the country's political parties. Under Article 222 of the 1999 constitution 'no association by whatever name called shall function as a political party, unless...the membership of the association is open to every citizen of Nigeria irrespective of his place of origin, circumstances of birth, sex, religion or ethnic grouping...the name of the association, its symbol or logo does not contain any ethnic or religious connotation or give the appearance that the activities of the association are confined to a part only of the geographical area of Nigeria and...the headquarters of the association is situated in the Federal Capital Territory, Abuja.'[29]

All political parties, upon pain of having their registration revoked or of being closed down, must allow any Nigerian who wishes to join them as a member to do so. Moreover, they cannot explicitly associate themselves with any one ethnic group or religious community, or promise to privilege its interests above those of any other. This obligation to represent as broad a spectrum of Nigerian society as possible is reinforced by Article 223 which insists 'that the members of the executive committee or other governing body of the political party reflect the federal character of Nigeria.' They will only be deemed to do so if they belong to at least 'two-thirds of all States of the Federation and the Federal Capital Territory, Abuja.'[30]

Of course an important divide still exists between what is done and what should be done. Formally, many of the rules, laws and guidelines needed to restrict and counter sectarianism are in place. Yet they are often ignored and broken. Indeed, the main problem is not a failure of understanding. Most of the country's political leaders, at all levels of government, recognise that sectarianism is a problem and appreciate the scale of the threat that it poses. Rather,

66 Nigeria Since Independence

the problem is one of implementation and enforcement, of making everyone follow the rules. For too long, the shorter-term gains which can be made from ignoring them have been allowed to outweigh the longer-term problems that can result from doing so.

Nevertheless, this does not mean that federalism has failed to have any effect. Far from it. While the country's politicians and political parties might not abide by all of the rules which have been introduced as part of it, they do follow some and often have to find ingenious ways of negotiating those they do not. In this way, federalism has gradually changed the political and social discourse in Nigeria, the popular narrative about how politicians and parties should behave, about what political life should be like. Moreover, through the changes federalism has made to the country's political structures and practices, it has made the task of the secessionist much harder to pursue.

Conclusions

'Next month,' wrote Brian Barder, Britain's High Commissioner to Nigeria, in his valedictory despatch to the United Kingdom's Foreign Secretary, Douglas Hurd, in January 1991, 'I leave Lagos and complete 17 years' involvement in African affairs, 10 of them dealing with west Africa or southern Africa in London, and 7 as head of mission in the two most populous countries of black Africa, Ethiopia and Nigeria. Tidily, I end where I began, with Nigeria, whose constitutional and political problems I first tried to grapple with as a new entrant in the Colonial Office in Great Smith Street a third of a century ago. I leave Nigeria with many of the same problems unresolved – not, I think, for any lack of effort by ourselves as the colonial power or by the Nigerians themselves, but chiefly because of the inherent difficulties we bequeathed when we gummed together such a big, unwieldy entity in such a casual manner 90 years ago.'[31]

Twenty years may have passed since Barder's final address as High Commissioner but much of what he says remains as true and valid today as it was when he first said it. Notwithstanding his lenient appraisal of the efforts of both Britain's imperial governments and the local leaders who took power once the Union Flag had been lowered for the last time, Barder's assessment highlights a critical truth; that modern Nigeria is still struggling to live with the ghosts of its past. Almost from the moment the country was created, those who have governed it, Britons and Nigerians alike, have struggled to master the powerful communal forces contained within its arbitrarily set borders. More than once these pressures have almost proved too much to bear and have come close to blowing the country apart. Yet in the interludes between such instances of high and bloody drama, these forces have persisted; at no point have they ceased to swell or press or threaten.

The challenge for those who govern Nigeria, therefore, has long been to identify and construct mechanisms that will either negate these pressures or allow for their safe release. That Britain's High Commissioner should still be speaking of the dangers they pose to the country's future development and prosperity some 31 years after it gained its independence, however, highlights the mixed results they have achieved in dealing with them. Certainly Nigeria is still in one piece but its people are not at peace. It has survived Biafra and is resisting the MEND but the suspicions and hostilities that gave rise to and are sustaining these secessionist movements still endure. Nigeria has seen off its challengers but it has not dealt with the causes of their anger – the very factors that are driving them to rebel.

One of the main ways in which the country's post-independence leaders, military and civilian, authoritarian and democratic alike, have sought to mitigate and diffuse these pressures is by engaging in a sustained programme of federalism. The programme has, over time, passed through various phases from planning and implementation, to expansion and entrenchment, to, most recently, maintenance and refinement. It has also been shaped by a wide range of short-term political, economic and social considerations as politicians of the day have used and adapted the programme to help them address whatever problems, dilemmas, threats and challenges they are facing at the time. Yet despite these shifts and changes successive governments have remained true to the programme, fully seized of its necessity and what it is trying to achieve.

This commitment was first made shortly after the country won its independence. Its early leaders very quickly embraced federalism as their preferred mechanism for extending the central government's authority over the sub-national political units and the politicians who headed them, and for eroding the strong, and on occasion overriding, loyalty felt by many Nigerians to their local ethnic and

68 *Nigeria Since Independence*

religious communities. The resolve of these early leaders was initially forged in direct response to the chaos, instability and bloodshed of the Dominion and the First Republic. Like many ordinary Nigerians, they looked to federalism to save them from the violence and volatility that so marked this early period. Such was the urgency of this task that federalism was quickly confirmed as the preferred solution and assumed to be vital to the country's future salvation and prosperity.

Rather than represent separate goals, the aims of strengthening the central government's authority and discouraging ethnic nationalism are mutually reinforcing. Extending and fortifying the powers of the centre have long been seen by the country's leaders as the most effective way of containing and countering the secessionism which can spring from unfettered regionalism. Simultaneously, strengthening Nigerians' loyalty to the nation-state so that it is at least equal to, and preferably stronger than, their devotion to their Hausa/Fulani or Yoruba or Igbo or Ijaw brethren will help ensure Nigeria's ongoing survival and long-term future. Federalism, then, is a grand political mechanism for altering society, for changing how Nigerians view themselves and each other.

Yet it has not been wholly successful. Still the Federal Government's authority is challenged. Still Nigeria is rejected by portions of its populace. Still there are Nigerians who would prefer to belong to some new state founded and dominated by their own ethnic group and carved out of Nigerian territory. Still Nigeria's future is shrouded in uncertainty, cloaked in a fog of doubt and threatened by forces that, concealed within, can loom large and dangerous at any given moment. Nevertheless federalism is trusted by the country's leaders as the solution, the most effective mechanism for dealing with the pressures that threaten Nigeria. But now it is also a factor in their manifestation; it helps explain their occurrence and shapes their expression.

The aim of this chapter has been to chart and explain this dualism, how federalism has both prevented Nigeria's disintegration and contributed to its failure. The chapter has argued that federalism has failed to achieve its intended goal of making Nigeria the primary focus of its citizens' loyalty above any devotion they may feel to their ethnic groups, religious communities or regions. This failure is due less to federalism's design, however, and more to its implementation.

For the successive iterations of federalism are, on the whole, well thought out. But they have been pursued with only partial commitment and have been modified to accommodate other considerations. These alterations have, on occasion, fundamentally compromised the programme's effectiveness. As a result, federalism has both discouraged and sustained the ethnic separatism and regionalism which so defined the Dominion and the First Republic and which have contributed to Nigeria's failure.

4

Fuel to the Flames: Oil and Political Violence in Contemporary Nigeria

Oil is contributing to Nigeria's failure in six main ways. First, its extraction undermines the quality of life and standards of living of tens of thousands of Niger Delta residents. The unsightly pipes, noisy pumping stations, frequent oil spills and constant gas flaring create an unpleasant and unhealthy environment to live in. Many of the streams and springs that provide drinking water are polluted. Much of the food produced locally is contaminated. The number of cases of certain types of cancer and respiratory illness are higher than the national averages. And the traditional industries of farming and fishing are in decline due to the damage caused to agricultural land and fish stocks leading to the impoverishment of those who work in them.

Second, oil is helping to fuel the insurgencies which are preventing the Federal Government from exercising direct and continuous control over the whole of Nigeria's territory. More specifically, it is the cause of two key grievances. The first is the hardships its extraction imposes on ordinary people. One of the main reasons the MEND, the NDVF and the NDPVF took up arms was to win environmental justice for the region's residents. They have long argued that the government and the oil companies must do more to clean up the pollution and improve local living standards. The second grievance is the proportion of the revenue generated from oil sales which is given to the region's inhabitants. These factions want that amount to be greatly increased if not for the entire sum to be handed over to the Niger Delta's residents.

Third, the oil sector has helped destroy much of the rest of Nigeria's economy resulting in greater poverty in many parts of the country. The sale of oil now provides the Federal Government with 95 per cent of its export earnings and 40 per cent of its total income.[1] The rapid growth in importance of this industry has been accompanied by a decline in official interest in the rest of the economy. The steady collapse of these other industries has resulted in rising levels of unemployment and falling standards of living throughout much of the country. And the economic hardships endured by millions of ordinary people have been magnified by the sustained overvaluation of the *Naira*. For the rapid expansion of the oil sector brought on a bad case of the Dutch Disease. The Federal Government's long-term macro-economic policy of privileging oil, therefore, has undermined the quality of life of millions of its citizens.

Fourth, oil money is fuelling much of the high-level corruption taking place in the country. The rapid enlargement of the oil sector over the past 40 years has transformed Nigeria into a rentier state. The income generated by oil pays not only for most public sector spending but also for many of the most lucrative contracts awarded to private companies. A majority of these continue to be granted by the Federal Government, which remains the country's most important economic actor. As one of the main sources of public and private finance, oil money makes up a significant portion of that which is stolen, embezzled and misappropriated by senior public figures. The theft and misuse of this money has significantly degraded the state's ability to provide its citizens with the public goods they deserve.

Fifth, oil has eroded Nigerian democracy. The development of the rentier economy and establishment of the state as the most important economic actor have made political position and influence vital to economic success and personal prosperity. Only through the state can an individual gain access to the oil revenue. Only by winning an election can an individual achieve political office. As a result, federal, state and local elections have all assumed significant economic importance thereby making it more tempting for those who compete in them to cheat. And oil revenue often provides those who hold office already with the means to do so. Elections are bought and sold and are seldom, if indeed ever, decided by the country's voters. This particular political right exists on paper but not in practice.

72 Nigeria Since Independence

Sixth, oil is driving the demands for secession made by groups in the Niger Delta and elsewhere. The MEND, the NDVF and the NDPVF have long asserted that the Niger Delta's inhabitants would be healthier, more prosperous and have better respected political and civil rights if the region established itself as an independent state. Such arguments are also central to the calls for independence made by groups and organisations in other parts of the country. Their leaders make the common argument that the Nigerian government is failing to provide the communities they represent with the rights, public services and opportunities that it should. Nigeria, these leaders assert, is curtailing the living standards and strangling the potential of their constituents.

Despite its contributions to Nigeria's failure, oil is also helping to keep the country together in two important ways. First, and most crucially, it is stifling the economic imagination of senior politicians and community leaders all over the country to such an extent that it is eroding their willingness to allow the country to break apart. The oil sector has assumed such a position of dominance within the economy that few of these figures are either prepared or able to look beyond it when considering the country's economic development and future. This lack of vision is undoubtedly hampering the diversification of the economy. Yet it is also strengthening the commitment of the non-oil producing states to Nigeria and redoubling their determination to prevent the Niger Delta from breaking away. Everyone needs the oil revenue, so everyone needs Nigeria.

Second, oil has helped fortify international support for Nigeria's continued unity. In truth, there has been no significant backing of any secessionist movement since the defeat of Biafra.[2] No reputable government or regime today is calling for Nigeria to break apart. The scale of this support for Nigeria's unity has grown in tandem with the expansion of the oil industry. With 37.5 billion barrels in proven oil reserves, Nigeria is one of the world's most important energy providers.[3] Under the terms of its agreement with the Organisation of the Petroleum Exporting Countries (OPEC), it is allowed to pump up to 2.2 million barrels of oil a day or 3 per cent of the total amount extracted worldwide.[4] Even though it consistently struggles to meet its allocation, its still sizeable contribution is vital to maintaining global supply. The international community is extremely anxious that nothing should disrupt the flow of this oil onto the global market.

The chapter is divided into three sections. The first traces the development of Nigeria's oil industry from independence to the present day. It pays particular attention to the industry's expansion and increasing domination of the country's economy. The second section then examines the ways in which oil is contributing to Nigeria's failure. It begins by looking at how oil is undermining the Federal Government's ability to promote the flourishing of all its citizens. The section then charts how the anger and frustration this is giving rise the insurgencies in the Niger Delta and north-east which are preventing the government from exerting its authority over the whole of Nigeria's sovereign territory. Finally, the third section looks at the ways in which oil is helping to keep the country together, at how it is fortifying national unity.

A brief history of the Nigerian oil industry

Nigeria's oil is deeply divisive. It is a major contributing factor to Nigeria's failure as a state. Not only is it helping to undermine the Federal Government's willingness and ability to promote the flourishing of all Nigerian citizens, but it is also driving the insurgencies. Partly, if not largely, as a result of these effects, oil continues to divide Nigerian public opinion over its desirability as a national resource. For some it is a blessing – a source of great wealth and international political prestige. But for others it is a curse – the root cause of many of the ills currently plaguing the country.

These opinions together form the nucleus of a dilemma which is alternately called the paradox of plenty, the resource curse, the curse of oil, the petro-Naira syndrome,[5] and the Dutch Disease. In truth, not all these concepts are the same. The Dutch Disease offers a much more sophisticated explanation for the economic stagnation and poverty often found in many resource-rich countries than the curse of oil which is little more than a pithy description.[6] Yet they all allude to the same seeming contradiction: that 'oil-rich countries tend to grow more slowly than their peers do, they are more authoritarian and conflict-ridden, and they lie nearer the bottom of Transparency International's famous corruption perceptions index.'[7]

74 *Nigeria Since Independence*

Many of the facts and figures on Nigeria and its oil industry are similarly contested. Such divergence is not particularly surprising given the difficulties often inherent in gathering accurate information in Africa. As Paul D. Williams notes in his recent study into the causes and consequences of conflict in the continent, 'not only is it sometimes dangerous to collect, there is no consensus on what analysts should be looking for. Simply put, our data about what goes on ... are poor.'[8] His observations can be applied equally to the study of most other human activities in the continent.

The data on the amount of oil Nigeria has, extracts, and sells is similarly contested. The Nigerian National Petroleum Corporation (NNPC), the state-owned company through which the Federal Government regulates Nigeria's oil industry, claims that the country has 28.2 billion barrels in proven reserves. But the OPEC and the U.S. Department of Energy (DOE) both place the figure much higher at 37.2 billion barrels. The NNPC maintains that Nigeria extracts up to 2.5 million barrels of crude oil each day. But the OPEC and the U.S. DOE place the amount at 2 million and between 1.7 and 2.1 million barrels a day respectively. The OPEC claims that Nigeria exports around 2.4 million barrels of crude oil each day, but the U.S. DOE places the figure lower at 1.8 million barrels a day.[9]

Such discrepancies also mark the latest data on the country's gas sector. The NNPC asserts that Nigeria has 165 trillion cubic feet in proven reserves. But the OPEC and the U.S. DOE claim that it has 180 and 187 trillion cubic feet in reserves respectively. The OPEC maintains that the country extracts 992 billion cubic feet of gas each day, but the U.S. DOE places that figure much lower at 820 billion cubic feet per day. The OPEC believes that the country exports 706 billion cubic feet of gas daily, but the U.S. DOE maintains that it exports no more than 565 billion cubic feet a day.[10]

Nigeria's oil and gas sectors are closely monitored by a range of domestic and international government agencies, companies and civil society groups. Yet, even so, significant disagreement still exists over how much oil and gas the country possesses, extracts and sells abroad. This makes the consistency of their appraisals of the centrality of these sectors to Nigeria's economy all the more surprising. The U.S. Department of State claims that fuels and mining products account for 97 per cent of the country's foreign currency earnings.[11] The U.S. DOE and World Bank similarly maintain that oil makes up 95 per cent of Nigeria's foreign currency income.[12] Seemingly, therefore, the differences over the precise amounts of oil and gas the country sells abroad have little impact on assessments of how important these sales are to Nigeria.

Few doubt the place of oil and gas at the heart of Nigeria's economy. Its movement there is the result of two closely connected processes. The first is the rapid growth in the size of the oil and gas industries over the past 40 years. Their massive expansion led to a corresponding rise in the money they brought into the country. The second process was their growth in size relative to the other parts of the economy. The oil and gas industries grew larger more quickly than did agriculture, food processing and manufacturing. In fact their growth caused the decline of these other sectors. Their contributions to the national coffers grew in proportion, therefore, to those of other industries.

Running throughout the development of Nigeria's oil and gas industries are two, as yet, unbroken threads. The first takes the form of a region – the Niger Delta. Nearly every drop of oil the country produces comes from fields located in the Delta and its coastal waters. It officially comprises of nine states – Abia, Akawa-Ibom, Bayelsa, Cross River, Delta, Edo, Imo, Ondo and Rivers. They are home to around 33 million people making it the most densely populated region in the country. Its inhabitants are divided into over 40 distinct ethnic groups which range dramatically in size. The smallest, such as the Ekoi, have just tens of thousands of members while the largest, such as the Ijaw, have many millions.[13] These ethnic divisions continue to shape the development and complexion of protest in the region.

The second unbroken thread takes the form of a company – Royal Dutch Shell. It has been involved in Nigeria's oil and gas sectors from the very earliest days. It was Shell's geologists who determined the likely presence of significant oil reserves in the Niger Delta. It was Shell's directors who secured the concession from the British colonial authorities to drill the initial exploratory wells. It was Shell's engineers who provided the technical expertise to build and operate them. And it was Shell's accountants and financial backers who provided the investment to develop and extend them. No other company or

76 Nigeria Since Independence

government agency has done more to develop Nigeria's oil and gas industries than Shell. No other company has made as much money from Nigerian oil and gas as Shell.

The precise date on which Nigeria's oil and gas industries were established is difficult to place mainly because there is no agreement as to what the criteria for deciding it should be. Exploration for the deposits, which later formed the nucleus of these sectors, began in the early years of the twentieth century. These searches were part of a global scramble for oil led by European and North American governments and industrialists. These early explorations were fitfully pursued and were interrupted by both the First and Second World Wars. It was not until the launch of Shell's five-year programme to aerially photograph the Niger Delta in 1948 that an attempt to systematically map the region's potential was made.

To help lead this new round of exploration, Shell and the Anglo-Iranian Oil Company established the Shell-D'Arcy Petroleum Development Company in September 1951.[14] Its main purpose was to refine their search and to undertake exploratory drilling.[15] The company sank its first deep well in October 1954 at Ihuo in what is today Imo State. This initial site proved a failure as did the dozen others which followed over the next five years. But in January 1956 the company discovered commercial quantities of oil at Oloibiri in Bayelsa State. This find was quickly followed by others at Agbada also in Bayelsa State; Krakama in Bendel State; Bormu, East and West Ughelli, and East Uzere in Delta State; Elenlenwa and Isoku in Ogun State; Apara in Oyo State; and Afam, Alakiri, Bonny, Buguma, Ebubu, Egbema, Ekulama, Korokoro, Soku, Umuechem and Yorla in Rivers State.

The first oil for export was pumped at Oloibiri in February 1958 just two years after it had been discovered there. The country's total output for that year was 1.8 million barrels. But production rose rapidly over the next decade. In 1960, the year Nigeria achieved independence, annual output stood at 6.2 million barrels of oil. In 1966, the year before the start of the Nigerian civil war, it was 152.4 million barrels. And in 1969, the last year of the conflict, it was 197.2 million barrels. Indeed, save for 1967 and 1968 when, as a result of the fighting, annual production slumped to 116.5 million and 51.9 million barrels, output grew rapidly with each year that passed.

And the rate of growth increased dramatically once the civil war was finally over. In 1970, the year in which the Biafran government formally surrendered, annual production climbed to 395.8 million barrels. In 1971, it rose to 558.6 million barrels, in 1972 to 643.2 million barrels, in 1973 to 750.5 million barrels, and in 1974 to 823.3 million barrels. This trend was interrupted in 1975 when output fell slightly to 651.5 million barrels, and it remained below the 1974 peak for the next two years. But, in 1979, a new production record was set when the yearly output climbed to 842.4 million barrels. This final surge meant that as the decade came to a close annual production was more than twice what it had been at the start.[16]

The 1970s was a golden decade for Nigeria's oil industry for three main reasons. First, Biafra's surrender brought an end to the fighting, which had caused the slump in production in 1967 and 1968. The restoration of peace and the reunification of the country removed a major impediment to the industry's development. Second, events in the Middle East helped ensure rising demand for Nigeria's output. In November 1978 workers at Iran's oil refineries went on strike as part of the prelude to the revolution of the following January in which the Shah, Mohammad Reza Pahlavi, was toppled from power by the followers of Grand Ayatollah Ruhollah Khomeini. This strike caused Iran's production to fall from 6 million barrels of oil per day to just 1.5 million barrels leading to increased global demand for supplies from other countries.[17]

Third, these events also pushed up the price of oil. As a result of the Iranian revolution the cost of a barrel of crude more than doubled from \$14.30 in 1978 to \$37.90 in 1980.[18] This increase came on top of the 70 per cent price rise forced through by the OPEC in October 1973. The catalyst for the organisation's actions was the outbreak of the Yom Kippur war earlier that month which pitted Egyptian, Jordanian, Iraqi and Syrian forces against those of Israel. In support of the Arab states, the OPEC's members suspended shipments of oil to the United States, Western Europe and Japan. This embargo caused prices to jump from \$3 a barrel on 16 in early October 1973 to \$12 a barrel by January 1974.[19]

Nigeria also benefitted greatly from the timing of each of these events. Its final victory over Biafra enabled it to regain total control of the country's oil industry just at the moment that global demand

78   *Nigeria Since Independence*

was beginning to soar. It then confirmed its membership of OPEC in July 1971 mere months before the organisation launched the embargo which triggered the rapid fourfold increase in oil prices. And it successfully expanded production throughout the 1970s to capitalise on the global surge in demand for oil from countries outside of the Middle East brought about by the Yom Kippur war and the Iranian revolution. Indeed, Nigeria could scarcely have timed the development of its oil industry any better.

Yet just as the 1970s had been a time of optimism and confidence for Nigeria's oil industry, so the 1980s proved to be one of despondency and doubt. During the course of the decade annual production rates slumped from 750 million barrels in 1980 to 525.6 million barrels in 1981, to 469 million barrels in 1982, and then to the 13-year low of 450.7 million barrels in 1983. Yearly output did climb slightly in 1984 and 1985 to 507.3 and 547.5 million barrels respectively, only to dwindle away again until 1989 when it rose to 625.9 million barrels. Annual production at the end of the decade was a full 125 million barrels lower than what it had been at the start.

The fall in production, however, was only part of the problem. For it coincided with a dramatic drop in global oil prices. Ironically, this decline sprang from, what is arguably still, the OPEC's greatest moment of triumph – the 1973 oil embargo. The sudden shortages this created in Europe and North America, and the accompanying rise in oil prices, plunged both regions into a deep recession from which they did not emerge until the mid-1970s. As a result of this economic slump, and the recession it triggered in other parts of the world, global demand for oil fell. By the mid-1980s, therefore, the supply of oil far exceeded demand thereby causing the price of a barrel of oil to plummet from $27.53 in 1985 to just $14.38 a year later.[20]

The harmful consequences this drop in price had on Nigeria were exacerbated by its massive dependence on its oil revenue. In 1966 the sale of oil abroad generated 32.39 per cent of the country's total export income. But by 1969 it brought in 41.13 per cent. This amount continued to grow over the next half decade. In 1970 it generated 57.56 per cent, in 1971 73.70 per cent, in 1972 82.01 per cent, in 1973 83.14 per cent, in 1974 92.60 per cent, and in 1975 95.88 per cent.

Fuel to the Flames 79

In the space of just ten years, Nigeria had become almost entirely dependent on oil for nearly all of its export earnings.

Nigeria's oil production continued to grow steadily throughout the 1990s and 2000s. In 1990 its annual output stood at 660.6 million barrels, in 1992 at 711.7 million barrels, in 1994 at 726.3 million barrels, in 1996 at 784.7 million barrels, in 1998 at 785.8 million barrels, in 2000 at 790.2 million barrels, in 2002 at 773 million barrels, in 2004 at 873 million barrels, in 2006 at 890.6 million barrels, in 2008 at 790.2 million barrels and in 2010 at 896 million barrels. From 1990 to 1999 yearly production rose by over 100 million barrels. Even though growth largely stalled between 2000 and 2009, annual output mostly remained above 800 million barrels.

This increase in production helped stabilise the country's oil revenue throughout the 1990s at an average of $12.14 billion per annum. But, just as crucially, the rise in output enabled Nigeria to benefit from the massive upswing in oil prices which began in 2000 and escalated rapidly from 2003 onwards. In 1999 its oil exports earned $12.58 billion. This amount climbed to $23.09 billion in 2000, $26.52 billion in 2003, $35.73 billion in 2004, $48.08 billion in 2005, $56.39 billion in 2006, and $65.00 billion in 2007 before peaking at $82.01 billion in 2008 the year in which the global price of oil reached a record high of $147.30 per barrel. It is estimated that as of 2004 Nigeria had earned around $400 billion from oil exports.[21]

While the huge rise in global prices greatly boosted Nigeria's income, it also reinforced the country's economic dependence on oil. In 1980 oil sales generated 96.01 per cent of the country's export revenue, in 1985 97.11 per cent, in 1990 97.03 per cent, in 1995 95.70 per cent, in 2000 97.00 per cent, in 2005 95.00 per cent, and in 2010 95.00 per cent also. Since 1974 these sales have brought in over 90 per cent of the country's export earnings each year. As a result, its economic and social development is now heavily dependent on three, key variables none of which the Federal Government fully controls.

The first variable is the amount of oil the country produces. Nigeria's output is heavily influenced by its obligations to the OPEC, the strength of global and domestic demand and the condition of its wells, pumping stations, pipes and other infrastructure. The second variable is how much oil Nigeria sells abroad. The amount it exports

80 *Nigeria Since Independence*

is shaped by its international responsibilities, domestic requirements and losses through illegal bunkering. And the third variable is the price of oil on the international market. Together, these variables determine how much oil Nigeria sells overseas, and the amount it makes from doing so. The country's dependence on them highlights the extent to which its economic, social and political stability are affected by volatile forces beyond the Federal Government's direct control.

Oil and its lubrication of Nigeria's failure

Oil is contributing to the Federal Government's failure to promote human flourishing in four main ways. First, the rapid expansion of the oil industry led to a fall in investment in other parts of the economy causing a drop in their output, revenue and size of their workforces. Second, the extensive pollution caused by the extraction and shipment of oil and gas is damaging the health, livelihoods and living environment of tens of thousands of Niger Delta residents. Third, as the main source of the country's export and foreign currency earnings, the oil revenue is helping to finance much of the corruption which takes place. And fourth, as the cause of Nigeria's transformation into a rentier state, the oil industry is undermining the country's democratic processes.

Damage to the economy

Over the past few years, the non-oil sectors of the economy have experienced strong growth. According to Nigeria's National Bureau of Statistics, they have increased in size by 8.49 per cent in 2010 and 8.84 per cent in 2011. The monetary value of its contribution to the country's gross domestic product (GDP) has climbed from N456.6 billion in 2006, to N510 billion in 2007, to N555.6 billion in 2008, to N601.9 billion in 2009, and to N652.6 billion in 2010.[22] Much of this growth has been driven by certain sectors such as wholesale and retail trade, and, in particular, telecommunications. It has achieved remarkable growth, expanding by 33.66 per cent in 2006, 33.84 per cent in 2007, 34.02 per cent in 2008, 34.18 per cent in 2009, and 34.47 per cent in 2010.[23]

But, not all of the country's non-oil sectors have performed quite so well. Manufacturing's contribution to Nigeria's GDP has declined steadily over the same period from 9.57 per cent in 2007 to 8.89 per cent in 2008, to 7.85 per cent in 2009, and to 7.64 per cent in 2010.[24] The main reason for this drop was the ongoing decay of the country's infrastructure and, in particular, of its power stations. Over the past decade they have failed to keep pace with the rise in demand. Today, Nigeria does not produce nearly enough power to meet its actual needs.[25] Its failure to do so and the frequent disruptions to supply are deterring investment in the country's economy and causing untold damage to its manufacturing base.[26]

Indeed, much of the economic progress that has been made over the past half decade has been achieved despite the Federal Government's efforts rather than because of them. The impressive growth of the telecommunications sector has been driven by the rapid expansion of the country's mobile phone network which is a response to the now total collapse of its terrestrial telephone system. Millions of Nigerians are using mobile phones because there is no other easy means of communication. The Federal Government's complete failure to maintain this vital piece of infrastructure has created a requirement which commercial companies are able to satisfy.

Moreover, the rapid growth of the telecommunications and wholesale and retail trade sectors has not significantly reduced the oil industry's importance to Nigeria's economy. The telecommunication industry's contribution to the country's GDP may have quadrupled between 2006 and 2010, but it still amounted to only 4.56 per cent of the whole.[27] Oil sales, on the other hand, made up 40.84 per cent of GDP in 2010. No other single sector contributes as much to the state's coffers or generates as much of Nigeria's export revenue and foreign currency earnings as it does.

The oil industry's contribution to Nigeria's GDP has grown rapidly over the past 50 years. Its growth has been matched by a concomitant decline in the size of the contributions made by other sectors of the economy. In 1960 agriculture contributed 64.1 per cent of GDP. But by 1990 it contributed 39 per cent and by 2010 35.4 per cent. In 1960 manufacturing contributed 4.8 per cent of GDP. By 1990 its contribution had risen to 8.2 per cent before falling to 7.64 per cent by 2010. In contrast, oil contributed just 0.3 per cent of GDP in 1960. But its contribution had risen sharply to 12.8 per cent by 1990 and to 40.84 per cent by 2010.[28]

82 *Nigeria Since Independence*

Yet the exponential growth in the size of the oil sector has not been matched by a similar increase in the number of people employed in it. Indeed, its importance is measured not by the size of its workforce, but the amounts of oil it produces and revenue it earns. While the total number of Nigerians working in the sector has of course increased over the years, they still amount to less than 10 per cent of the country's total labour force. The vast majority of people, around 70 per cent, still work in agriculture. Most Nigerians work not in the sector which has proven to be the most dynamic and economically important, but that which has suffered serious, sustained decline.

This decline has been caused, in part, by the rise of oil. Not only has the oil sector received the largest share of all public and private investment in the country's economy, but its rapid expansion gave Nigeria a bad dose of the Dutch Disease. During the 1970s the country was flooded with foreign currency which raised the value of the *naira* to artificially high levels. As a result, imported goods became cheaper, and were highly sought after by the *nouveaux riches* because of the status attached to them. This led to a decrease in demand for local agricultural and manufactured products sending these sectors of the economy into decline. Their stagnation was both stimulated and hastened by the flight of huge numbers of people from the countryside to the cities seeking to make their fortunes on the back of the oil bonanza.

Damage to the environment

The manner in which the oil is extracted imposes significant environmental hardships on tens of thousands of ordinary people. Unsurprisingly the brunt of this burden continues to be borne by those living closest to the oil wells – the inhabitants of the Niger Delta. Yet the privations they endure are due not to an absence of appropriate regulation, but a failure to rigorously interpret and enforce it. Indeed, numerous laws, guidelines and standards have been passed, set and established over the past 40 years. But they continue to be either ignored or only partially implemented, or interpreted in ways that permit significant pollution to be made and not cleared up.

The foundations of the legal framework governing the oil industry were laid in the closing months of the civil war. In 1969 the Federal Military Government of General Yakubu Gowen passed what remains the country's most significant piece of oil legislation – the Petroleum Act. It included two critical provisions. The first was Nigeria's absolute right of ownership of all oil and gas located within its sovereign borders.[29] This claim was reinforced by the 1979, 1989 and 1999 constitutions that declared 'all minerals, mineral oils and natural gas' to be the property of the Federal Government.[30]

In accordance with this provision, all companies seeking to engage in the exploration, extraction, storage, refinement or transportation of oil must be licensed by the Department of Petroleum Resources (DPR). But licenses are only awarded to either Nigerian citizens or companies that are registered in Nigeria. For a foreign company to operate in the country, it must first either take on a Nigerian partner or establish a local subsidiary. Not only does this requirement further enhance the Federal Government's authority over its oil industry and encourage foreign companies to appoint Nigerians to senior positions on their boards of directors, but it also ensures that a significant portion of any profits they make or technology they import remain in the country.

Yet this provision also forms part of the bedrock on which the grievances of the Niger Delta factions are built. For it denies completely the competing claims of ownership made by the region's inhabitants. It insists that every drop of oil found in Nigeria belongs to the Federal Government. The citizens of Bayelsa State and the Ijaw have no greater right to the oil found under their lands than do the residents of Kano or the Fulani. The Delta factions want to end the primacy of the Federal Government's claim. They are fighting to transfer ownership of the oil from Abuja to the peoples of the Niger Delta.

The second important provision of the Act was the regulations it established for producing oil. To retain their licences, oil companies must engage in 'good oil field practice.' What this entails is laid out by the Mineral Oils (Safety) Regulations which were first introduced by the 1963 Mineral Oils Act, the precursor to the Petroleum Act. The regulations do not detail how oil companies should behave but rather compel them to adhere to the 'appropriate current Institute of Petroleum Safety Codes... American Petroleum Institute Codes, or... American Society of Mechanical Engineers Codes.'[31] All oil companies operating in Nigeria must conform to the most up-to-date operating procedures set down by one of these bodies.

84 *Nigeria Since Independence*

This means that, legally at least, good practice in Nigeria is indistinguishable from that in the United States.

Oil companies are also subject to other restrictions. First, before they start exploring or drilling for oil, they must consider what impact their actions will have on the local environment in accordance with the 1992 Environmental Impact Assessment Act. Second, before the work has begun and while it is taking place they must 'adopt all practicable precautions' to prevent pollution; take 'prompt steps to control' any that should occur; and cause 'as little damage as possible to the surface of the … area [in which they are operating] and to the trees, crops, buildings, structures and other properties' found there.[32] Third, they must comply with all planning laws; give local residents access to any roads or paths they build; and protect any land, building or other object of devotional significance they encounter.

The Petroleum Act and its associated legislation – the 1956 Oil Pipelines Act, the 1968 Oil in Navigable Waters Act, the 1979 Associated Gas (Reinjection) Act, the 1988 Federal Environmental Protection Agency Act, and the 1992 Environmental Assessment Act – established both the environmental standards oil companies must meet and the regulatory apparatus to monitor their compliance. Central to this oversight structure are the DPR and the Federal Environmental Protection Agency (FEPA). The DPR has responsibility for supervising the behaviour of oil companies and can revoke a company's licence if it does not exhibit good oil field practice. The FEPA has responsibility for setting water, land and air quality levels and ensuring that oil companies meet them.

That the Nigerian authorities have long struggled to maintain these standards is now largely beyond question. In the mid-1990s the NNPC estimated that around 14,500 barrels of oil were spilled each year in 300 separate incidents. Given the consistent under-reporting of both the size and number of spills, it is highly likely that these figures are too low.[33] And the same is probably true of the DPR's estimate that around 2.5 million barrels of oil were spilled in 4,835 separate incidents between 1976 and 1996.[34] Certainly Darren Kew and David Phillips suggest the amount to be far higher as they estimate that around 12.75 million barrels of oil were spilled between 1957 and 2007.[35]

Even if the NNPC's and DPR's figures are accepted without question, they still mean that millions of barrels of oil have been spilled in the Niger Delta. And, just as crucially, very little of what has been spilled has been cleaned up. Indeed, the DPR estimates that only 600,000 barrels of the 2.5 million that it said were spilled have been recovered.[36] One of the reasons the authorities have failed to fully enforce the legislation they have introduced is because 'most state and local government institutions involved in environmental resource management lack funding, trained staff, technical expertise, adequate information, analytical capability and other pre-requisites for implementing comprehensive policies and programmes' while the 'overlapping mandates and jurisdiction between FEPA and the DPR frequently contribute to counterproductive competition.'[37]

As a result of these spills, the Niger Delta is now one of the five most polluted places on the planet. Oil leaks 'affect creeks, streams...mangrove forests...soil plots, and...aqua life' while the constant gas flaring creates 'sulphuric acid mists [which] damage plants and forests...[and] pollut[e] rainwater.' The region's 'traditional sources of livelihood' have been adversely affected and a high portion of its inhabitants suffer from oil poisoning in addition to other waterborne diseases like malaria, dysentery, tuberculosis, typhoid and cholera.[38] The Federal Government's failure to fully enforce its oil laws and ensure that the industry complies with the environmental standards it sets is undermining the quality of life of tens of thousands of Niger Delta inhabitants and significantly limiting their opportunities for self-betterment.

Damage to democracy

The rapid expansion of the oil industry and its increasing domination of the economy have turned Nigeria into a rentier state. This means that most of the Federal Government's revenue comes from sources outside of the country rather than within it. Abuja does not depend on either the taxes it imposes on its citizens, the duties it levies on some of the services it provides, or on the loans it take out from domestic lenders for its income. Indeed, since the 1970s, much of its revenue has come from the '"rents" paid to it through licences and royalties from multinational petroleum corporations.'[39]

86   *Nigeria Since Independence*

The Federal Government's general disinterest in either taxing its people or sorting out the chaotic and barely functioning national tax system is one of the few ways in which ordinary Nigerians benefit from their oil industry.[40] Shell, Agip and Chevron are made to pay, not they. Yet this financial benefit has significant social and political costs. First, the Federal Government is not maximising its income; it is not fully exploiting every possible revenue stream. The additional income that it could raise through more efficient taxation could be spent on strengthening and expanding public services. A better organised and more rigorously enforced tax system could generate the extra revenue that the Federal Government needs to improve its provision of public goods.

Second, because the Federal Government does not depend on its citizens for its income, it is less inclined to listen to their views or respond to their demands. The democratic contract which binds taxation to political representation has been severely damaged. And Nigerians' political rights have been compromised further by the electoral fraud rentierism continues to give rise to. In Nigeria, as in other rentier states, the central government is the primary recipient of the rents that are collected. This concentration of wealth and economic power in the hands of a few gives them both the means and the motive to abuse the democratic process,[41] to stuff ballot boxes, to intimidate voters and to rig elections.

The means are provided by the vast sums of money, much of it in hard foreign currencies, flowing into the state's coffers. Those government figures with access to them have at their disposal the resources they need to fix elections. And the motive to do so is furnished by both the existence of this wealth and the knowledge that access to it only comes with being in government. Only by winning and retaining office can these figures exploit the rents paid to the Federal Government. There are no similar opportunities elsewhere in Nigeria because the state is the focus of economic activity. As a result elections are seen as being simply too important to be left to the vagaries of the electorate.

The refusal of political figures and many of the main parties to allow parliamentary, presidential, state and even local elections to proceed unmolested is evidenced by international assessments of recent votes. In the build-up to the 2007 presidential election, the U.S. State Department noted 'significant human rights problems' including 'the abridgement of citizens' right to change their govern-ment ... [and] restrictions on freedom of speech, press, assembly ... and movement.'[42] Of the election itself, the European Union noted that 'polling procedures were often poorly followed and the secrecy of the vote was not guaranteed in the majority of ... stations.'[43] While Human Rights Watch observed that voting 'was marred by the late opening of polls, a severe shortage of ballot papers, the widespread intimidation of voters, the seizure of ballot boxes by gangs of thugs, vote buying and other irregularities.'[44]

Corruption

The spread of corruption in Nigeria occurred in tandem with the growth of the oil industry. More specifically, it was driven by two main processes. First, the country's increasing dependence on its oil revenue. Second, the Federal Government's steady expansion of state control over the oil industry. Together these processes turned the state into Nigeria's primary economic actor. It collected the rents and royalties paid by the oil companies. It received the income from the sale of oil abroad. It set many of the taxes on oil-related activity. As a result, rent-seeking steadily replaced agriculture as the main means by which individuals earned their fortunes and achieved prestige.

During the oil boom of the 1970s, many of those with access to the vast wealth brought in by oil built and developed clientelist networks in order to increase their power, extend their influence and enhance their status. In this way, money from the state and the upper reaches of society was distributed down to the lower levels of both the government and the population. But when the price of oil fell sharply in the mid-1980s this flow of money was reduced to little more than a trickle with two important consequences. First, it made the competition to gain and retain control of the state more ferocious than ever. This led to an increase in corruption as senior figures bribed lavishly in order to maintain their posi-tions and thwart their rivals. Second, it forced those lower down the networks to act corruptly in order to make up the shortfalls in their income.

Further evidence of the intimate relationship between oil and corruption is provided by Nigeria's four oil refineries. Over the past two decades they have each suffered numerous serious breakdowns

88 *Nigeria Since Independence*

leading to either a drop in production or the total suspension of it. Moreover, there have been times when all four refineries have been out of action at once. On these occasions, Nigeria has had to import all of its petrol, diesel and kerosene. The embarrassing paradox of one of the world's main oil producing countries having to buy its gasoline abroad is not lost on most Nigerians. But the primary cause of their anger is the government's ongoing failure to fix these problems despite spending hundreds of millions of dollars on solutions and remedies. As they suspect, much of this money has simply been wasted or stolen.[45]

Failure to promote human flourishing and the spread of armed violence

The rapid expansion of the oil sector has stymied the development of other parts of the economy, caused significant damage to the environment in the Niger Delta, encouraged and facilitated corruption and graft, and compromised and eroded the country's democratic processes and structures. The oil industry has undermined the Federal Government's ability to promote the flourishing of all its citizens and, in so doing, is helping to sustain the insurgencies in the Niger Delta and the north-east. All of the armed factions currently at large in Nigeria claim to be fighting to curb corruption, win political rights and justice for ordinary people, and improve their economic prospects. And these groups also want to end the pollution which is blighting the lives of the region's inhabitants.

The links between the Federal Government's failure to take care of its citizens and the insurgent groups, which by their actions are preventing it from exercising total control over the country's sovereign territory, are clear from the goals these factions have adopted. In January 2012, the spokesman for Boko Haram, Abu Qaqa, declared that 'the secular state…is responsible for the woes we are seeing today.…We are not saying we have to rule Nigeria, but we have been motivated by the stark injustice in the land.…Poor people are tired of the injustice, people are crying for saviours and they know the messiahs are Boko Haram. People are singing songs in Kano and Kaduna saying "we want Boko Haram."'[46]

The goals of winning justice for ordinary people and punishing the government feature prominently in the numerous statements of intent issued by the MEND. Indicative of them was the announcement it made in February 2012 claiming responsibility for the attack at Ogbobagbene in Burutu Local Government Area of Delta State, on the compound of the Minister for the Niger Delta, Godsday Orubebe. In its statement the group promised to 'reduce the Nigerian oil production to zero and drive off our land, thieving oil companies. British Petroleum is prepared to pay $25 billion compensation for the Gulf of Mexico oil spillage. Yet for worse spillages in the Niger Delta, our people are paid with death at the hands of the Nigerian military.... MEND understands the negative impact our assault on the Nigerian oil industry will have on the ordinary citizen in a country which relies almost entirely on one source of revenue. Unfortunately, the extremely irresponsible, floundering government of Nigeria is more concerned with enriching themselves and family members than attending to the problems of the Niger Delta and the continuously depreciating standard of living of the ordinary Nigerian. A government incapable of managing roads, refineries, power stations and other basic infrastructure is again squandering valuable public funds on a committee tasked with investigating the viability of nuclear energy for electricity generation. In this new phase of our struggle for justice ... MEND will pay considerable attention to dealing with the security forces and traitorous indigenes of the Niger Delta.'[47]

This statement leaves no doubt as to who the enemy is, what their crimes are, what the MEND wants to achieve, and what it is prepared to do in pursuit of its goals. Of course, the group has made many such proclamations over the past seven years, some highlighting different issues than this. But there are sufficient similarities between them to identify the faction's core objectives. These remain 'to obtain a greater share of, if not exclusive rights to, the Niger Delta's oil and gas revenues; to end corruption in the delta; and to gain the release of key leaders from prison.'[48] By undermining the Federal government's ability and willingness to promote the flourishing of all its citizens, Nigeria's oil industry is helping to sustain the various insurgencies which are preventing it from exercising total control over all of the country's territory.

Secessionism

One of the fiercest debates in Nigeria today is over the distribution of the oil revenue. Since independence its dispersal has been determined

90　*Nigeria Since Independence*

by the derivation formula. The formula has been revised many times over the years, but its three basic functions have remained unchanged. The first is to divide the revenue from the rents and royalties paid by the oil companies between the federal, state and local governments. The second is to distribute the portion of the revenue allocated to states between the state governments. And the third is to divide the taxes levied on oil and gas and the revenue generated by their sale abroad between the Federal Government and the Niger Delta states.

Given that the oil sector is the country's most important source of revenue, the derivation formula determines a significant portion of the federal, state and local governments' income. At present 58 per cent is given to the Federal Government, 30 per cent to the state governments, 12 per cent to the local governments and 13 per cent to the special projects fund which is managed by the Federal Government.[49] The distribution of the 30 per cent set aside for the states between their governments is based on five considerations – the principle of equality, population size, territory size and make-up, social development and own-income generation. By custom, equality and population size are given the most weight. Every state can expect to receive some of the oil-rent revenue. The amount they receive is mostly determined by how many people live there.

Many people in the Niger Delta, however, are unhappy with this arrangement. In particular, they resent having to share this income with everyone else since the oil is under their lands, and it is they who have to live with the consequences of its extraction. To assuage their anger the Delta states are granted a portion of the tax and sales revenue made from oil. No other states receive this. Moreover, they receive other sizeable payments from the special projects fund. Yet the division of the tax and sales revenue is another cause of anger in the Niger Delta. Politicians and ordinary people alike insist that the 13 per cent the region receives is too low and must be increased.

This anger is helping to sustain the separatist impulses which are threatening to tear the country apart. The discovery of commercial quantities of oil in the late 1950s and early 1960s encouraged the eastern region, where much of it was found, to declare its secession from Nigeria as the independent state of Biafra. The alleged iniquity of the derivation formula continues to fuel the demands for independence made by the MEND and other Niger Delta factions. Oil and the allocation of the revenues it generates are helping to drive the insurgencies in the Niger Delta which are preventing the Federal Government from exercising total control over the region and placing the country's long-term future in doubt.

On troubled waters: oil and its contribution to Nigeria's unity

Yet, paradoxically, the issues of oil ownership and income derivation are also helping to keep the country together in two important ways. First, and most crucially, the growth of the oil sector has stifled the economic imagination of the country's politicians and community leaders. The larger the sector has grown and the more money it has brought into country, the less able these leaders have become to envisage an economic future beyond or without it. The main dispute over oil today is not about the wisdom of depending so heavily on one industry, but the division of the revenue it generates, how much the different tiers of government and parts of the country get.

The development and entrenchment of Nigeria's rentier economy mean that the 30 non-oil producing states depend on the Niger Delta and Abuja for much of their income. Quite clearly, they will only continue to receive this revenue so long as the country remains intact. And their dependence on oil will continue for as long as Nigeria remains a rentier state. For only the Federal Government can instigate the macro-economic reforms needed to end its rentier status. The whole country's reliance on oil, therefore, is fortifying the determination of the 30 states to stop the Niger Delta from breaking away. The economic necessities generated by rentierism are helping to maintain this broad commitment to preserving Nigeria's unity.

The international community is just as unwilling to see the country break apart. To begin with, key foreign governments and global institutions have shown a real reluctance to recognise new states in Africa. They would much prefer the existing states to stay together. And in Nigeria's case, this aversion is heightened by its importance as an energy provider. The country has 37.5 billion barrels in proven reserves although this figure will almost certainly rise as further discoveries are made offshore. It pumps between 1.6 and 2 million barrels of oil a day. This represents 2 per cent of the total amount

92 Nigeria Since Independence

produced daily worldwide. Of this slightly more than 60 per cent is shipped directly to the United States, Canada and Europe.[50]

Nigeria's importance as an energy provider is raised still further by the quality of the oil it produces. First, its oil is described by industry experts as light and sweet. This means that it is ideally suited to refinement into motor fuels. Second, the country's close proximity to the Atlantic sea lanes facilitates the shipment of its oil to refineries in North America and Europe. Third, the ongoing disruption to supplies from other important oil-producing countries in North Africa and the Middle East means that it is more important than ever to maintain the flow from Nigeria. The country's oil, then, is one of the main reasons why a majority of Nigerian and international politicians want the country to remain together.

Conclusions

Oil is undermining the Federal Government's ability to promote the flourishing of all its citizens in four main ways. First, the extraction, transportation, storage and shipment of oil are causing significant damage to the environment of the Niger Delta. The many thousands of barrels of oil which have been spilled, and not cleared up, over the years pollute many of the region's waterways and forests, and much of its arable land. The constant gas flaring creates a noxious miasma which then falls as acid rain. And the unsightly pipes and whirring pumping stations provide an ugly and noisy backdrop to everyday life. In these ways the oil industry is damaging the health and destroying the livelihoods of tens of thousands of Niger Delta residents.

Second, the growth of the oil industry has severely damaged the non-oil parts of the economy. Its rapid expansion led to the overvaluation of the *naira* which undermined the competitiveness of the local manufacturing and agricultural industries. The jobs that were inevitably lost in them were not replaced by new ones in the oil sector. Its importance is measured not by the size of its workforce but by the amounts of oil it produces and revenue it earns. While the total number of people working in it has increased, they still amount to only a small percentage of the entire labour force. Most Nigerians still work on the land, in a neglected and decaying industry.

Third, Nigeria's transformation into a rentier state has damaged democracy. The Federal Government receives much of its income from the rents and royalties paid by foreign oil companies. This means that it does not depend on the taxes paid by its citizens making it less inclined to listen to their views and opinions. Moreover, the concentration of wealth and economic power in the Federal Government provides its members with both the means and the motive to abuse the democratic process. The means are provided by the vast sums of money flowing into the state's coffers, and the motive to do so is furnished by the existence of this wealth and the knowledge that access to it only comes with being in government. Elections, therefore, are simply far too important to be left to the electorate.

Fourth, the vast revenue generated by the oil industry is both encouraging and facilitating corruption. Nigeria has the unenviable reputation of being one of the most corrupt places on the planet, and the level of corruption is getting worse, not better. As the country's most important source of income, the oil sector provides much of the money which is stolen, embezzled and misappropriated by senior public figures. Moreover, the enormous sums it brings in represent a huge temptation to those tasked with managing and spending them.

The Federal Government's ongoing failure to promote the flourishing of all its citizens is helping to sustain the insurgencies in the Niger Delta and the north-east. Both Boko Haram and the MEND claim to have taken up arms in order to bring an end to the corruption, poor governance, economic mismanagement and environmental neglect which are so compromising the standards of living and quality of life of many millions of Nigerians. They are seeking to both punish the Federal Government for its failure to take better care of its people and remove it from power, either nationally or locally, so that a more caring and considerate regime can be put in place. And unless the inhabitants of the Niger Delta are given a much greater, if not total, control over the revenue generated by oil, the MEND wants the region to break away from the rest of Nigeria.

Yet oil is also helping to keep Nigeria together in two important ways. First, it is stifling the economic imagination of members of the Federal Government and political leaders of the non-oil producing states. Oil revenue makes up a large portion of the budgets they manage. They accept the oil sector's economic primacy and exhibit no great desire to end it. They and their states will only continue to

94 Nigeria Since Independence

benefit from this revenue so long as Nigeria remains together. They are all determined to prevent the Niger Delta from breaking away. And, in this, they are supported by the international community. Nigeria's importance as an energy provider means that Washington, London, Paris and Brussels are extremely anxious to make sure that nothing disrupts the flow of oil from the Niger Delta onto the international market.

5

Of the People but for the People? Nigeria and Its Armed Forces

On 7 February 2011 Nigeria's Supreme Court overturned former Rear Admiral Francis Agbiti's conviction for negligence and disobedience. The five judges unanimously declared his sentence unsafe on the grounds that his original trial had not been fair. In summing up on the court's behalf, Justice Olufunlola Adekeye paid particular attention to Agbiti's opening argument that the members of the panel that tried him were either unqualified to do so, known to be prejudiced against him before the trial started, or acted inappropriately during its course. Two of its members, Major General Akpa and Air-Vice Marshal Odesola, were too junior to have sat upon it. Its president, Rear Admiral Ajayi, was known to have disliked Agbiti from old while its other senior member, Rear Admiral Oni, sponsored the publication of an article critical of Agbiti while the trial was still taking place.[1]

Agbiti's downfall had been brought about by the disappearance of the Russian oil tanker, *MT African Pride*, from Nigerian custody in August 2004.[2] It had been seized, and its 13-man crew arrested, on suspicion of engaging in illegal oil bunkering.[3] In its hold were found 11,000 barrels of unaccounted oil worth an estimated $2.1 million. The vessel had been intercepted by the NNS *Beecroft* as it tried to leave Nigerian territorial waters. After it had been safely shepherded into dock, Agbiti, the officer in overall command of the *Beecroft*, was ordered by the Chief of the Naval Staff to release the impounded vessel into police custody.[4] Yet Agbiti refused to do so, immediately before the ship, still with its valuable cargo on board, disappeared.

96 Nigeria Since Independence

News of the *African Pride*'s loss was greeted with a storm of incredulous outrage at home and knowing bemusement abroad,[5] and served only to strengthen the widely held belief that senior officials, military officers and political figures were directly involved in the bunkering racket. A host of urgent questions now jostled for answers. Why had the oil not been unloaded? Why had the ship not been properly guarded? How had it been able to sail away undetected? Why had no one stopped it escaping? The vessel's subsequent discovery a few weeks later just a short distance out of Port Harcourt, one of Nigeria's busiest ports and the capital of the Niger Delta region, merely fortified these popular suspicions.[6] Either the navy was so grossly incompetent that it could not track the movements of a 30,000 tonne ship, or key personnel within the organisation were directly involved in its disappearance.

To assuage public anger and assert some control over the situation, the House of Representatives launched an official enquiry. Led by the Chairman of the House Committee on the Navy, Anthony Aziegbemi, its objective was to investigate what had happened to the *African Pride* and to identify and prosecute those who were involved in taking it. Unsurprisingly the committee's suspicions fell very quickly on Agbiti and two of his fellow Rear Admirals, Samuel Kolawole and Antonio Bob-Manuel. Agbiti clearly had questions to answer over his refusal to obey the Chief of the Naval Staff's direct order to hand the *African Pride* over to the police. While it had been Kolawole's responsibility to ensure that the ship was properly secured, and Bob-Manuel had commanded one of the coastal sectors through which the vessel was assumed to have passed when making its escape.

After a lightning investigation, the committee decided that there was sufficient evidence to charge all three officers. The collective court-martial that followed lasted two months and culminated in Bob-Manuel being acquitted, Agbiti being found guilty of negligence and disobedience and Kolawole being convicted of negligence, disobedience, lying and, the more serious crime, of conspiracy. Rear Admiral Ajayi and his fellow judges decided that his failure to secure the vessel had been deliberate and that he should have acted more decisively on the intelligence he received from a reliable source warning of its likely theft.[7] The delivery of these final verdicts came barely three months after the House of Representatives had launched its enquiry. Rarely before had Nigeria's justice system acted with such speed.

The Federal Government hoped that these convictions would bring this unhappy and deeply embarrassing episode to a close.[8] Yet the approbation it won from the general public and international community for its swift and decisive action was more than offset by the opprobrium it earned as a result of the sentences handed down to Agbiti and Kolawole by the court. Despite the seriousness of the charges of which they were both convicted neither man was sent to prison or even fined. Moreover they both received the same punishment – dishonourable discharge from the navy – even though Kolawole was found guilty of conspiracy and Agbiti was not. The Federal Government may have found its sacrificial lambs, but the Nigerian public was not nearly satisfied with the amount of blood that was let.

The relative leniency of the punishments handed down to Agbiti and Kolawole merely compounded the cynicism felt by many ordinary Nigerians that there was much more to this case than met the eye, that it represented just a tiny part of the sprawling under-world of bunkering and smuggling. These suspicions were sustained and nurtured by the remarkable and disturbing revelations that emerged during the course of the court martial. Bob-Manuel alleged that he had been offered, and refused, a £60,000 bribe by the brother of a former Minister of Defence to organise the release of the ship. Moreover, Aziegbemi discovered that at least three leading Nigerian banks, with connections to financial institutions in Switzerland, had traded in bunkered oil, and that seven state governors were also implicated in its theft and sale.[9]

More damaging though to the Federal Government's claim that Agbiti's and Kolawole's conviction and subsequent expulsion from the navy struck a decisive blow against the oil smugglers' and their ability to engage in their nefarious trade was the steady stream of reports claiming that bunkering was as rife and profitable as it had always been. In its 2005 annual report, Shell – the longest operating, largest and most notorious of the oil companies working in the Niger Delta[10] – estimated that between 20,000 and 40,000 barrels of oil were stolen each day throughout the course of that year.[11] That represented a total annual amount of 100 to 250 million barrels of oil worth between $1.5 and $4 billion.[12]

Just over a year after the *African Pride* trial had finished, Human Rights Watch published a report detailing both the extent of the

98 *Nigeria Since Independence*

bunkering still taking place and the scale of the political, social, economic and environmental problems its occurrence caused.[13] It claimed that 'expatriate and local businessmen, high-level politicians and military personnel, and even employees of the oil companies themselves' were directly involved.[14] Agbiti's and Kolawole's conviction and discharge from the navy had not delivered, it seemed, the body blow to this illicit trade that some members of the Federal Government claimed it had. Moreover, there appeared to be little prospect of it ever coming to an end as long as so many powerful and influential people had a stake in it continuing.

From the moment the legal drama surrounding the *African Pride* began with the vessel's seizure, right up until the Supreme Court's annulment of Agbiti's conviction, Nigeria's military was cast in multiple and, at times, conflicting roles. Through those personnel who, for a variety of reasons, found themselves directly involved in this rapidly unfolding drama, the military played a myriad of different parts. Sometimes simultaneously sometimes alternately, it appeared to be the unassuming yet doughty defender of Nigeria's interests; an uncaring and abusive usurper of the people's rights and inheritance; an innocent victim of civilian greed and duplicity; a hapless and ineffective incompetent; and the exonerated martyr, ennobled by the crosses it had been unfairly forced to bear over the preceding months and years.

The drama surrounding the *African Pride* has undoubtedly helped expose and draw attention to the military's multiple personalities. The armed forces have, since independence, trod an ambiguous path. At times they have played a crucial role in preserving the country's unity, strengthening its institutions, establishing and enforcing the rule of law, stabilising the West Africa sub-region and improving the quality of life and standards of living of ordinary Nigerians. On other occasions though, they have abused human and civil rights, engaged in and helped entrench corruption, alienated ethnic and religious minorities and outraged the country's traditional international allies and near neighbours. Perhaps understandably, therefore, the military continues to provoke strongly held and contrasting opinions.

The aim of this chapter is to highlight and examine these multiple personalities to show how the military has hastened Nigeria's failure and resisted its breakup. The chapter argues that the armed forces have helped preserve the country's unity and counter its failure in three distinct ways. First, they have fought to keep it whole, to prevent regions like Biafra, the Niger Delta and the Sultanate of Sokoto from breaking away. Second, they have brought much-needed stability to Nigerian politics and society at critical moments and helped renew public trust in their leaders. And third they have helped to bring together different ethnic groups and communities and foster greater understanding between them.

It has been through their efforts to keep the country intact, however, that the armed forces have made their first important contribution to Nigeria's failure. By denying the want-away regions their independence and preserving the borders the country inherited from the departing British, the military has ensured that there is a state called Nigeria to fail. In addition to this passive and unintentional contribution, the military has also played a more active role. By failing to defeat the insurgent groups ranged against it and abusing the civil, political and human rights of ordinary Nigerians, it has stoked popular anger and antipathy towards the state driving some individuals and communities into the arms of groups like the MEND and Boko Haram, which are undermining the Federal Government's ability to control its sovereign territory. Moreover, by abusing these rights the armed forces have compromised the flourishing of some Nigerian citizens.

To sustain this argument, the chapter is divided into four main sections. The first examines the contradictory roles played by the military, paying particular attention to the actions and behaviour of its leaders and officers. The second identifies and analyses the ways in which the military has contributed to and furthered Nigeria's failure to control and failure to promote human flourishing. This leads, in the third, to an examination of the ways in which the armed forces have helped to preserve and strengthen Nigeria's unity and also counteract its failure. Finally, the fourth offers up some concluding comments.

The legacy and reputation of Nigeria's armed forces

'With monotonous predictability,' wrote Wole Soyinka at the height of the Abacha regime, 'every military junta will be heard to declare its iron resolve to keep the nation together. Very good. But suppose every act of the same military in government can be proved to have

100   *Nigeria Since Independence*

headed the nation in the opposite direction? What price its commitment? All that is served by the chest-thumping rhetoric is the right of the military to do anything, adopt and execute any policy no matter where it leads. A bugle rouses the nation to its mission of keeping the nation together while a mailed fist and studded boot silence the protestations, the warnings that the act of the military contradicts its glorious aim.'[15]

What was clear to Soyinka, as it doubtless was to tens of thousands of his fellow Nigerians, was that the military played an ambiguous and, at times, self-defeating role. That what its commanding officers said while in high political office did not always match, or was even flatly contradicted by, what they did, was only part of the matter. Such tensions between word and deed, between what those in charge say and do, are a central feature of political life all over the world. More crucial, and where Nigeria does differ from other places, is the size of the gap between the stated aims of these soldier–politicians and the consequences of their actions in pursuit of them.

One of the main goals of these soldier–politicians, which they all shared and of which Soyinka wholeheartedly approved, was the preservation of Nigeria's unity. Each of them justified their seizure or assumption of power on the grounds that the country was in mortal danger and only they could save it.[16] Yet, crucially, Soyinka's main aim is not to challenge either the validity of these claims or the strength of the military's belief in them. That Nigeria has faced numerous existential threats is beyond question. Likewise, the vital role played by the armed forces in meeting at least some of them cannot be disputed. Biafra's unilateral declaration of independence was only overturned after two-and-a-half years of armed struggle. The military has proven its commitment to Nigeria's unity in the blood it has spilt.

Soyinka is concerned instead with the ways in which successive military regimes have gone about maintaining this unity and the consequences of its actions. The cost to ordinary Nigerians has been extremely high. Lives have been lost, political rights compromised and civil liberties suspended. These abuses have long given rise to resentment among certain ethnic groups, religious communities and the populations of particular regions and states. So unhappy are some of these peoples so disillusioned with military rule and with being Nigerian citizens that they dream and agitate for their own

Of the People but for the People? 101

homelands, for Biafra, for Ogoniland, for the Sultanate of Sokoto. The considerable human cost attached to the military's repeated efforts to safeguard Nigeria's unity, therefore, help sustain at least some of the challenges which threaten to tear the country asunder and are causing its failure now.

The military's self-defeating behaviour is, in part, a result of the importance it places on the task of preserving Nigeria's integrity. Not surprisingly or unreasonably, it privileges the pursuit of this high politics aim above all others. The defence of the nation-state from enemies and threats from both within and without is the primary function, if not the very *raison d'être*, of all official armed forces.[17] Yet the Nigerian military places such importance on this undertaking that it subordinates all other concerns, including the civil and political rights and economic well-being of the country's citizens, to its pursuit. The quest for unity is allowed to take precedence over everything else and to legitimise all actions. All too often, the military has allowed itself to become preoccupied with the individuals, organisations, groups and communities which it thinks are threatening Nigeria's unity, to the detriment of the overall effect it is trying to achieve.

Yet the armed forces have not been guilty of mere over enthusiasm or of simply losing sight of what they are trying to achieve amid the cut and thrust of trying to achieve it. Certainly there have been instances of well-meant but ultimately counterproductive exuberance. General Buhari's 'war against indiscipline' comprised of numerous initiatives which enjoyed wide public backing and, if implemented fully as their architects intended, may well have altered the behaviour of both individuals and society in ways that would have largely benefitted everyone. On many other occasions, however, members of the armed forces have been driven not by altruism or a desire to serve the public, but by naked self-interest. Senior officers, as well as personnel of other ranks, have abused their positions to enrich and empower themselves, their friends, their families and their supporters.

This Dr Jekyll and Mr Hyde duality has shaped and permeated the very fabric of the country's capital. Its streets, its buildings and even its populace bear the marks of the military's selfless commitment to public service and self-interest. To begin with, the decision to establish a new seat of government was taken by General Murtala Mohammed

102 *Nigeria Since Independence*

during the first weeks of his brief, yet popular, administration.[18] He supported the growing body of opinion which held that Lagos was simply too crowded, too congested and too closely associated with one ethnic group (the Yoruba) to continue as the nation's capital. He agreed that a new centre was needed in which all Nigerians felt they had an equal stake, which highlighted the country's aspirations to be a dominant force in Africa and beyond, and which emphasised Nigeria's ambition, dynamism and forward-thinking drive.

By establishing a new capital, General Mohammed hoped to neutralise it as a source of contention between the country's main ethnic groups and transform it into a place which encouraged popular belief in and commitment to Nigeria. His goal was nothing less than to use the capital – its location, buildings and layout – to further the process of nation building, to unite and inspire Nigerians in their nationhood. It was for these reasons, therefore, that he and his immediate successor, General Olusegun Obasanjo, decided to build the new capital from scratch (rather than bestow the title on some other, existing settlement), locate it on the near-virgin site of Abuja (at the geographical heart of the country), and place it within the newly established Federal Capital Territory (so that no one ethnic or religious group had a greater claim to it than any other).

The new capital's ethnic neutrality was scrupulously preserved throughout the main planning and building phases. The contract for the city's master plan was put out to international tender and eventually won by the American firm Wallace McHarg Roberts and Todd, while the contract for the city centre was awarded to the celebrated Japanese architect Kenzo Tange. Much of the work on their designs was carried out by the German-Nigerian construction company Julius Berger Nigeria, a subsidiary of the Mannheim-based firm, Bilfinger Berger. By bringing in this outside expertise, the Obasanjo, Buhari and Babangida regimes, which together commissioned and oversaw much of the planning and building work as well as the formal transfer of the capital from Lagos to Abuja, were able to prevent any one ethnic group from claiming proprietary rights over the city.[19]

The same level of care has not been taken, however, to ensure that the capital is just as open, accessible and welcoming to all classes of citizen. From its inception, Abuja was envisioned as a global city, an African rival to London, New York, Paris and Berlin. Indeed one of Abuja's roles, part of its purpose as a place, was declaratory, to make

Of the People but for the People?   103

a statement, in bricks and mortar, of Nigeria's intent on becoming a leading power in Africa and beyond. The city's founding fathers were determined, therefore, to keep the chaos and confusion that have for so long defined Kano, Lagos and many other African urban centres well at bay. They were determined that Abuja was going to be different.

This resolution helps account for the special emphasis the city's founding fathers and governing ministers have consistently placed on aesthetics, on what Abuja looks like. Indeed they were absolutely convinced that appearances mattered, that assuming the airs of a global hub was crucial to Abuja becoming one, that the city could only truly realise its international ambitions if it looked the part. This faith in the importance of appearance, however, has not manifested itself architecturally. The city is not renowned for either its striking buildings, or innovative structures or dramatic public spaces. Rather it has resulted in a series of social campaigns, spaced over several years, to rid the city of the unappealing manifestations of poverty and human suffering.[20]

Successive FCT ministers have enacted legislation to banish all structures and individuals they deem incompatible with their common vision of Abuja as a wealthy, ordered and modern city. Slum neighbourhoods are bulldozed, shanty dwellings razed to the ground, makeshift stalls and workshops cleared, and, since October 2006, *okadas*, the small engine motorcycles that are the main means of transport for millions of ordinary Nigerians, have been banned from the city's streets. These measures represent not an assault on poverty but on the appearance of poverty, on the structures, objects, practices and people who represent poverty. Indeed Abuja is no place for the poor. By ensuring that rents and house prices are kept high and preventing the construction of low-cost homes, FCT ministers have stopped the poor, who make up around 60.9 per cent of the country's total population, from living within the city's limits. Abuja is their capital but not their home.

Of course, the elitism that has long defined the governance of Abuja has not been practiced by the military alone. The ordinance outlawing the use of *okadas*, for example, was issued by the civilian FCT administration of Nasser el-Rufai.[21] Yet, he, and the territory's other civilian ministers, was only continuing along the path already laid down by their military counterparts and the military-dominated

104 *Nigeria Since Independence*

governments on which they served. The type of city Abuja was to be, and the place of the poor within it, was mainly decided by soldiers. The new capital remains, by origins, a marshal town, a product of the vision, ambition and drive of Generals Mohammed, Obasanjo, Buhari and Babangida.

What they have created is a city that provides testament to their ambition for Nigeria but which is riven by schism between rich and poor, and rulers and ruled. Abuja highlights the armed forces' efforts to both keep Nigeria together and take it forward, and the ways in which they have contributed to its failure. These schisms are not only evidence of successive governments' failure to promote the flourishing of all its citizens, they also point to the socio-economic and political dissatisfaction of many ordinary Nigerians. Frustration such as this drives on the various insurgencies and separatist movements currently operating in the country.

The armed forces' contribution to Nigeria's failure

Since becoming a republic on 1 October 1963,[22] Nigeria has had 14 heads of state including the current incumbent, Goodluck Jonathan. Of these, eight were serving officers in the Nigerian army at the same time they held political power.[23] In every instance, their assumption of high office was a direct result of both their service in the military and their rank.[24] They each became head of state, in practice if not formally in name, precisely because they had command over tens of thousands of armed men and women.[25] These eight soldiers together ruled Nigeria for around 30 years. Their civilian counterparts will not match their collective term in office until 2020 and will only do so then if there are no more *coups d'état* in the meantime.

The armed forces, then, have played a central and multifaceted role in Nigerian public life since independence. In addition to the routine military tasks they were established to perform, they have launched numerous other political initiatives, economic programmes and social campaigns. Indeed, a large portion of their cumulative post-independence activity has been non-military. This body of undertakings includes all those enterprises and assignments which the armed forces have either pursued by non-military means (they have engaged and employed civilian agents and institutions to carry

Of the People but for the People? 105

them out) or which have the achievement of non-military goals (be they political, economic, social or cultural) as either their main or sole priority.

The armed forces' contribution to Nigeria's failure is similarly multi-faceted. To begin with, its failure has only been made possible because of the military's success in helping keep it together. One of the reasons why Nigeria is a failed state is because the Federal Government does not fully control all of the territory under its nominal authority. Both now and in the past, regions and areas have defied and resisted its control. If they had successfully seceded from the republic, Nigeria would have ceased either to exist (in which case there would be no state of that name to fail) or it would have been shorn of the troublesome areas which are, in part, responsible for its failure today. Nigeria is not failed despite its unity but because of it.

This contribution to Nigeria's failure is clearly unintentional insomuch that it is the result of a series of actions which, on many notable occasions, were pursued with precisely the opposite objective in mind. A distinction must be drawn, therefore, between passive and active contributions to Nigeria's failure, between behaviour that has helped create the permissive environment which has made failure possible and that which has directly hastened its occurrence. Since independence, the armed forces have contributed to Nigeria's failure in both ways. They are still fighting hard to keep the country together but the way they go about this is, in part, counterproductive. For the abuses perpetrated by their officers, personnel and units are helping to drive the insurgent groups whose actions are compromising the Federal Government's ability to fully control its territory and look after its citizens.

A failure to defend

Arguably the most important active contribution the military has made to Nigeria's failure is its inability to defeat the various insurgent groups currently waging war on Abuja. Based on the characteristics they exhibit – their membership, their goals and how they go about realising them – these factions can be arranged into two broad categories. The first consists of, what will be termed, local insurgent groups. These predominate in the south, unlike the regional insurgents of the second category who are concentrated in the north.

106 *Nigeria Since Independence*

Most local insurgents are Niger Delta militants and include the fighters of the MEND, the NDVF, and the NDPVF. They are so termed because, for the moment at least, they have no ambitions beyond Nigeria and draw no great ideological strength or military assistance from elsewhere. That is not to suggest that these factions have no international connections. All three exploit the extremely porous border that separates the Delta from Cameroon to evade the attention of the Joint Task Force troops sent against them. Moreover, the MEND, for one, has been armed with weapons purchased in South Africa and smuggled through Angola.[26]

Yet, even so, these factions remain resolutely parochial in both their outlook and objectives, and the support they receive. Indeed, it was the proven strength of the MEND's provincialism that made its attack in Abuja so unexpected and shocking. Although it had threatened to bring the fight to the capital many times before over the previous few years,[27] it never had. Even if this attack represents the opening of new, and for the MEND, more remote front, the group's main area of operations remains relatively confined. In fact, this shift to include locations in the centre of the country highlights the limit of the MEND's ambition to spread the fight. And, in truth, and despite what it might say, the group is unlikely to carry out many more attacks outside of the south–south since that is the territory it is fighting over and where its main base of support is located.

As the largest and best known of the Delta factions, even the MEND's relatively limited reach exceeds that of the NDVF and NDPVF. Even so, that does not make the threat they pose either individually or collectively to the security, economic development and territorial integrity of Nigeria any less significant. The political and economic goals of these and the other Delta factions broadly overlap. And central to them is winning autonomy for some or all of the various ethnic groups who inhabit the six states that make up the south–south sub-region. The largest of these ethnicities is the Ijaw who form the mainstay of the MEND's support and focus of its actions. For one of the group's principal goals is to establish an independent Ijaw homeland centred on the territory that forms the Bayelsa, Delta and Rivers states.

The dangers this ambition present Abuja places it on a collision course with the MEND. For a start, its realisation would result in Nigeria's territory and population being reduced, its access to the

Of the People but for the People? 107

Gulf of Guinea being impaired and its economic development being severely damaged in both the short to medium terms. For, today, the export of Niger Delta oil provides the Nigerian Federal Government with 95 per cent of its export earnings and 40 per cent of its total income.[28] Given this, the Federal Government will not countenance either giving in to the MEND's demands or accepting any comprise that jeopardises this vital revenue stream. And its resolve has only been hardened by the violence the MEND has unleashed against the Joint Task Force and other civilian targets.

It is this violence, coupled with the MEND's proven track record of dispensing it, that makes the group such a threat to Nigeria's national security. From the moment it first emerged in the winter of 2005, the organisation carried out numerous attacks against oil installations and shipping in the Niger Delta and Gulf of Guinea as well as the security forces sent to protect these assets and kill and capture its militants. And in the weeks and months which followed its high-profile bombing campaign in Abuja, the group's fighters raided two oil rigs in the Gulf of Guinea in separate assaults, kidnapping seven foreign nationals during the first offensive,[29] and seven Nigerians during the second.[30]

Yet the danger the MEND poses to Nigeria's internal security and stability is more profound than even this. One of the reasons the group has survived this long, despite the extensive military campaign waged against it by the Federal Government, is its ability to corrupt the soldiers and officers sent against it as well as the politicians who ordered them into battle. Over the past few years, there have been several high-profile courts-martial of serving military personnel who have sold government-owned weapons and ammunition to the MEND fighters and other insurgents.[31] Although the group is neither the sole cause of corruption nor the only body to exploit and perpetuate it, the organisation is helping to downgrade the efficacy and trustworthiness of the country's armed forces. In this way, it is undermining the ability and resolve of the institution most central to safeguarding Nigeria's security and territorial integrity.

It is not just the local insurgent groups that are weakening Nigeria's ability to protect itself, so too are regional factions like Boko Haram. Unlike their local counterparts, most of these groups are based in the north. They are so called because they draw their support from like-minded bodies and sympathetic governments elsewhere and are

108　*Nigeria Since Independence*

starting to develop cross-border ambitions as they look to operate in both neighbouring countries and further afield. Indeed, just like the international organisations that are providing them with assistance, achieving regional or even global reach is an increasingly important objective for them. And, as a result of the help they receive, it seems that some of them may soon have the capacity to undertake transnational operations.[32]

That these northern groups are less parochial in their focus than either the MEND or the NDVF or the NDPVF is to be expected given their embrace of Islamism. For a start, this doctrine is shared by organisations all over the world. And at its core is a requirement for those who embrace it to propagate its beliefs and values. Indeed, it is Islamism's will to universalism which accounts for the breadth of the doctrine's spread. Pivotal to its journey to Nigeria are the men who established the country's various Islamist groups. Nearly all of them spent some time living in other parts of the Muslim world where they were exposed to Islamist views and ideas. They then brought what they had learned abroad back to Nigeria and set about disseminating it.

The abuse of human rights

The armed forces have a long and inglorious history of abusing human rights. General Abacha's imprisonment of Shehu Yar'Adua and judicial murder of Ken Saro-Wiwa, General Buhari's abduction of Umaru Dikko, and the MOPOL's summary execution of Mohammed Yusuf are just a few of the more notorious highlights in this roll call of infamy. Such incidents serve as grisly reminders of what the armed forces are capable of. Its soldier–statesmen and commanding officers, enlisted personnel and fighting units have routinely ignored domestic public opinion and international concerns to commit one atrocity after another. Based on the evidence of past behaviour, some of it extremely recent, there is very little Nigeria's military are not prepared to do.

Some of these abuses have had a profound influence on Nigeria's failure. Saro-Wiwa's execution inspired scores of angry young Delta inhabitants to take up arms against the state and capitalise on the newfound international interest in the region. Likewise, Yusuf's death has, in light of the string of attacks mounted by Boko Haram since it occurred, only galvanised his supporters into stepping up their armed struggle. Just as damaging have been those occasions when the military has abused the rights of whole groups of citizens. These wholesale abuses are instrumental in turning entire communities against the military and state and help create reservoirs of sympathy and support for the various groups and organisations currently challenging the Federal Government's authority.

Most of these larger-scale abuses are perpetrated in those parts of the country in which the armed forces are conducting active operations: the Niger Delta, Maiduguri and the surrounding area, and the city of Jos. Indeed Jos has witnessed many of the worst atrocities committed in recent years. It experienced major unrest in 2001, 2004, 2008, and, most recently, in 2010. On each occasion far more people died as a result of the security forces' efforts to restore order than during the disturbances themselves. Time and again, the armed forces have shown themselves to be quite willing to use lethal force against unarmed civilians, including women and children.[33]

The armed forces' efforts to prevent Nigeria's failure and disintegration

Inevitably Nigeria's armed forces have shaped and influenced the country in ways far beyond what their counterparts elsewhere, who have not exercised political power to the same extent as they, have been able to. The long years its senior personnel held high office afforded it numerous opportunities, not open to many other armed forces, to resist, prevent and reverse the state's failure. Its efforts to stop Nigeria from failing have also, therefore, taken the form of political initiatives, economic programmes and social campaigns as well as more customary, and expected, military activities. Its broad contribution to Nigeria's failure is matched, and must be balanced against, its similarly expansive attempts to stop the country from falling apart and failing.

The measures enacted by the armed forces to prevent Nigeria's failure can, on the basis of their primary purpose, be separated out under three function-describing headings: maintaining and preserving security, strengthening public participation and trust in the political process and promoting social integration and harmony. Each of these groupings can themselves be broken down into two distinct subsections. The maintaining and preserving security category has internal

110 *Nigeria Since Independence*

and external dimensions; the strengthening public participation and trust in the political process category has structural and practical elements; and the promoting social integration and harmony category has military-specific and broader-society aspects.

Maintaining and preserving security

Arguably the most important contribution the armed forces have made to resisting Nigeria's failure is to fight those insurgent groups and rebel movements seeking to either reduce or end the Federal Government's authority over a particular community or part of the country. The largest and most successful military campaign ever mounted by Nigerian forces, either at home or abroad, was against the breakaway region of Biafra which unilaterally declared its independence on 30 May 1967. Fighting between what remained of the Nigerian army and those units which sided with the rebels began ten days later on 6 July 1967. The conflict continued until 13 January 1970 and ended with Biafra's complete and unconditional surrender.

During the course of this two-and-a-half years war somewhere between one and three million people lost their lives.[34] Of those who died, a large majority were Biafran although the Nigerians still counted their dead in the hundreds of thousands. More civilians perished than combatants, killed not in, the at times, bitter fighting between the two warring factions, but by the famine which quickly followed on its heels. The mass starvation to which Biafra succumbed was caused in part by the Nigerian army's deliberate blockade of the fledgling republic. Food, fuel, medicines and other essential goods became ever scarcer as General Gowon and his commanders tightened their grip. Attrition – wearing down the Biafrans' resolve and ability to continue fighting – was central to the Nigerian armed forces' strategy of reasserting their control over the recalcitrant province.

That the war lasted for as long as it did and claimed so many lives was due in no small part to the assistance given to both sides by outside forces. In the beginning, General Gowon turned to Britain and the United States for help and military supplies. While London and Washington were sympathetic to his efforts to restore Nigeria's territorial integrity, they refused to provide him with any military equipment on the grounds that it would simply prolong the conflict.[35] With the flow of weapons from Nigeria's traditional suppliers now closed off, Gowon turned instead to the Soviet Union, which was only too willing to break the embargo put in place by Britain and the United States. On 25 August 1967, his forces took delivery of four Czech-built Delphin L-29 training aircraft which were accompanied by 153 technicians.[36] This was to be the first of several arms shipments from the Soviet Union and its Warsaw Pact allies to Nigeria.

Despite the embargo, the Biafrans were also able to secure at least some of the weapons they needed from abroad. Their main suppliers were international arms dealers, who furnished them with everything from automatic rifles to combat aircraft.[37] They often did so with the tacit support of certain foreign governments. For just as the Soviet Union was keen to increase its influence in Nigeria at the expense of Britain and the United States, so too was France. But, unlike its Soviet counterpart, Charles De Gaulle's government backed the Biafrans instead of General Gowon. As did, and in direct violation of the OAU's official stance that the conflict was an entirely internal matter for the Nigerian government alone to resolve,[38] Côte d'Ivoire, Gabon, Tanzania and Zambia.[39]

Even with this help and support though, the Biafrans were quickly forced onto the defensive. So, in an effort to redress the balance, they turned to, and came increasingly to rely on, foreign mercenaries. Arguably the most famous of these was Rolf Steiner, a veteran of the *Wermarcht*, the French Foreign Legion, and the Secret Army Organisation (Organisation Armée Secrète, OAS).[40] He, along with a handful of other Europeans, led the Fourth Commando Brigade (FCB) of the Biafran army. Many of the men recruited into the FCB were armed with weapons manufactured in Europe and funnelled into Biafra through neighbouring Gabon, and the Portuguese colony of São Tomé and Principe.[41]

Yet neither this support nor the various strategic and operational blunders made by the Nigerians during the course of the war were enough to prevent General Gowon's eventual, decisive victory. In truth, the odds had been heavily stacked against Biafra from the outset. That it was able to maintain its struggle for as long as it did was due to the astute politicking of its leaders, the ingenuity of its commanders, and the fortitude and forbearance of its population. General Gowon's triumph though put an end to Igbo hopes of establishing an independent homeland for two or three generations. Moreover his resolute response to Biafra's secession allied to the scale of the suffering endured by its people during and immediately after

112 *Nigeria Since Independence*

the war offered a powerful warning to other communities and ethnic groups of what to expect should they too try to quit the republic.

Strengthening public participation and trust in the political process

The armed forces have also worked hard, on occasion, to reinvigorate the political process and restore public trust in it. Attempts to reform the country's political institutions and processes, and even adapt its political culture, have been made by several soldier–statesmen. The packages of reforms implemented have varied in both form and ambition, and some have clearly been more successful than others. The most serious attempts to overhaul the country's political structures were made in the years during and immediately following the civil war. Perhaps unsurprisingly, the fighting, bloodshed and devastation it unleashed on the country added a new level of urgency to this requirement. Indeed, the political settlement the country had inherited from the departing British had permitted and exacerbated the inter-communal tensions which eventually led Biafra to declare its independence.

In an attempt to weaken the Biafran cause from the outset, General Gowon announced the replacement of the northern, western, midwestern and eastern regions with 12 new federal states on 27 May 1967,[42] three days before Colonel Odumegwu Ojukwu declared the unilateral withdrawal of Biafra from the Nigerian Republic. Gowon's goal was to drive a wedge between Biafra's Igbo majority and its significant non-Igbo minority. By creating a series of smaller states, Gowon offered groups like the Ijaw, Ibibio and Efik the chance to gain far greater political influence than they had enjoyed before. For the position of the boundaries of each new state helped ensure that these communities formed a large portion, if not an outright majority, of their inhabitants and voters. As such, they would enjoy significant representation in the new congresses and other political institutions each state was formally endowed with.

Of course, the three states that replaced the old eastern region (which became Biafra during the civil war) existed only on paper until the conflict was over.[43] Even so, their establishment created a dilemma for the ethnic minorities who lived within them. Either they could be citizens of a large multi-ethnic state in which they could enjoy a fair degree of political power at the local and state levels, or

Of the People but for the People? 113

they could belong to a smaller state that was quiet clearly dominated by one ethnic group, the Igbo. Partly as a result of General Gowon's actions, the Biafran cause was viewed with considerable suspicion, and even hostility, by many members of the Niger Delta minority communities. So successful was he in driving a wedge between the Igbo and other ethnic groups, that his programme of state creation became a template for future leaders eager to win support from some of the country's smaller communities and reduce the power and influence of its bigger groups.

Once the fighting was over General Gowon and his immediate successors, Generals Mohammed, Obasanjo and Buhari, worked hard to stabilise political life in the country and to dampen the inter-ethnic tensions that had led inexorably to the onset of civil war. To that end, all three leaders were careful not to vilify or persecute the defeated Igbo. The tone was set in the weeks immediately following the conclusion of the fighting by General Gowon who declared that there was 'no victor' and 'no vanquished' in what had been a 'war of brothers.' As well as granting a blanket amnesty to all those who had fought for Biafra he launched the three Rs policy of reconstruction, rehabilitation and reconciliation. The three Rs initiative built on General Gowon's state creation programme and formed part of the broader policy of federalism which was pursued by successive military and civilian governments.

As part of this policy, these soldier–statesmen made a concerted effort to clean up Nigerian politics and clamp down on some of the most egregious abuses of power. Their goals were to restore public confidence in their leaders, and to make the political process operate more efficiently and effectively. Indeed, making the political system more responsive to and better able to deliver the needs of the people was one of the main ways they hoped to win back the trust of ordinary Nigerians. Perhaps the most concerted, and certainly the most high profile and well known, campaign was General Buhari's war against indiscipline which he launched by decree shortly after he seized power in December 1983.

The war against indiscipline was launched expressly to 'correct the ills of government.' To achieve that, General Buhari and the ruling National Council of State (NCS), which he headed, 'agreed that the programme should meaningfully begin with the leadership of the various segments of society and be extended down

114 Nigeria Since Independence

to the grassroots, to also include its introduction in the mosques and churches, family units and schools... [and] be launched by the military governors in all the states of the federation and be vigorously pursued as an on-going policy of the Federal Military Administration.'[44] In so doing, General Buhari and the NCS aimed to fundamentally change how Nigerians behaved, to force them to become better, more responsible citizens.

To enforce these changes in behaviour, the NCS devised a code of conduct for virtually all aspects of public life, from the important to the downright trivial. Draconian punishments were handed out to anyone caught breaking it. Public-sector workers who turned up late for work could expected to be beaten or summarily dismissed from their jobs or forced to clean the streets. The death penalty was introduced for such crimes as drug smuggling, interfering with oil pipelines and electricity cables, and counterfeiting money. Buildings constructed without planning permission were torn down, street hawkers were barred from public spaces and the homeless were driven from the city centres. General Buhari and the NCS placed a great deal of emphasis on appearances, on making Nigeria look more orderly and organised.[45]

Despite the hardships it imposed on many ordinary Nigerians, the war against indiscipline proved to be extremely popular (initially at least) with many of them. The code of conduct that lay at its core was clear and unambiguous, and left people in little doubt as to what behaviour was acceptable and what was not. Its vigorous enforcement, and emphasis on improving the aesthetics of urban landscapes, helped ensure that its impact was quickly seen and felt. And General Buhari's determination to hold members of the country's political and business elite to account won him the admiration of many ordinary people and helped cement his reputation as a tough, no-nonsense leader and organiser who got things done.

Through the war against indiscipline, General Buhari helped restore the public's trust in its leaders and political process. Finally, the state seemed to care about ordinary Nigerians and displayed a new determination to provide them with at least some public services. This newfound energy and commitment only enhanced the pride that the war's code of conduct had helped stimulate in the chests of many individuals and communities. The purpose and

Of the People but for the People? 115

dynamism of the war, and those who initiated and led it, seemed to speak of a brave, prosperous and more peaceful future for Nigeria.

Promoting social integration and harmony

Finally, the military has worked hard to improve relations between the country's various ethnic groups and religious communities. Over the past 40 years, its commanding officers, including several soldier–statesmen, have launched a range of initiatives to foster greater trust and understanding between the Hausa/Fulani and the Yoruba, the Igbo and the Ijaw, Muslims and Christians. Together, these schemes represent the most coherent programme of social integration ever launched in Nigeria. For they outline a series of measures that are at once both sensible and feasible, financially inexpensive, politically acceptable (in the main), and with numerous potential side benefits. Most crucially, though, these initiatives hold out the possibility of achieving fundamental change, of transforming popular attitudes and beliefs for the better.

Nearly all of the initiatives launched by the armed forces have been introduced in the decades since the end of the civil war. Perhaps unsurprisingly, the violence, bloodshed, trauma and destruction visited on the country by that conflict helped instil in General Gowon and many of the armed forces' other senior officers a renewed sense of urgency about tackling the animosity and hatred that had long defined relations between the country's main ethnic groups. Of course the military had played its part in stoking the acrimony that had led Biafra to declare its independence. The 1966 *coup* and counter-*coup*, led by Igbo and Hausa officers respectively, highlighted the considerable distrust with which the various communities viewed one another and seemed to confirm their respective fears of being marginalised and exploited by their rapacious compatriots. Nevertheless, once the fighting was over, General Gowon and his immediate successors, Generals Mohammed and Obasanjo, set about using the armed forces to promote inter-communal harmony.

Most of the initiatives they introduced, and certainly all the major ones, share certain core characteristics. The similarities enable them to be grouped together and described as a programme, and from which they derive at least some of their strength. First, these initiatives are all specific to the armed forces. That is, they seek to use the institution of the military to strengthen social cohesion by making

116 *Nigeria Since Independence*

changes to how it is organised and how it goes about at least some of its business. Second, the primary objective of these initiatives is to demystify the various religious groups and ethnic communities. They seek to make these communities seem less alien and threatening to each other by providing some of their members with opportunities to interact. Third, they also attempt to fortify the participants' national identity, to develop their sense of Nigerian-ness and loyalty to Nigeria above that to their local group.

Arguably the most important initiative launched and sustained by the armed forces to promote social integration and harmony has been the National Youth Service Corps (NYSC) programme. Introduced by General Gowon on 22 May 1973, it obliges all Nigerian graduates, upon completion of their term of study at either university or polytechnic, to complete one year of non-military national service. The programme's core goals have remained largely unchanged. They were formally codified by General Babangida on 16 June 1993 and include 'develop[ing] common ties among...Nigerian youths and promot[ing] national unity and integration; remov[ing] prejudices, eliminate[ing] ignorance and confirm[ing]...the many similarities among Nigerians of all ethnic groups; and...develop[ing] a sense of corporate existence and common destiny of the people of Nigeria.'[46]

To achieve these, and its other, goals, the NYSC programme recommends 'the equitable distribution of members of the service corps and the effective utilisation of their skills...; that as far as possible, youths are assigned to jobs in States other than their States of origin; that...youths...work together...as representative[s] of Nigeria...; that the...youths are exposed to the modes of living of the people in different parts of Nigeria; that the...youths are encouraged to eschew religious intolerance by accommodating religious differences; that members of the service corps are encouraged to seek at the end of their one year national service, ...employment all over Nigeria...; that employers are induced...to employ more readily and on a permanent basis, qualified Nigerians, irrespective of their States of origin.'[47]

Two of the main goals of the NYSC programme are to encourage interaction between young Nigerians of different ethnic groups and to make their allegiance to the nation stronger than their loyalty to their individual communities. These are also objectives of the

Of the People but for the People? 117

military's recruitment and stationing policies. Members of all the country's main ethnic groups, and a good number of its smaller ones, can be found in the officer corps, and non-commissioned and enlisted ranks of all three services. Perhaps unsurprisingly, some groups are over-represented in certain services. The Hausa and Fulani of the landlocked north, for example, traditionally provide the navy with only a handful of its personnel. And the Igbo have only recently witnessed a restoration of their numbers in the army's upper echelons as the memory of the Biafran war fades.

It is also now standard practice for troops to be garrisoned in towns and areas outside of their home states and regions. This is another legacy of the civil war and is a response to the relative ease with which Colonel Odumegwu Ojukwu and the other Biafran commanders were able to put together a military force to resist the Federal troops sent against them simply by taking control of the Igbo units already stationed in Biafra. As well as increasing the exposure of armed forces personnel to peoples of other ethnic groups, this stationing policy has the added advantage of making it harder for any one region to marshal its forces quickly in support of any unilateral declaration of independence. Just as this policy seeks to strengthen the bonds between service personnel from different parts of the country and between units made up of soldiers, sailors and airmen, and the inhabitants of the regions they are garrisoned in, it also attempts to weaken slightly the loyalty they feel to the communities they have left behind. Some allegiances are encouraged; others are discouraged.

Official wariness of the bonds of allegiance that exists between members of the armed forces and their local communities and regions helps explain the composition of the Joint Task Forces sent to combat the MEND and the other Delta insurgents, and Boko Haram. It has long been alleged that the MEND has received both intelligence and material support from some of the service personnel and units sent to fight it. The country is periodically rocked by the news that yet more soldiers, sailors and airmen have been arrested and will stand trial for aiding and abetting the enemy.[48] Such acts raise urgent questions as to where the loyalties of certain units lie, and whether they can be truly trusted at critical moments.

These concerns are perhaps inevitable in a country where corruption is endemic. To reduce the risk of individuals and units giving

118   *Nigeria Since Independence*

into temptation or allowing their loyalty to a particular community to override their duty to the state, the armed forces' high command tries, whenever possible, to use troops with few personal ties to the region they are called on to operate in. Not only does practice reduce the likelihood of service personnel being asked to confront either people they know or are members of communities to which they might belong, but it also lessens the risk of their being exposed to blackmail and threats. For it is far harder for the MEND to locate and kidnap or threaten the friends and family of a soldier from Sokoto than it is one from Port Harcourt or even Lagos.

Using troops from outside the area of operations has the added benefit of making them less likely to disobey orders that require them to confront local people especially when they are called upon to use lethal force. Soldiers, sailors and airmen with familial links to an area may be less willing to fire on the people who live there than those with none. Such measures only improve the operational effectiveness of Nigeria's armed forces making them better able to cope with the threats to the Federal Government's authority and the country's continued territorial integrity which they must confront. Paradoxically, the military's, now standard, garrisoning and force generation policies on some occasions seek to foster stronger bonds of understanding between service personnel and the peoples of other ethnic groups and on others to exploit the lack of familiarity between them. Both approaches help ward off and counter act Nigeria's failure (albeit in markedly different ways).

Conclusions

Goodluck Jonathan's tortuous journey from Aguda House to Aso Rock marked a critical moment in Nigeria's development as a civilian-led democracy. His ordeal began the moment his predecessor, Umaru Yar'Adua, was spirited out of the country to receive medical treatment in Saudi Arabia, and it continued until days after his eventual victory in the 2011 presidential election. During that time he had to navigate a series of daunting political and social obstacles any one of which could have halted his progress indefinitely and, in so doing, escalate Nigeria's crisis. His fate was tied, from the outset, to that of the country as a whole. Should he have faltered then it too would have suffered. Civil war was an ever-present danger.

Of the People but for the People? 119

The starting shot that both launched Jonathan on his way and triggered the crisis he immediately found himself embroiled in was Yar'Adua's enforced withdrawal from public life. In the same instant that his medical evacuation became necessary, he ceased to be able to discharge the duties of his office effectively, with grave consequences for the Federal Government. Both the constitution and convention dictated that his direct and heavy involvement was critical to its function. In the very least he was required to shape and resolve policy debates; instruct his ministers and senior state functionaries and monitor their actions; and review and approve all new legislation. In Yar'Adua's absence, the uppermost echelons of the Federal Government were left all but paralysed.

This damaging and dangerous situation was brought about by the confluence of four distinct developments. The first, and most enduring, was the steady concentration of political power in the hands of the president. The executive continues to dominate the political system thereby ensuring that very little can happen without its involvement and agreement. The second was the length of time Yar'Adua spent out of the country: three months and a day. In itself his absence was not a problem even if it was highly unusual and could hardly be considered appropriate. The third was Yar'Adua's isolation. Very few people, and certainly no members of the Nigerian public, had access to him or could even speak with him directly.[49] Finally, the fourth was Yar'Adua's apparent refusal to relinquish power to Jonathan or some other stand-in. Together these developments helped ensure that Yar'Adua was unable to do his job while preventing anyone else from taking it on instead.

The first serious and overt attempt to resolve this situation was made in early December 2009 by the Nigerian Bar Association, which called on Yar'Adua to relinquish his powers to Jonathan.[50] While the Association's request was soundly ignored by the president, it helped draw public attention to both the severity of his illness and growing absence from the country. The Association's appeal was followed on 22 January 2010 with the Supreme Court's more robust demand to the Cabinet that it decide, within the next 14 days, whether Yar'Adua was fit enough to discharge his duties.[51] This order was similarly ignored although it heightened the mounting pressure on the other parts of the Federal Government to take the matter out of the president's hands given his seeming reluctance to step aside voluntarily.

120   *Nigeria Since Independence*

Finally, on 9 February 2010, the Senate ordered that Jonathan be sworn in as Acting President until Yar'Adua was well enough to take up the reins of office once again.[52] He never did.

While the Senate's decision helped bring some much needed stability to Nigerian politics and an end to the embarrassing fiasco of Yar'Adua's prolonged absence and incapacity, it also created the possibility of another, equally serious constitutional crisis. Despite the obvious need to resolve Yar'Adua's status, the Senate did not have the legal authority to strip him of his powers and invest them in Jonathan. In good faith, without bloodshed and with the strong backing of most of the country's international allies and many of its citizens, the Senate had devised and executed a *coup d'état* which had Jonathan, as its main beneficiary, squarely at its heart.

In times past, and not so very long ago, the circumstances leading up to Jonathan's assumption of power would have greatly tempted groups of military officers to intervene in the political process. With the president out of the country and incapacitated, confusion at home as to what was happening and who was in charge, and growing frustration among the general public with the ongoing paralysis of the Federal Government both the impetus and opportunity for a military takeover was strong. It is hard to imagine either Sani Abacha, or a young IBB or Buhari allowing such a situation to continue for as long as it did. Little wonder then that, throughout the long months of Yar'Adua's absence, Abuja was alive with speculation over whether the armed forces would intervene again.[53]

These concerns did not end, however, with Jonathan's assumption of power. Questions remained over what would happen should Yar'Adua return and try to reclaim his office. That he did not, and died shortly afterwards, spared Nigeria the agony and dangers of having to make a decision. But the issue of regional rotation remained unresolved. After Obasanjo's two terms in office, many in the north felt that it was their turn, through Yar'Adua, to occupy Aso Rock. Jonathan's ascension to the presidency, and subsequent victory in the election the following year, clearly cut this short. Throughout this period, and to this day, albeit in diminished form, doubts smouldered over the reliability of the armed forces' northern officers and the level of popular frustration in their home region.

That such concerns have proven to be ill founded both bodes well for civilian rule and democracy and highlights the military's

Of the People but for the People?   121

complex and ambiguous legacy. Its history, forged through its collective actions and by individual officers like Gowon, Obasanjo, Buhari and Abacha, is interwoven with that of Nigeria's drawn out and ongoing tussle with failure. Now, as in the past, the military has simultaneously and alternately worked against and facilitated the state's failure to control and failure to promote human flourishing. It has also striven to preserve the country's unity and stimulated or ignored the separatist impulses that threaten to tear it asunder. The armed forces remain Nigeria's greatest defender and one of its most dangerous threats.

Conclusions

On 16 April 2011, former Delta State governor and Special Advisor to the President of Nigeria, James Ibori, appeared before the City of Westminster magistrate in London. In a short hearing that lasted barely five minutes, he was formally charged with 25 counts of money laundering, financial fraud and larceny.[1] His request for bail was refused on the grounds that he was a flight risk. No bond, it was thought, was sufficiently large to prevent him from fleeing the country. Instead, he was remanded in custody at Wandsworth Prison until the start of his trial 12 days later at Southwark Crown Court.

These proceedings were the latest in a series of trials to be held at Southwark involving Ibori and his close associates. Indeed, over the previous 12 months four people had been tried and convicted of committing crimes on his behalf. On 22 November 2010, his wife, Theresa Ibori, was sentenced to five years in prison after being found guilty of money laundering.[2] Then, on 9 March 2011, his former lawyer, Bhadresh Gohil, was given a seven-year prison sentence after being convicted of fraud.[3] Finally, on 7 June 2011, his sister, Christine Ibie-Ibori, and mistress, Udoamaka Okoronkwo, were both given five-year prison terms after being found guilty of money laundering.[4]

Yet for much of the time the case against James Ibori was being prepared, it seemed unlikely to ever come to court. Not, as his supporters claimed, because it was built of straw. Indeed, it was sufficiently developed for the Metropolitan Police to trace its threads back to Nigeria and repeatedly petition Abuja for access to certain records.[5] Rather, it was the reluctance of the former Attorney-General of Nigeria, Michael Aondoakaa, to help his British counterparts. Time and again, he made a mockery of both President Yar'Adua's public support for the case and private assurances to the British government that he would do what he could to advance it, by refusing to give investigators in London the documents they were asking for.[6] Gone, it seemed, was the fruitful working relationship that had existed between the Metropolitan Police and the Economic and Financial Crimes Commission (EFCC) under President Obasanjo.[7] It was not until Aondoakaa was finally removed from office by President Goodluck Jonathan that Ibori's arrest was able to go ahead.[8]

Yet, even then, Ibori's journey to Westminster Magistrates' Court was far from straightforward. To begin with, the Nigerian police found it extremely difficult to enforce the arrest warrant for him. When rumours of its issue first began to circulate, Ibori quickly retreated to his hometown of Oghara in Delta State. There, he surrounded himself with hundreds of armed area boys who forcibly prevented police officers from approaching his compound.[9] Backed up by military units drawn from the Joint Task Force and State Security Service personnel, they mounted several raids to try to capture him.[10] But on each occasion they were driven back. Almost overnight, Oghara was turned into a no-go zone for the security forces.

The acute embarrassment this failure caused Nigeria's Federal Government was soon compounded by the stunning news that Ibori had escaped. Despite being wanted on both domestic and international arrest warrants, an easily recognisable public figure with a global profile, surrounded by hundreds of police officers, soldiers and SSS personnel, he had somehow managed to slip out of his compound and flee the country. To do this, he almost certainly received help from individuals in positions of authority such as immigration officers, customs officials, air traffic controllers and others. The Federal Government found itself in the unfortunate position, therefore, of being undermined in its efforts to apprehend Ibori by some of its own employees. And it was a blow for the new president personally. For he had flexed muscles and been found wanting.

For a short period after Ibori's disappearance, no one knew where he had gone. There was, of course, plenty of rumour and speculation. But the mystery was not fully solved until he resurfaced in Dubai some days later.[11] Not for him the fugitive's life of the Delta insurgent. Not for him the seclusion and dangers of the mangrove

124 *Nigeria Since Independence*

swamps and steaming creeks. Not for him the wearisome discomfort of the constant movement and temporary camps that came with such an existence. Indeed, his was to be an altogether more comfortable exile. A banishment of pampered luxury and five-star ease in the indulged and indulgent surroundings of this playground of the world's rich and famous. A gilded and air conditioned cage where he could hide from his pursuers.

Yet, unfortunately for Ibori, his time as a cosseted runaway was short-lived as he was picked up by the local police on 13 May 2010 on the outstanding international warrant for his arrest. Over the next 11 months, his lawyers fought a series of legal battles with the Dubai authorities and Metropolitan Police over his ongoing incarceration and proposed extradition to the United Kingdom. Time and again they argued vehemently for his release on bail and once succeeded in getting it granted.[12] But it was quickly revoked on the grounds that his past behaviour suggested that he might try to flee the country.[13] Ibori's lawyers employed a range of tactics and arguments to prevent his deportation to Britain. In addition to presenting his claim for political asylum in Dubai,[14] they also alleged that he was medically unfit to travel.[15]

The start of Ibori's trial represented a notable triumph for both the British government and the hard-pressed inhabitants of Delta State. For at long last one of the key architects of their misfortune and impoverishment, who, until so very recently, had enjoyed high level protection, was finally being asked to account for his actions. The frantic energy with which Ibori had resisted extradition evaporated almost the moment his trial began. And contrary to his earlier declarations of defiance he did not refute the legitimacy of the court or even contest the charges.[16] On 17 April 2012, he was sentenced to 13 years in prison and stripped of millions of pounds worth of assets.[17]

Yet Ibori's trial and subsequent conviction provided moments of sombre reflection for Nigerians. That he, a senior politician who for many years had occupied positions of considerable trust and responsibility, had been convicted of such crimes was deeply distressing. The discomfort this realisation caused was compounded by that generated by the difficulties the British and Nigerian governments encountered in trying to bring him to justice and the fact that his eventual trial was held not in Delta State or even Nigeria, the scenes

Conclusions   125

of his crimes, but in London. So great were his wealth and power that it took a concerted international effort to apprehend him. Even then, he was too big for Nigeria to handle. The depth of his pockets and extent of his reach meant that there was every chance that he might manipulate the country's justice system to suit his own ends.

Indeed, the remarkable drama of Ibori's rise and fall says much about the causes and consequences of Nigeria's failure as a state. Not only is Ibori strongly suspected of retaining and bankrolling some of the insurgents operating there, but his repeated raids on the Delta State treasury's coffers have helped ensure that there is a steady stream of hopeless young men willing to take up arms and engage in crime for want of anything else to do. Indeed, Ibori's actions have contributed to both Nigeria's failure to control and failure to promote the flourishing of its citizens in the Delta and elsewhere.

The spiralling violence and worsening instability of the past few years are sustaining a fierce debate over the extent and severity of Nigeria's failure as a state. That it is failed rather than failing is now beyond question, present tense not future. Nigeria is a failed state in two main ways. First, its government does not exercise total control over all parts of its sovereign territory. There are areas in the Niger Delta and in and around the north-eastern city of Maiduguri that lie beyond Abuja's direct and continuous authority. Second, it is failing to promote the flourishing of all its citizens. It does not provide all Nigerians with the public goods and social services that it should, including basic health care, primary education, law and order, impartial justice, sufficient electricity and properly maintained roads.

Despite its failure, Nigeria has avoided breaking up. There is, of course, a close relationship between state failure and state disintegration. For a start, many failed states have multiple, competing centres of authority within their borders. A government's inability to exercise total control over its territory does not necessarily mean an absence of governance in those areas that lie beyond its writ, but that the governance is exercised by some other authority. Indeed, and somewhat paradoxically, most failed states suffer from having too many governments rather than too few. These alternative poles of power often stimulate and give structure to the secessionist demands voiced by the region or community over which they have control.

126 *Nigeria Since Independence*

In Nigeria, the most serious threat of secession confronting the Federal Government is by the MEND which continues to whip up and marshal anti-Abuja sentiments in the Niger Delta. It is doing so for two main reasons. First, it wants to punish the federal authorities for not taking better care of the people who live in there. Second, it wants to give the region's inhabitants much greater control over the oil that is extracted from beneath their lands and the revenue it generates. Cleaving the Niger Delta from the rest of Nigeria and establishing it as an independent state is one way in which the group could achieve both these goals.

The MEND's sometime desire to break Nigeria apart is a key point of difference between the group and Boko Haram. For Boko Haram is not fighting to liberate a particular region or province from Abuja's authority. On the contrary, it wants to keep Nigeria together and impose sharia law throughout its entire territory. As the group's spokesman, Abu Qaqa, recently stated 'we will consider negotiation only when we have brought the government to their knees. Once we see that things are being done in accordance to the dictates of Allah, and our members are released [from prison], we will put aside our arms.'[18]

Nigeria's failure and continued unity are the result of three key mechanisms – federalism, oil, and the armed forces. Both individually and collectively these mechanisms play complex and contradictory roles. The revenues generated by the oil sector, for example, are a major motivating factor for those fighting both for and against the Delta's independence. The armed forces, the institution that has arguably done more than any other to keep Nigeria together, continue to stimulate resentment and separatist challenges as a result of its abuses of human rights, and the corruption engaged in by some of its senior officers. In such instances, Nigeria's endurance is not because of the state and its institutions but despite them.

These mechanisms help keep Nigeria together by affecting the behaviour of different groups and sections of society. Some help strengthen the state. They buttress and rehabilitate its institutions and agencies, improve its operation and make it more effective. They enhance its ability to provide Nigerians with the public goods they are due. Others contribute to the ongoing project of building a Nigerian nation. They promote ideas of a unified nation-state and seek to inculcate in the population a loyalty to it above and beyond that to other imagined communities of kith, kin, locale and religion. Others still facilitate the pursuit of self-interest. They exist to benefit select groups within society who currently have more to gain from Nigeria remaining intact than they do from it breaking up.

The book, then, had two main aims. First, to chart and examine the paradoxical effects of each of the three mechanisms in order to explain why Nigeria is failed yet intact and how it is a 'successful failed state.'[19] The second is to contribute to the ongoing debates over state failure. In particular, the book shows that chronic and persistent failure does not automatically lead to collapse and disintegration, and that there can be political and economic utility in failure for certain sections of society, most notably members of the political and business elites. Of course, the benefits they accrue are offset by other costs. Yet they are insufficient to totally cancel out the gains. Especially given the political, economic and social outlay attached to changing those factors causing Nigeria's failure, making Nigeria a failed state.

Notes

Introduction

1. Flora Shaw first proposed the name 'Nigeria' in an essay published in *The Times* on 8 January 1897. She married Sir Frederick Lugard in June 1902. Lugard first served as High Commissioner of the Protectorate of Northern Nigeria from its creation on 1 January 1900 until November 1906. He was later Governor-General of the Colony and Protectorate of Nigeria from 1 January 1914 to 8 August 1919. For a thoroughgoing account of Shaw's life see E. Morberly Bell, *Flora Shaw (D.B.E.)* (London: Constable, 1947).

2. In her essay to *The Times*, Shaw argued that 'the name Nigeria applying to no other part of Africa may without offence to any neighbours be accepted as co-extensive with the territories over which the Royal Niger Company has extended British influence, and may serve to differentiate them equally from the colonies of Lagos and the Niger Protectorate on the coast and from the French territories of the Upper Niger.' *The Times*, 'Nigeria', 8 January 1897, Issue 35095, p. 6, col. A.

3. At the time Flora Shaw's article was published, the British government had authority over two territories in the area that was to become Nigeria – the Lagos Colony and the Niger Coast Protectorate. The Lagos Colony had been established in 1862 and the Niger Coast Protectorate in 1891 as the Oil Rivers Protectorate. Its name was changed on 12 May 1893. A further larger territory, covering much of central and northern Nigeria, was administered by the Royal Niger Company.

4. On that date, the Protectorate of Northern Nigeria was combined with the Colony and Protectorate of southern Nigeria to form the Colony and Protectorate of Nigeria. It was renamed the Federation of Nigeria on 1 October 1954.

5. Eghosa E. Osaghae, *Nigeria since Independence: Crippled Giant* (London: Hurst, 1998), p. 2.

6. The term 'south–south' refers to the Niger Delta region.

7. Fund for Peace, *Failed State Index Scores 2011*, 2011, available at http://www.fundforpeace.org/global/?q=fsi-grid2011 (accessed 17 February 2012) and Fund for Peace, *Failed State Index Scores 2010*, 2010, available at http://www.fundforpeace.org/web/index.php?option=com_content&task=view&id=452&Itemid=900 (accessed 18 February 2011).

8. Fund for Peace, *Failed State Index Scores 2009*, 2009, available at http://www.fundforpeace.org/web/index.php?option=com_content&task=view&id=391&Itemid=549 (accessed 18 February 2011).

9. Fund for Peace, *Failed States Index Scores 2008*, 2008, available at http://www.fundforpeace.org/web/index.php?option=com_content&task=view&id=292&Itemid=452 (accessed 18 February 2011).

Notes 129

10. Fund for Peace, *Failed States Index Scores 2007*, 2007, available at http://www.fundforpeace.org/web/index.php?option=com_content&task=vie w&id=229&Itemid=366 (accessed 18 February 2011).
11. Fund for Peace, *Failed States Index Scores 2006*, 2006, available at http://www.fundforpeace.org/web/index.php?option=com_content&task=vie w&id=104&Itemid=324 (accessed 18 February 2011).
12. Fund for Peace, *Failed States Index Scores 2005*, 2005, available at http://www.fundforpeace.org/web/index.php?option=com_content&task=vie w&id=103&Itemid=325 (accessed 18 February 2011).
13. The World Bank defines absolute poverty as living on $1.25 or less a day and moderate poverty as living on $2 or less a day.
14. Cited in BBC, *Nigerians living in poverty rises to nearly 61%*, 13 February 2012, available at http://www.bbc.co.uk/news/world-africa-17015873 (accessed 18 February 2012), p. 1.
15. These countries are second, tenth, fifteenth and thirtieth respectively in the Fund for Peace's 2011 Failed State Index. Fund for Peace, *Failed State Index Scores 2011*.
16. The six states in question are Akwa Ibom, Bayelsa, Cross River, Delta, Edo and Rivers.
17. For a fuller explanation of the concept of imagined communities see Benedict Anderson, *Imagined Communities* (2nd ed.) (London and New York: Verso, 1991).

1 Fear of Failure: Negative Sovereignty and the Birth of State Failure

1. The population of each is Benin 9,211,700; Burkina Faso 16,268,700; Cameroon 19,958,400; the Central African Republic 4,505,900; Chad 11,506,100; Côte d'Ivoire 21,570,700; the Democratic Republic of the Congo 67,827,500; Gabon 1,501,300; Madagascar 20,146,400; Mali 13,323,100; Mauritania 3,365,700; Niger 15,891,500; Nigeria 158,258,900; the Republic of the Congo 3,758,700; Senegal 12,860,700; Somalia 9,358,600; and Togo 6,780,000. United Nations, *Country Profiles and Human Development Indicators*, 2010, available at http://hdr.undp.org /en/countries/ (accessed 23 May 2011).
2. The five sub-regions are North, East, Southern, Central and West. The only sub-region not represented was the southern.
3. British Somaliland gained its independence on 26 June 1960 and Italian Somaliland five days later on 1 July 1960.
4. Two car bombs exploded outside the Ministry of Justice on 1 October 2010. Reuters, *Bombs Rattle Independence Day in Nigeria*, 1 October 2010, available at http://af.reuters.com/article/worldNews/idAFTRE6902IJ20101001 (accessed 24 May 2011), p. 1.
5. For example, descriptions of Côte d'Ivoire, the DRC and Somalia as failed can be found in Thomas Dempsey, *Counter-Terrorism in African Failed States: Challenges and Potential Solutions* (Carlisle, Pennsylvania: U.S. Army

130 *Notes*

War College Strategic Studies Institute, 2006), p. 12, and Robert I. Rotberg (ed.), *When States Fail* (Princeton, New Jersey: Princeton University Press, 2004), p. 5.

6. Joel S. Migdal, *Strong Societies and Weak States: State-Society Relations and State Capabilities in the Third World* (Princeton, New Jersey: Princeton University Press, 1988), p. 4.

7. I. William Zartman (ed.), *Collapsed States: The Disintegration and Restoration of Legitimate Authority* (Boulder, Colorado: Lynne Rienner Publishers, 1995), p. 5.

8. Robert H. Jackson, *The Global Covenant: Human Conduct in the World of States* (Oxford: Oxford University Press, 2000), p. 296.

9. Rotberg, *When States Fail*, p. 1.

10. Jean-Germain Gros, 'Towards a Taxonomy of Failed States in the New World Order: Decaying Somalia, Liberia, Rwanda and Haiti,' *Third World Quarterly*, September 1996, Vol. 17, No. 3, p. 456.

11. Weber defines the ideal state as 'a compulsory association with a territorial base ... [where] the use of force is regarded as legitimate only so far as it is either permitted by the state, or prescribed by it. ... The claim of the modern state to monopolize the use of force is essential to its character of compulsory jurisdiction and of continuous organization.' Max Weber, *The Theory of Social and Economic Organization* (New York: The Free Press, 1947), p. 143.

12. Robert H. Jackson, *Quasi-States: Sovereignty, International Relations and the Third World* (Cambridge: Cambridge University Press, 1990), p. 29.

13. Ibid.

14. Ibid.

15. Ibid., 27.

16. Robert H. Jackson and Carl G. Rosberg, 'Why Africa's Weak States Persist: The Empirical and the Juridical in Statehood,' *World Politics*, October 1982, Vol. 35, No. 1, p. 2.

17. This argument is developed and outlined by Jackson over the course of a number of works. See Jackson and Rosberg, 'Why Africa's Weak States Persist'; Robert H. Jackson and Carl G. Rosberg, 'Sovereignty and Underdevelopment: Juridical Statehood in the African Crisis,' *The Journal of Modern African Studies*, 1986, Vol. 24, No. 1, pp. 1–31; Jackson, *Quasi-States*; Robert H. Jackson, 'Juridical Statehood in Sub-Saharan Africa,' *Journal of International Affairs*, 1992, Vol. 46, No. 1, pp. 1–16; and Jackson, *The Global Covenant*.

18. Perhaps nowhere is this wait-and-see policy better highlighted than in Algeria. Concerned that Algeria might slip into the Soviet Union's sphere of influence if and when it achieved independence, the U.S. government pushed its French counterpart to cut a deal with the National Liberation Front's (NLF). Paris found itself in the unenviable position, therefore, of being harangued by its friends and foes alike. For an excellent analysis of the impact of Cold War politics on Algeria's quest for independence see Matthew J. Connelly, *A Diplomatic Revolution: Algeria's Fight for*

Notes 131

Independence and the Origins of the Post-Cold War Era (Oxford: Oxford University Press, 2002).

19. Jackson, *Quasi States*, p. 40.
20. Ibid., 85.
21. United Nations General Assembly, *1514 Declaration on the Granting of Independence to Colonial Countries and Peoples*, 14 December 1960, available at http://daccess-dds-ny.un.org/doc/RESOLUTION/GEN/NR0/152/88/IMG/NR015288.pdf?OpenElement (accessed 25 May 2011).
22. Organisation of African Unity, *OAU Charter*, 25 May 1963, available at http://www.au.int/en/sites/default/files/OAU_Charter_1963_0.pdf (accessed 25 May 2011), Article III.
23. Mohammed Ayoob, *The Third World Security Predicament: State Making, Regional Conflict and the International System* (Boulder, Colorado: Lynne Rienner Publishers, 1995), p. 78.
24. United Nations General Assembly, *1541 Principles Which Should Guide Members in Determining Whether or Not an Obligation Exists to Transmit the Information Called for Under Article 73e of the Charter*, 15 December 1960, available at http://daccess-dds-ny.un.org/doc/RESOLUTION/GEN/NR0/153/15/IMG/NR015315.pdf?OpenElement (accessed 25 May 2011).
25. South Sudan was finally recognised as an independent sovereign state on 9 July 2011.
26. The other is Eritrea which won its independence from Ethiopia in the early 1990s. Yet even then there was still a two-year gap between when it achieved independence (24 May 1991) and when it was recognised as a sovereign state (24 May 1993) by the international community.
27. John A. A. Ayoade, 'States without Citizens: An Emerging African Phenomenon,' in Donald Rothchild and Naomi Chazan (eds.), *The Precarious Balance: State and Society in Africa* (Boulder, Colorado: Westview Press, 1988), pp. 100–118.
28. Gros, 'Towards a Taxonomy of Failed States in the New World Order,' p. 461.
29. Ibid.
30. Rotberg, *When States Failed*, pp. 17–19.
31. Ibid., 5.
32. Ibid., 9.
33. Rotberg, *When States Failed*, p. 9.
34. International Commission on Intervention and State Sovereignty, *The Responsibility to Protect*, December 2001, available at http://www.iciss.ca/report2-en.asp (accessed 10 June 2011).
35. Paul D. Williams, *State Failure in Africa: Causes, Consequences and Response*, 2007, available at http://elliott.gwu.edu/assets/docs/research/williams07.pdf (accessed 3 May 2011), p. 2.
36. Ibid.
37. United Nations General Assembly, *2005 World Summit Outcomes*, 15 September 2005, available at http://www.who.int/hiv/universalaccess2010/worldsummit.pdf (accessed 10 June 2011), p. 31.

132 *Notes*

38. Williams, *State Failure in Africa*, p. 2.
39. The UK's 2009 National Security Strategy argued that 'Al Qa'ida affiliates will develop more autonomy...[and] will continue to gravitate towards fragile and failing states.' UK Cabinet Office, *The National Security Strategy of the United Kingdom: Update 2009: Security for the Next Generation*, June 2009, available at http://www.official-documents.gov.uk/document /cm75/7590/7590.pdf (accessed 21 July 2011), p. 44.
40. The UK's 2010 National Security Strategy asserted that 'fragile, failing and failed states around the world provide the environment for terrorists to operate as they look to exploit ungoverned or ill-governed space.' UK Cabinet Office, *A Strong Britain in an Age of Uncertainty: The National Security Strategy*, October 2010, available at http://www.direct.gov.uk/prod_consum_dg/groups/dg_digitalassets/@dg/@en/documents/digitalasset /dg_191639.pdf?CID=PDF&PLA=furl&CRE=nationalsecuritystrategy (accessed 21 July 2011), p. 28.
41. This concern was expressed most clearly by the UK's former Secretary of State for International Development Hilary Benn. In June 2004 he made a speech to the Centre for Global Development in Washington warning that 'states that are unable or unwilling to sustain strong public health systems can become reservoirs of communicable diseases – HIV/AIDS, polio and malaria.' Hilary Benn, *A Shared Challenge: Promoting Development and Human Security in Weak States*, 23 June 2004, available at http://www.cgdev. org/doc/weakstates/WeakStates_Benn.pdf (accessed 21 July 2011), p. 3.
42. Jack Straw, *Failed and Failing States*, speech delivered 6 September 2002 at the European Research Institute, University of Birmingham, available at http://www.mafhoum.com/press3/111P3.htm (accessed 6 August 2012).
43. For example, U.S. officials have applied the term failing state to the Italian region of Calabria. This usage is at odds with its original academic meaning which applied to states alone, not subsections of them. *The Economist*, 'Failed States: Where Talk Is Cheap and Talk Is Loose', 17 May 2011, available at www.economist.com/node/18396240 (accessed 3 June 2011), p. 1.

2 The Enemy Within: Insurgency and the Failure of the Nigerian State

1. Ojo Maduekwe, *Lest we Forget*, public lecture delivered 30 September 2004.
2. BBC, *Nigeria Nearing a 'Failed State,'* 18 August 2009, available at http: //news.bbc.co.uk/go/pr/fr/-/1/hi/world/africa/8207736.stm (accessed 15 February 2011), p. 1.
3. The Independent, *Nigeria Is Falling Apart, Says Nobel Prize-Winning Author*, 16 March 2010, available at http://www.independent.co.uk/news/world /africa/nigeria-is-falling-apart-says-nobelprizewinning-author-1921835. html (accessed 15 February 2011), p. 1.

Notes 133

4. Punch, *Kidnappings: Nigeria May become a Failed State – ASUU*, 1 February 2011, available at http://www.punchontheweb.com/Articl.aspx?theartic= Art201102013433382 (accessed 15 February 2011), p. 1.
5. Sunday Tribune, *Nigeria Is Showing Symptoms of a Failed State – Okei-Odumakin*, 31 July 2011, available at http://tribune.com.ng/sun /interview/4665-nigeria-is-showing-symptoms-of-a-failed-state-okei-odumakin (accessed 20 April 2012).
6. J.N.C. Hill, *Sufism in Northern Nigeria: A Force for Counter Radicalisation?* (Carlisle, Pennsylvania: Strategic Studies Institute US Army War College, 2010) and Abimbola Adesoji, *The Boko Haram Uprising and Islamic Revivalism in Nigeria*, Africa Spectrum, 2010, Vol. 45, No. 2, pp. 98–99.
7. The Guardian, *Boko Haram Vows to Fight until Nigeria Establishes Sharia Law*, 27 January 2012, available at http://www.guardian.co.uk/world/2012 /jan/27/boko-haram-nigeria-sharia-law (accessed 23 April 2012).
8. This Day, *Boko Haram – Death Toll Now 700, Says Security Commander*, 2 August 2009, available at http://www.thisdayonline.info/nview. php?id=150423 (accessed 3 December 2010).
9. Daily Trust, *Boko Haram – Why We Executed Them*, 22 September 2009, available at http://allafrica.com/stories/200909221140.html (accessed 3 December 2010) and BBC, *Nigeria Sect Head Dies in Custody*, 31 July 2009, available at http://news.bbc.co.uk/1/hi/8177451.stm (accessed 3 December 2010).
10. This Day, *Nigeria: Borno ANPP Chairman Killed in Suspected Boko Haram Attack*, 7 October 2010, available at http://allafrica.com /stories/201010080326.html (accessed 27 April 2012).
11. BBC, *'Boko Haram' Gunmen Kill Muslim Cleric Birkuti*, 7 June 2011, available at http://www.bbc.co.uk/news/world-africa-13679234 (accessed 27 April 2012).
12. Amnesty International, *Nigeria: Armed Groups Targeting Civilians in Latest Bombings*, 27 June 2011, available at http://www.amnesty. org/en/for-media/press-releases/nigeria-armed-groups-targeting-civilians-latest-bombings-2011–06–27 (accessed 28 April 2012).
13. BBC, *Nigeria Boko Haram Islamists 'Bomb Maiduguri Drinkers'*, 27 June 2011, available at http://www.bbc.co.uk/news/world-africa-13920980 (accessed 28 April 2012).
14. New York Times, *Suicide Bomber Attacks U.N. Building in Nigeria*, 26 August 2011, available at http://www.nytimes.com/2011/08/27/world /africa/27nigeria.html?pagewanted=all (accessed 27 April 2012).
15. In this instance, the Federal Capital Territory is included as a state.
16. Nigerian Tribune, *Suspected Boko Haram Members Ambush Police Patrol Team in Damaturu*, 19 January 2012, available at http://www.tribune.com. ng/index.php/news/34589-suspected-boko-haram-members-ambush-police-patrol-team-in-damaturu – cp (accessed 29 April 2012).
17. BBC, *Nigeria Jailbreak: Boko Haram Claims Kogi Prison Attack*, 16 February 2012, available at http://www.bbc.co.uk/news/world-africa-17059895 (accessed 29 April 2012).

134 *Notes*

18. Reuters, *Islamists Kill Dozens in Nigeria Christmas Bombs*, 25 December 2011, available at http://www.reuters.com/article/2011/12/25/us-nigeria-blast-idUSTRE7BO03020111225 (accessed 29 April 2012).
19. Reuters, *Suicide Car Bombs Hit Nigerian Newspaper Offices*, 26 April 2012, available at http://www.reuters.com/article/2012/04/26/us-nigeria-bomb-idUSBRE83P0NR20120426 (accessed 29 April 2012).
20. Vanguard, *Boko Haram Bombs Kano Afresh*, 24 January 2012, available at http://www.vanguardngr.com/2012/01/boko-haram-bombs-kano-afresh/ (accessed 29 April 2012).
21. Jane's, *Movement for the Emancipation of the Niger Delta (MEND)*, 10 May 2012, available at http://articles.janes.com/articles/Janes-World-Insurgency-and-Terrorism/Movement-for-the-Emancipation-of-the-Niger-Delta-MEND-Nigeria.html (accessed 2 May 2012).
22. Ibid.
23. Alamieyeseigha was arrested by the UK's Metropolitan Police in September 2005 on charges of money laundering. He fled the country, allegedly by disguising himself as a woman, after he was released on bail. When police officers raided his flat in the Water Gardens district of West London, they found nearly one million pounds in cash in various currencies along with an assortment of other treasures. Indeed so wealthy was Alamieyeseigha, he could afford to forfeit these valuables and his considerable bail bond. Michael Peel, *A Swamp Full of Dollars: Pipelines and Paramilitaries at Nigeria's Oil Frontier* (London and New York: I.B. Tauris, 2009), pp. 105–106. On 26 July 2007 he was sentenced to two years in prison by a Nigerian court after pleading guilty to charges of theft and money laundering. He was released almost straight away due to the amount of time he had already served.
24. Vanguard, *MEND Proposes 11-Point Agenda for Peace in the Niger Delta*, 18 February 2008, available at http://www.vanguardngr.com/index.php?option=com_content&task=view&id=2490&Itemid=43 (accessed 18 February 2008).
25. The Daily Telegraph, *Car Bomb Attacks on Nigeria's Independence Day Kill 10*, 1 October 2010, available at http://www.telegraph.co.uk/news/worldnews/africaandindianocean/nigeria/8037584/Car-bomb-attacks-on-Nigerias-independence-day-kill-10.html (accessed 12 October 2010).
26. Michael Watts, 'Blood Oil: The Anatomy of a Petro-Insurgency in the Niger Delta, Nigeria,' in Andrea Behrends, Stephen P. Reyna and Günther Schlee (eds.), *Crude Domination: An Anthropology of Oil* (Oxford: Berghahn Books, 2011), p. 61.
27. Ibid.
28. Nigerian Guardian, *Gunmen Strike in N'Delta, Kill Three Naval Officers*, 4 February 2008, available at http://www.guardiannewsngr.com/news/article04//indexn3_html?pdate=040208&ptitle=Gunmen%20strike%20in%20N'Delta,%20kill%20three%20naval%20officers&cpdate=040208 (accessed 2 April 2008).
29. Punch, *Militants Abduct Lawmaker's Sister*, 8 January 2008, available at http://www.punchontheweb.com/Articl.aspx?theartic=Art2008010813

Notes 135

62242 (accessed 10 January 2008) and The Daily Telegraph, *British Oil Contractor Kidnapped by Gunmen in Nigeria*, 20 February 2006, available at http://www.telegraph.co.uk/news/worldnews/africaandindianocean /nigeria/1510983/British-oil-contractor-kidnapped-by-gunmen-in-Nigeri a.html (accessed 3 May 2012).

30. Houston Press, *The Cost of Doing Business*, 21 September 2006, available at http://www.houstonpress.com/2006-09-21/news/the-cost-of-doing-business/ (accessed 3 May 2012).

31. John Campbell, 'Nigeria on the Brink: What Happens if the 2011 Elections Fail?' *Foreign Affairs*, 9 September 2010, available at http://www.foreignaffairs.com/articles/66746/john-campbell/nigeria-on-the-brink?page=show (accessed 15 July 2011), p. 1.

32. Indeed, and as Graf puts it, 'if the Federal Government did not exactly provide a textbook lesson in how to conduct a *war* – stories of inefficiency, indiscipline among the ranks, lost opportunities and the like were rampant – it did in some measure demonstrate how a lasting *peace* could be made.' William D. Graf, *The Nigerian State* (London: James Currey, 1988), p. 44. Yet these inefficiencies aside, Gowon did win the war and, in the process, stopped Nigeria from breaking up.

33. Somewhat bizarrely IBB once referred to himself as the 'Evil Genius.' Karl Maier, *This House Has Fallen: Nigeria in Crisis* (London: Penguin Books, 2000), p. 43.

34. Vanguard, *Army Court-Martials 15 Officers over Missing Arms*, 14 January 2008, available at http://www.vanguardngr.com/index.php?option=com_ content&task=view&id=4474&Itemid=0 (accessed 18 January 2008), p. 1.

35. BBC, *Can Nigeria's Police be Reformed?* 30 July 2009, available at http: //news.bbc.co.uk/1/hi/world/africa/8034141.stm (accessed 5 May 2012).

36. Senior member of the British High Commission Abuja, interview by author, Abuja, 13 December 2008.

37. Oga is a Pidgin word meaning 'big-man'.

38. Daniel Jordan Smith, *A Culture of Corruption: Everyday Deception and Popular Discontent in Nigeria* (Princeton and Oxford: Princeton University Press, 2007), pp. 171–174.

39. BBC, *Nigeria Rescue Bid: Kidnapped Briton and Italian Killed*, 8 March 2012, available at http://www.bbc.co.uk/news/uk-17305707 (accessed 5 May 2012).

40. Vanguard, *Nigeria: Army/Police Clash, Which Way Forward*, 3 June 2011, available at http://allafrica.com/stories/201106030868.html (accessed 5 May 2012).

41. Smith, *A Culture of Corruption*, p. 171.

42. Amnesty International, *Tens of Thousands Caught in Crossfire in Niger Delta Fighting*, 21 May 2009, available at http://www.amnesty.org/en /news-and-updates/news/tens-thousands-caught-crossfire-nige r-delta-fighting-20090521 (accessed 6 July 2011), p. 1.

43. Human Rights Watch, *Nigeria: Arbitrary Killings by Security Forces in Jos*, 19 December 2008, available at http://www.unhcr.org/refworld /docid/49509c061a.html (accessed 6 July 2011), p. 1.

136 *Notes*

44. U.S. Department of State, *2010 Human Rights Report: Nigeria*, 8 April 2011, available at http://www.state.gov/g/drl/rls/hrrpt/2010/af/154363.htm (accessed 6 July 2011), p. 1.
45. Amnesty International, *Annual Report 2011: Nigeria*, 2011, available at http://www.amnesty.org/en/region/nigeria/report-2011 (accessed 6 July 2011).
46. The Guardian, *Nigerian Churches Targeted by Christmas Day Bombs*, 25 December 2011, available at http://www.guardian.co.uk/world/2011/dec/25/nigerian-church-bombed-christmas-prayers (accessed 6 May 2012).
47. BBC, *Nigeria Church Hit by Deadly Gun Attack in Gombe*, 5 January 2012, available at http://www.bbc.co.uk/news/world-africa-16436112 (accessed 6 May 2012).
48. BBC, *Nigerian Christians Hit by Fresh Islamist Attacks*, 7 January 2012, available at http://www.bbc.co.uk/news/world-africa-16442960 (accessed 6 May 2012).
49. BBC, *Nigeria Violence: Scores Dead after Kano Blasts*, 21 January 2012, available at http://www.bbc.co.uk/news/world-africa-16663693 (accessed 6 May 2012).
50. BBC, *German Engineer Kidnapped in Kano Nigeria*, 26 January 2012, available at http://www.bbc.co.uk/news/world-africa-16745509 (accessed 6 May 2012).
51. BBC, *Nigeria Unrest: 'Suicide Attack' on Kaduna Barracks*, 7 February 2012, available at http://www.bbc.co.uk/news/world-africa-16931981 (accessed 6 May 2012).
52. The Guardian, *Pirates Attack Cargo Ship off Nigeria*, 13 February 2012, available at http://www.guardian.co.uk/world/2012/feb/13/pirates-attack-cargo-ship-nigeria (accessed 6 May 2012).
53. The Guardian, *Nigerian Prison Raid Frees 118 Inmates*, 16 February 2012, available at http://www.guardian.co.uk/world/2012/feb/16/attack-nigerian-prison-escape-118-inmates (accessed 6 May 2012).
54. BBC, *Nigeria Rescue Bid*.
55. Ibid.
56. BBC, *Deadly Attack on Nigeria's Bayero University in Kano*, 30 April 2012, available at http://www.bbc.co.uk/news/world-africa-17886143 (accessed 6 May 2012).
57. United Nations, *Nigeria*, 2011, available at http://data.un.org/Country Profile.aspx?crName=NIGERIA#Social (accessed 26 June 2011), p. 1.
58. Then it stood at 40 years of age. United Nations Children's Fund, *Nigeria*, 2 March 2010, available at http://www.unicef.org/infobycountry/nigeria_statistics.html#78 (accessed 6 July 2011), Demographics.
59. United Nations, *Nigeria*, 2010, available at http://hdrstats.undp.org/en/countries/profiles/NGA.html (accessed 26 June 2011), p. 1.
60. World Bank, *Nigeria*, 2011, available at http://web.worldbank.org/WBSITE/EXTERNAL/COUNTRIES/AFRICAEXT/NIGERIAEXTN/0,,contentMDK:22553025~pagePK:141137~piPK:141127~theSitePK:368896,00.html (accessed 6 July 2011), p. 1.

Notes 137

61. Department for International Development, *Nigeria*, June 2008, available at www.dfid.gov.uk/countries/africa/Nigeria-facts.asp (accessed 11 February 2009), p. 1.
62. World Health Organisation, *Nigeria: Health Profile*, 4 April 2011, available at http://www.who.int/gho/countries/nga.pdf (accessed 6 July 2011), p. 2.
63. United Nations, *Adult Literacy Rates both Sexes (% Aged 15 and Above)*, 2011, available at http://hdrstats.undp.org/en/indicators/101406.html (accessed 7 May 2012).
64. The World Bank, *Education: Data and Statistics*, 2011, available at http://web.worldbank.org/WBSITE/EXTERNAL/TOPICS/EXTEDUCATION/0,,contentMDK:20573961~isCURL:Y~menuPK:282412~pagePK:148956~piPK:216618~theSitePK:282386,00.html (accessed 7 May 2012).
65. Ibid.
66. Thomas Hylland Eriksen, 'A Non-Ethnic State for Africa? A Life-World Approach to the Imagining of Communities,' in Paris Yeros (ed.), *Ethnicity and Nationalism in Africa: Constructivist Reflections and Contemporary Politics* (Basingstoke, Hampshire: Palgrave MacMillan, 1999), p. 56.
67. Ibid.
68. For example, 10,560 Nigerian nationals were granted British citizenship in 2007 and 2008 alone. UK Home Office, *British Citizenship Statistics United Kingdom, 2008*, 20 May 2009, available at http://www.homeoffice.gov.uk/publications/about-us/non-personal-data/Passports-immigration/citizenship-statistics-1998–2008/british-citizenship-stats-2008?view=Binary (accessed 13 July 2011), p. 7.
69. Chief Ralph Uwazuruike, The Aba Declaration: Birth of New Biafra, public speech delivered 22 May 2000.
70. Immigration and Refugee Board of Canada, *Nigeria: Treatment of Members of the Movement for the Actualisation of the Sovereign State of Biafra (MASSOB); availability of State Protection (August 2004–June 2005)*, 27 June 2005, available at http://www.unhcr.org/refworld/country,,IRBC,,NGA,,440ed73221,0.html (accessed 7 May 2012).
71. The two men, Chris McManus and Franco Lamolinara, had been working for an Italian construction firm, B Stabilini, on a road project in Kebbi State in the north-west of the country. They were abducted from McManus's home in the city of Birnin Kebbi. A third man, a German, escaped when the raid took place and a fourth, a Nigerian, was shot and wounded and left behind.
72. News of the failed raid was reported all over the world: Al Jazeera, *Western Hostages Killed in Nigeria*, 9 March 2012, available at http://www.aljazeera.com/news/africa/2012/03/20123820234528508.html (accessed 25 March 2012); The Financial Times, *Italy Attacks UK Over Nigeria Hostage Rescue*, 9 March 2012, available at http://www.ft.com/cms/s/0/f371d0fa-6a04–11e1-b54f-00144feabdc0.html#axzz1q8acTm1G (accessed 25 March 2012); The Independent, *Raid was 'Best Chance' to Rescue Nigeria Hostages*, 13 March 2012, available at http://www.independent.co.uk/news/world/africa/raid-was-best-chance-to-rescue-nigeria-hostages-7565498.html

138 *Notes*

(accessed 25 March 2012); France 24, *European Hostages Killed in Joint Rescue Attempt*, 9 March 2012, available at http://www.france24.com /en/20120308-european-hostages-killed-nigeria-rescue-attempt-british-italian-cameron (accessed 25 March 2012); Irish Times, *Foreign Hostages Killed in Nigeria*, 8 March 2012, available at http://www.irishtimes.com /newspaper/breaking/2012/0308/breaking50.html (accessed 25 March 2012); USA Today, *British, Italian Hostages Killed in Nigeria Rescue*, 8 March 2012, available at http://www.usatoday.com/news/world/story/2012–03–08 /nigeria-hostages/53417830/1 (accessed 25 March 2012); Vanguard, *British, Italian Hostages Killed in Failed Rescue in Nigeria*, 8 March 2012 available at http://vanguardngr.com/2012/03/british-italian-hostages-killed-in-failed-rescue/ (accessed 25 March 2012).

73. Robin Hughes and Matthew Maguire, for example, was held captive by the MEND for several months in 2008 and 2009. The Guardian, *Niger Delta Militants to Release British Hostage*, 19 April 2009, available http://www.guardian.co.uk /world/2009/apr/19/robin-hughes-hostage-nigeria-release (accessed 4 May 2012).

3 The Emperor's New Clothes? Federalism, the Decline of Old Loyalties and the Rise of New Jealousies

1. Eghosa E. Osaghae, *Nigeria since Independence: Crippled Giant* (London: Hurst, 1998), p. 34.
2. The federal parliament comprised of 312 seats: 174 of these were filled by representatives elected by northern voters, 73 by eastern, 62 by western and 3 by Lagosian. Osaghae, *Nigeria since* Independence, p. 32.
3. The National Council of Nigeria and the Cameroons changed its name to the National Council of Nigerian Citizens in January 1962 after the British mandate territory of Southern Cameroons became part of the independent Republic of Cameroon on 1 October 1961.
4. C.M. Ngou, 'The 1959 Elections and Formation of the Independence Government,' in Peter Ekeh (ed.), *Nigeria since Independence: The First 25 Years* (Ibadan: Heinemann, 1989), p. 100.
5. William D. Graf, *The Nigerian State* (London: James Currey, 1988), p. 36.
6. Ibid.
7. Ibid.
8. The AG's other most important figure, Samuel Akintola, who was premier of the western region, supported the NPC thereby causing a serious split in the party.
9. The remaining five seats were all taken by independent candidates.
10. The remaining 36 seats of the NNA's haul were won by the NNDP, the renamed rump of the AG led by Samuel Akintola, in the west. This was 21 more than the AG, the traditional power in the region.
11. Walter Schwarz, *Nigeria* (New York: Praeger, 1968), p. 178.

Notes 139

12. His murder by the second group of conspirators was not officially confirmed until 4 January 1967.
13. Osaghae, *Nigeria since Independence*, p. 63.
14. Lagos first became a crown colony on 5 March 1862.
15. Kalu N. Kalu, *State Power, Autarchy, and Political Conquest in Nigerian Federalism* (New York: Lexington books, 2008), p. 189.
16. Federal Republic of Nigeria, *Constitution of the Federal Republic of Nigeria* (5 May 1999), Article 8(1 a i, ii, iii, b, c and d).
17. Federal Republic of Nigeria, *Constitution of the Federal Republic of Nigeria* (1979), Article 277(1), Federal Republic of Nigeria, *Constitution of the Federal Republic of Nigeria* (1989), Article 329(1), and Federal Republic of Nigeria, *Constitution of the Federal Republic of Nigeria* (5 May 1999), Article 318(1).
18. Human Rights Watch, *Arbitrary Killings by Security Forces: Submission to the Investigative Bodies on the November 28–29, 2008*, July 2009, available at http://www.hrw.org/sites/default/files/reports/nigeria0709web.pdf (accessed 2 April 2012), p. 3, and John Boye Ejobowah, *Recognition in the Nigerian Public Sphere: A Liberal Argument about Justice in Plural Societies* (Lanham, Maryland: Lexington Books, 2001), p. 140.
19. Federal Republic of Nigeria, *Constitution of the Federal Republic of Nigeria* (5 May 1999), Article 15(3 a, b, c, and d).
20. This commitment to rotate the top jobs between the members of different ethnic groups is set down in the constitution of the ruling People's Democratic Party (PDP) to which both Yar'Adua and Jonathan belong. It states that 'in pursuance of the principle of equity, justice and fairness, the party shall adhere to the policy of rotation and zoning of party and public elective offices and it shall be enforced by the appropriate executive committee at all levels.' People's Democratic Party, *Constitution*, 28 July 1998, available at http://www.peoplesdemocraticparty.net/attachments/article/7 /PDP%20constitution.pdf (accessed 7 August 2012), Article 7 (7.2 c).
21. Under the provisions of the constitution, he was obliged to step down having nearly completed the second of his two permitted terms in office. To free himself from this requirement, Obasanjo attempted to have the constitution changed. In May 2006, he placed a motion before the Senate calling for the removal of all limits on the length of time an individual could serve as president. And to smooth its passage through the house, he allegedly offered Senators huge cash bribes (in some instances up to $750,000) in return for their support. Despite his best efforts, Obasanjo failed to secure the votes he needed. Jean Herskovits, 'Nigeria's Rigged Democracy,' *Foreign Affairs*, July/August 2007, Vol. 86, No. 4.
22. Aso Rock is the name given to the president's compound in Abuja. This was not the only reason why Nigerians were keen to see Obasanjo step down, but it was one of them.
23. General Obasanjo, as he was then, was head of the Federal Military Government from 13 February 1976 to 1 October 1979.

140 *Notes*

24. Federal Republic of Nigeria, *Constitution of the Federal Republic of Nigeria* (5 May 1999), Article 146.
25. 'The President shall vacate his office at the expiration of a period of four years commencing from the date.' Federal Republic of Nigeria, *Constitution of the Federal Republic of Nigeria* (5 May 1999), Article 135(2).
26. Transparency International, *Corruption Perceptions Index 2011*, 2011, available http://cpi.transparency.org/cpi2011/results/ (accessed 12 March 2012). Demands for better government must be heeded.
27. Federal Republic of Nigeria, *Constitution of the Federal Republic of Nigeria* (5 May 1999), Articles 90, 91 92(1), 93, 176(1), 186, 197(1 a, b, c and 3).
28. Federal Republic of Nigeria, *Constitution of the Federal Republic of Nigeria* (5 May 1999), Article 133 and 132.
29. Federal Republic of Nigeria, *Constitution of the Federal Republic of Nigeria* (5 May 1999), Article 222(a, b, e and f).
30. Federal Republic of Nigeria, *Constitution of the Federal Republic of Nigeria* (5 May 1999), Article 223 (1 b and 2 b).
31. Cited in Matthew Parris and Andrew Bryson, *Parting Shots* (London: Viking, 2010), pp. 282–283.

4 Fuel to the Flames: Oil and Political Violence in Contemporary Nigeria

1. U.S. Department of Energy, *Country Analysis Briefs: Nigeria*, August 2011, available at http://www.eia.gov/EMEU/cabs/Nigeria/pdf.pdf (accessed 23 February 2012).
2. During the civil war, France, Israel, Portugal, South Africa and a number of other African states backed the Biafrans.
3. U.S. Department of Energy, *Nigeria*.
4. Cited in Andy Rowell, James Marriott and Lorne Stockman, *The Next Gulf* (London: Constable, 2005), p. 105.
5. This term is perhaps the least common and, unlike all the others, relates to Nigeria alone. It is used by William D. Graf, *The Nigerian State* (London: James Currey, 1988), p. 223.
6. Coined in the late 1970s by the *Economist* magazine to explain the collapse of manufacturing in the Netherlands following its discovery of natural gas a decade earlier, the term 'Dutch Disease' refers to those instances when a country suffers from exchange rate problems resulting from its sudden overdependence on the export of a single commodity usually an unrefined or unprocessed natural resource of some description. John Ghazvinian, *Untapped: The Scramble for Africa's Oil* (London: Harcourt, 2007), pp. 96–98.
7. Nicholas Shaxson, *Poisoned Wells: The Dirty Politics of African Oil* (Basingstoke, Hampshire: Palgrave Macmillan, 2007), p. 6.
8. Paul D. Williams, *War and Conflict in Africa* (Cambridge: Polity Press, 2011), p. 5.
9. All these figures have been drawn from the following sources: Nigerian National Petroleum Corporation, *Oil Production*, 23 February 2012,

available at http://www.nnpcgroup.com/NNPCBusiness/UpstreamVentures /OilProduction.aspx (accessed 23 February 2012), Organisation of Petroleum Exporting Countries, *Nigeria*, 2012, available at http://www.opec.org/opec_ web/en/about_us/167.htm (accessed 23 February 2012) and U.S. Department of Energy, *Nigeria*.

10. The figures provided by the OPEC were in cubic metres. They were converted into cubic feet by the author to facilitate their comparison with those provided by the NNCP and the U.S. DOE. The amount of gas the U.S. DOE believes Nigeria exports is determined by subtracting the amount Nigeria consumes each year from that which it produces. Nigerian National Petroleum Corporation, *Oil Production*, 23 February 2012, available at http://www.nnpcgroup.com/NNPCBusiness/UpstreamVentures/ OilProduction.aspx (accessed 23 February 2012), Organisation of Petroleum Exporting Countries, *Nigeria*, 2012, available at http://www. opec.org/opec_web/en /about_us/167.htm (accessed 23 February 2012) and U.S. Department of Energy, *Nigeria*.

11. U.S. Department of State, *Background Note: Nigeria*, 20 October 2011, available at http://www.state.gov/r/pa/ei/bgn/2836.htm (accessed 23 February 2012).

12. World Bank, *Nigeria: Country Assistant Strategy*, 2011, available at http://web.worldbank.org/WBSITE/EXTERNAL/COUNTRIES/AFRICAEXT /NIGERIAEXTN/0,,menuPK:368909~pagePK:141132~piPK:141105~theSi tePK:368896,00.html (accessed 23 February 2012) and U.S. Department of Energy, *Country Analysis Briefs: Nigeria*, August 2011, available at http://www.eia.gov/EMEU/cabs/Nigeria/pdf.pdf (accessed 23 February 2012).

13. There are currently thought to be around 90,000 Ekoi and 15 million Ijaw.

14. This new venture was named after William Knox D'Arcy who founded one of the companies which later became part of the Anglo-Iranian Oil Company.

15. In 1954, the Anglo-Iranian Oil Company changed its name to British Petroleum. As a result, the joint venture also changed its name to the Shell – BP Petroleum Development Company.

16. All figures are drawn from: BP, *Annual Report and Accounts* (London: BP, various years); BP, *Statistical Review of World Energy* (various years); and Central Bank of Nigeria, *Annual Reports and Statement of Accounts* (various years).

17. Time Magazine, *Iran: Another Crisis for the Shah*, 13 November 1978, available at http://www.time.com/time/magazine/article/0,9171,946149,00. html (accessed 1 March 2012).

18. Tim Niblock, *Saudi Arabia: Power, Legitimacy and Survival* (Abingdon, Oxon: Routledge, 2006), p. 70.

19. Robert O. Keohane, *After Hegemony: Cooperation and Discord in the World Political Economy* (Princeton, New Jersey: Princeton University Press, 1984), p. 223.

20. Forbes, 2012, available at http://www.forbes.com/static_html/oil/2004 /oil.shtml (accessed 1 March 2012).

142   *Notes*

21. Peter Lewis, 'Getting the Politics Right: Governance and Economic Failure in Nigeria,' in Robert Rotberg (ed.), *Crafting the New Nigeria: Confronting the Challenges* (Boulder, Colorado: Lynne Rienner Publishers, 2004), p. 99.
22. Nigeria National Bureau of Statistics, *2010 Review of the Economy* (2010), available at http://www.nigerianstat.gov.ng/ext/latest_release/2010_Review_of_the_Nigerian_Economy.pdf (accessed 15 March 2012), p. 12.
23. Ibid., 14.
24. Ibid.
25. BBC, *Nigeria Power Shortage to Persist*, 30 May 2008, available at http://news.bbc.co.uk/1/hi/world/7426593.stm (accessed 16 March 2012), p. 1.
26. BBC, *Nigeria Needs $85 Billion to Fix Power*, 26 June 2008, available at http://news.bbc.co.uk/1/hi/7475284.stm (accessed 16 March 2012), p. 1.
27. In 2006, the sector's revenue made up 1.83 per cent of the country's GDP. Nigeria National Bureau of Statistics, *2010 Review of the Economy*, p. 14.
28. Overseas Development Institute, *The Impact of Oil on Nigeria's Economic Policy Formulation*, 16 June 2004, available at http://www.odi.org.uk/events/docs/117.pdf (accessed 7 August 2012), p. 1 and Nigeria National Bureau of Statistics, *2010 Review of the Economy*, p. 14.
29. Section one of the Act declared that 'the entire ownership and control of all petroleum in, under or upon any [of Nigeria's] lands...shall be vested in the state.' Federal Republic of Nigeria, Petroleum Act (27 November 1969), Article 1 (1).
30. For example, see Federal Republic of Nigeria, *Constitution of the Federal Republic of Nigeria* (5 May 1999), Article 44 (3).
31. Federal Republic of Nigeria, *Mineral Oils (Safety) Regulations*, 1963, available at http://www.lexadin.nl/wlg/legis/nofr/oeur/arch/nig/mineraloilsreg.pdf (accessed 7 August 2012), Part III – Duties of Managers, Article 7.
32. Federal Republic of Nigeria, *Petroleum Act* (27 November 1969), Part 1, Article 37 (e).
33. David Moffat and Olof Lindén, 'Perception and Reality: Assessing Priorities for Sustainable Development in the Niger River Delta,' *Ambio* (A Journal of the Human Environment), December 1995, Vol. 24, No. 7–8, p. 532.
34. Human Rights Watch, *The Price of Oil: Corporate Responsibility and Human Rights Violations in Nigeria's Oil Producing Communities*, January 1999, available at http://www.hrw.org/reports/1999/nigeria/nigeria0199.pdf, pp. 54–55.
35. The amounted quoted by Kew and Phillips was 1.5 million tons. Darren Kew and David L. Phillips, 'Seeking Peace in the Niger Delta: Oil, Natural Gas and Other Vital Resources,' *New England Journal of Public Policy*, 2007, Vol. 21, No. 2, pp. 159–160. The author has converted this to barrels to facilitate comparison with the other figures cited. The author used BP's conversion formula of 1 ton equalling 8.5 barrels. The formula can be found at BP, 1999 – 2012, available at http://www.bp.com/conversionfactors.jsp (accessed 8 March 2012).
36. Human Rights Watch, *The Price of Oil*, p. 55.

37. Environmental Resources Managers Ltd, *Niger Delta Environmental Survey Final Report Phase I; Volume I: Environmental and Socio-Economic Characteristics* (Lagos: Niger Delta Environmental Survey, 1997), p. 263.
38. Kew and Phillips, 'Seeking Peace in the Niger Delta', pp. 159 – 160.
39. Toyin Falola and Matthew M. Heaton, *A History of Nigeria* (Cambridge: Cambridge University Press, 2008), pp. 183–184.
40. The other main benefit ordinary Nigerians gain from their oil industry is cheap, subsidised fuel. But, recently, even this has been under threat. In January 2012, President Jonathan announced its removal. He later was forced to reverse his decision in the face of widespread anger and protests. BBC, *Nigerians Protest at Removal of Fuel Subsidy*, 3 January 2012, available at http://www.bbc.co.uk/news/world-africa-16390183 (accessed 7 May 2012).
41. Hazem Beblawi, 'The Rentier State in the Arab World,' in Giacomo Luciani (ed.) *The Arab State* (Berkeley and Los Angeles: University of California Press, 1990), pp. 87–88.
42. US Department of State, *Nigeria*, 6 March 2007, available at http://www.state.gov/g/drl/rls/hrrpt/2006/78751.htm (accessed 25 February 2011), p. 1.
43. European Election Observation Mission, *Nigeria Final Report: Gubernatorial and State Houses of Assembly Elections 14 April 2007 and Presidential and National Assembly Elections 21 April 2007*, 23 August 2007, available at http://ec.europa.eu/external_relations/human_rights/eu_election_ass_observ/nigeria/report_final_annex_23–08–07_en.pdf (accessed 20 May 2009), p. 4.
44. Human Rights Watch, *Nigeria: Presidential Election Marred by Fraud, Violence*, 25 April 2007, available from http://www.hrw.org/en/news/2007/04/24/nigeria-presidential-election-marred-fraud-violence (accessed 25 May 2009), p. 1.
45. Daniel Jordan Smith, *A Culture of Corruption: Everyday Deception and Popular Discontent in Nigeria* (Princeton and Oxford: Princeton University Press, 2007), p. 116.
46. This statement is part of an interview between Abu Qaqa and the Guardian newspaper. The Guardian, *Boko Haram Vows to Fight until Nigeria Establishes Sharia Law*, 27 January 2012, available at http://www.guardian.co.uk/world/2012/jan/27/boko-haram-nigeria-sharia-law (accessed 18 March 2012).
47. A large portion of the statement was reproduced in the national, daily newspaper, the Nigerian Tribune. The Nigerian Tribune, *MEND Vows to Attack MTN, SACOIL, Others: Claims Responsibility for Agip Pipeline Attack*, 5 February 2012, available at http://tribune.com.ng/index.php/front-page-news/35458-mend-vows-to-attack-mtn-sacoil-others-claims-responsibility-for-agip-pipeline-attack (accessed 18 March 2012).
48. Jane's, *The Movement for the Emancipation of the Niger Delta (MEND)*, 2009, available at http://articles.janes.com/articles/Janes-World-Insurgency-and-Terrorism/Movement-for-the-Emancipation-of-the-Niger-Delta-MEND-Nigeria.html (accessed 18 March 2012).

144 Notes

49. John Campbell, *Nigeria: Dancing on the Brink*, (New York: Rowman and Littlefield Publishers, 2011), p. 26.
50. U.S. Department of Energy, *Nigeria*.

5 Of the People but for the People? Nigeria and Its Armed Forces

1. Vanguard, *The Supreme Court Had Voided the Conviction of Rear Admiral Francis Agbiti by a General Court Martial*, 7 February 2011, available at http://community.vanguardngr.com/forum/topics/the-supreme-court-has-voided (accessed 31 August 2011), p. 2.
2. BBC, *Missing Tanker 'Shame' in Nigeria*, 20 September 2004, available at http://news.bbc.co.uk/1/hi/world/africa/3672264.stm (accessed 31 August 2011), p. 1.
3. Oil bunkering 'is the illegal tapping... [of] oil pipelines, often at manifolds or well-heads, and the extraction of crude oil which is piped into river barges that are hidden in small tributaries. The crude is then transported to ships offshore for sale.' Human Rights Watch, *Rivers and Blood: Guns, Oil and Power in Nigeria's Rivers State*, 4 February 2005, available at http://www.hrw.org/legacy/backgrounder/africa/nigeria0205/nigeria0205.pdf (accessed 6 September 2011), p. 4.
4. This Day, *Missing Ship: Supreme Court Nullifies Agbiti's Trial*, 7 February 2011, available at http://allafrica.com/stories/201102070609.html (accessed 6 August 2012), p. 1.
5. The persistence of oil bunkering was well known to policy makers, researchers and academics throughout Europe and North America before this incident took place. Twelve months before the *African Pride*'s disappearance, Human Rights Watch had published a report detailing the scale of the problem and its impact on the safety and well-being of the Niger Delta people. Human Rights Watch, *The Warri Crisis: Fuelling Violence*, November 2003, Vol. 15, No. 18, available at http://www.hrw.org/sites/default/files/reports/nigeria1103.pdf (accessed 5 September 2011), pp. 17–21.
6. The ship was discovered along with the *MT Jimoh*, which had disappeared at the same time as the *African Pride*. The *Jimoh* had been renamed the *MT Lord* in an attempt to disguise its identity. BBC, *Missing Tanker Found in Nigeria*, 24 September 2004, available at http://news.bbc.co.uk/1/hi/world/africa/3686284.stm (accessed 5 September 2011), p. 1.
7. The Times, *Nigerian Admirals Pay the Price for Stealing Captured Oil Tanker*, 8 January 2005, available at http://www.timesonline.co.uk/tol/news/world/article409606.ece (accessed 1 September 2011), p. 1.
8. Daily Telegraph, *Embarrassment as Nigerian Navy 'Loses' Impounded Tanker*, 21 September 2004, available at http://www.telegraph.co.uk/news/worldnews/africaandindianocean/nigeria/1472282/Embarrassment-as-Nigerian-navy-loses-impounded-tanker.html (accessed 5 September 2011), p. 1.

Notes 145

9. Ibid.
10. Domestic opposition and international criticism of Shell and its Nigerian subsidiary, Shell Nigeria, have grown steadily, albeit unevenly, over the past 20 years. Much of the opprobrium levelled at the company has been stimulated and generated by one man – Ken Saro Wiwa. In 1992 he founded the Movement for the Survival of the Ogoni People to pressure Shell and the Federal Government into compensating the Ogoni people for the grinding poverty and wretched environmental conditions they were forced to endure. MOSOP launched a highly effective two-pronged strategy to press its case. At home, its activists took part in mass demonstrations and sabotaged pipes and equipment belonging to Shell and the Nigerian National Petroleum Corporation. Overseas, Saro-Wiwa embarked on a relentless public relations campaign to highlight the plight of the Ogoni and other Niger Delta peoples. So successful was he that the Abacha regime had him arrested and executed on trumped up murder charges. Yet, even in death, Saro-Wiwa was still able to embarrass Shell as the company was heavily criticised for not doing more to save his life. Misty L. Bastin, '"Buried beneath Six Feet of Crude Oil": State-Sponsored Death and the Absent Body of Ken Saro-Wiwa,' in Craig W. McLuckie and Aubrey McPhail (eds.), *Ken Saro-Wiwa: Writer and Political Activist* (Boulder, Colorado: Lynne Rienner Publishers, 2000), p. 133.
11. Shell Petroleum Development Company, *Shell Nigeria Annual Report 2005: People and the Environment* (Nigeria: Shell Petroleum Development Company, August 2006), pp. 4–8.
12. WAC Global Services, *Peace and Security in the Niger Delta: Conflict Expert Group Baseline Report for Shell Petroleum Development Company*, December 2003, available at http://shellnews.net/2007/shell_wac_report_2004.pdf (accessed 6 September 2011), p. 46.
13. Human Rights Watch, *Rivers and Blood*, pp. 8–9.
14. Ibid., 8.
15. Wole Soyinka, *The Open Sore of a Continent: A Personal Narrative of the Nigerian Crisis* (Oxford and New York: Oxford University Press, 1996), p. 33.
16. In a speech made shortly after his seizure of power, General Babangida justified his actions by arguing that 'when in December 1983, the former military leadership, headed by Major General Muhammadu Buhari, assumed the reins of government, its accession was heralded in the history of this country. ... Since January 1984, however, we have witnessed a systematic denigration of that hope. ... The initial objectives were betrayed and fundamental changes do not appear on the horizon. Because the present state of uncertainty, suppression and stagnation resulted from the perpetuation of a small group, the Nigerian Armed Forces could not as a part of that government be unfairly committed to take responsibility for failure. Our dedication to the cause of ensuring that our nation remains a united entity worthy of respect and capable of functioning as a viable and credible part of the international community dictated the need to arrest the situation.' Cited in Ndaeyo Uko, *Romancing the Gun: The Press as a Promoter of Military Rule* (Trenton, New Jersey: Africa World Press, 2004), pp. 180–181.

146 *Notes*

17. Clause 217 of the constitution stipulates that 'the Federation shall ... maintain the armed forces as may be considered adequate and effective for the purpose of – (a) defending Nigeria from external aggression; (b) maintaining its territorial integrity and securing its borders from violation on land, sea or air; (c) suppressing insurrection and acting in aid of civil authorities to restore order when called upon to do so by the President, but subject to such conditions as may be prescribed by an Act of the National Assembly; and (d) performing such other functions as may be prescribed by an Act of the National Assembly.' Federal Republic of Nigeria, *Constitution of the Federal Republic of Nigeria* (1999).

18. The decree establishing the Federal Capital Territory of Abuja and the Federal Capital Development Authority, the body charged with developing the new capital, was passed on 4 February 1976. Francine Rodd, Jewell Kidd, Willie Cohen and Taniko Noda *Around and About Abuja* (Ibadan: Spectrum Books, 2005), p. 5. General Mohammed was killed nine days later in a failed *coup d'état* led by Lieutenant Colonel Buka Suka Dimka.

19. Abuja replaced Lagos as Nigeria's capital on 12 December 1991.

20. BBC, *Life of Poverty in Abuja's Wealth*, 13 February 2007, available at http://news.bbc.co.uk/1/hi/world/africa/6355269.stm (accessed 25 September 2011), p. 1.

21. El-Rufai served as FCT Minister from 17 July 2003 until 27 July 2007.

22. For the first three years of its independence, Nigeria was a dominion. As a result its head of state was Queen Elizabeth II of Great Britain and Northern Ireland. She was represented in country by a governor-general. This role was performed first by Sir James Robertson (1 October 1960–16 November 1960) and then Nnamdi Azikiwe (16 November 1963–1 October 1963). Azikiwe was Nigeria's last governor-general and its first president.

23. These soldier–statesmen were Johnson Aguiyi-Ironsi (16 January 1966–29 July 1966), Yakubu Gowan (1 August 1966–29 July 1975), Murtala Mohammed (29 July 1975–13 February 1976), Olusegun Obasanjo (13 February 1976–1 October 1979), Muhammadu Buhari (31 December 1983–27 August 1985), Ibrahim Badamasi Babangida (27 August 1985–26 August 1993), Sani Abacha (17 November 1993–8 June 1998) and Abdulsalami Abubakar (8 June 1998–29 May 1999).

24. Nigeria's first *coup d'état* was led by five army majors – Kaduna Nzeogwu, Emmanuel Ifeajuna, Donatus Okafor, Christian Anuforo and Adewale Ademoyega – and was only partially successful. While it did result in the collapse of the First Republic, largely because important political figures like the Prime Minister, Abubakar Tafewa Balewa, and Premier of the Western Region, Obafemi Awolowo, were executed, none of *coup* ever assumed power. That passed instead to Major-General Aguiyi-Ironsi, the most senior army officer not directly implicated in the *coup* who had not been executed by the conspirators. Eghosa E. Osaghae, *Nigeria since Independence: Crippled Giant* (London: Hurst, 1998), pp. 56–57.

25. Nigeria's soldier–statesmen adopted a range of titles. Aguiyi-Ironsi, Gowon, Mohammed and Obasanjo each assumed the title of Head of the Federal Military Government. Buhari, on the other hand, was known as the Chairman of the Supreme Military Council, IBB as the President of the Armed Forces Ruling Council, and Abacha and Abubakar as Chairman of the Provisional Ruling Council. Despite their different titles, these soldier–statesmen all assumed the same political and representational powers.

26. Alex Perry, *Falling off the Edge: Globalization, World Peace and Other Lies* (London: Pan Books, 2010), p. 127.

27. For example, on 4 August 2008, the MEND issued a statement threatening attacks against the Abuja-based staff and property of the German construction company Julius Berger. Agence France-Presse, *Nigerian Armed Group Threatens German Construction Firm Unit*, 4 August 2008, available at http://www.thefreelibrary.com/Nigerian+armed+group+th reatens+German+construction+firm+unit-a01611602841 (accessed 16 August 2008), p. 1.

28. U.S. Department of Energy, *Nigeria: Country Analysis Brief*, July 2010, available at http://www.eia.doe.gov/cabs/Nigeria/Background.html (accessed 18 November 2010), p. 1.

29. Reuters, *Gunmen Kidnap Crew from Afren Oil Rig in Nigeria*, 8 November 2010, available at http://www.alertnet.org/thenews/newsdesk/LDE6A708L.htm (accessed 18 November 2010), p. 1.

30. Reuters, *Militants Kidnap 7 from Exxon Platform Off Nigeria*, 16 November 2010, available at http://www.alertnet.org/thenews/newsdesk/LDE6AE 188.htm (accessed 18 November 2010), p. 1.

31. J.N.C Hill, 'Thoughts of Home: Civil–Military Relations and the Conduct of Nigeria's Peacekeeping Forces,' *The Journal of Military Ethics*, Vol. 8, No. 4 (November 2009), p. 298.

32. Certainly this is the claim made by the U.S. House of Representatives Committee on Homeland Security. U.S. House of Representatives Committee on Homeland Security Subcommittee on Counterterrorism and Intelligence, *Boko Haram: Emerging Threat to the U.S. Homeland*, 30 November 2011, available at http://homeland.house.gov/hearing/sub-committee-hearing-boko-haram-emerging-threat-us-homeland (accessed 22 May 2012).

33. Human Rights Watch, *World Report 2011: Nigeria*, January 2011, available at http://www.hrw.org/world-report-2011/nigeria (accessed 11 August 2012), Human Rights Watch, *Nigeria Prosecute Killings by Security Forces*, 26 November 2009, available at http://www.hrw.org/news/2009/11/26 /nigeria-prosecute-killings-security-forces (accessed 11 August 2012), and Vanguard, *Nigeria: Army Court-Martials Two Colonels, 12 Others for Alleged Misconduct*, 28 May 2012, available at http://allafrica.com/stor-ies/201205290252.html (accessed 11 August 2012).

34. Toyin Falola and Matthew M. Heaton, *A History of Nigeria* (Cambridge University Press, Cambridge 2008), p. 158.

148   *Notes*

35. Robert B. Shepard, *Nigeria, Africa, and the United States: From Kennedy to Reagan* (Bloomington, Indiana University Press, 1991), p. 40.
36. Cited in Olayiwola Abegunrin, *Nigerian Foreign Policy under Military Rule, 1966–1999* (Westport and London, Praeger, 2003), p. 52.
37. Indeed, the Biafrans were able to acquire several World War II vintage American B-26 bombers. Ibid. p. 53.
38. Thomas D. Musgrave, *Self-Determination and National Minorities* (Oxford, Oxford University Press, 2000), p. 198.
39. Gérard Kreijen, *State, Sovereignty, and International Governance* (Oxford, Oxford University Press, 2002), p. 351.
40. The OAS was established in January 1961 with the goal of keeping Algeria French. To do that, it embarked on a terror campaign in both Algeria and France that claimed the lives of hundreds of people.
41. Time, *The Mercenaries*, 25 October 1968, available at http://www.time. com/time/magazine/article/0,9171,900387,00.html (accessed 14 May 2009).
42. The dozen states created were Benue Plateau, East-Central, Kano, Kwara, Lagos, Mid-Western, North Central, North Eastern, North Western, Rivers, South Eastern and Western.
43. The three states that replaced the eastern region were East-Central, Rivers and South Eastern.
44. Cited in William D. Graf, *The Nigerian State* (London: James Currey, 1988), p. 164.
45. Toyin Falola and Matthew M. Heaton, *A History of Nigeria* (Cambridge: Cambridge University Press, 2008), pp. 214–215 and Daniel Jordan Smith, *A Culture of Corruption: Everyday Deception and Popular Discontent in Nigeria* (Princeton and Oxford: Princeton University Press, 2007), p. 113.
46. Federal Government of Nigeria, *National Youth Service Corps* (2011), available at http://www.nysc.gov.ng/history2.php (accessed 14 October 2011), Objectives of the Scheme 1f, 1g and 1h.
47. Ibid. Objectives of the Scheme 1a, 1b, 1c, 1d, 1e, 1f and 1g.
48. On 14 January 2008 the courts-martial of 14 army officers (three colonels, two lieutenant-colonels and nine non-commissioned officers) began at the Infantry Centre and School in Jaji. All were accused, and later convicted, of stealing weapons from the Nigerian Army Central Ordinance Depot (NACOD) in Kaduna, and selling them on to militants in the Niger Delta. Vanguard, *Army Court-Martials 15 Officers over Missing Arms*, 14 January 2008, available at http://allafrica.com/stories/200801150105. html (accessed 15 October 2011), p. 1.
49. Nigerian Tribune, *Yar'Adua: Unravelling the Secrecy*, 20 May 2010, available at http://www.tribune.com.ng/index.php/editorial/5628-yaradua-unravelling-the-secrecy (accessed 25 September 2011), p. 1.
50. ThisDay, *NBA Backs Akerdolu over Yar'Adua's Health*, 14 December 2009, available at http://allafrica.com/stories/200912150767.html (accessed 8 September 2011), p. 1.

Notes 149

51. BBC, *Nigeria Cabinet Told to Rule on Sick President Yar'Adua*, 22 January 2010, available at http://news.bbc.co.uk/1/hi/world/africa/8474669.stm (accessed 8 September 2011), p. 1.
52. Agence France Presse, *Nigeria's VP Takes over from Ailing President*, available at http://www.google.com/hostednews/afp/article/ALeqM5i8DQEN tzQXmEbHeJQbS9ZAlpVg1g (accessed 8 September 2011), p. 1.
53. Many national, and some international, newspapers carried articles arguing for and against both the likelihood and desirability of another military-led *coup d'état*. For example, see ThisDay, *SNG Warns against Military Intervention*, 26 February 2010, available at http://allafrica.com /stories/201002260391.html (accessed 9 September 2011), ThisDay, *Yar'Adua's Return Has Compounded Our Political Crisis*, 2 March 2010, available at http://allafrica.com/stories/201003030458.html (accessed 9 September 2011), Daily Champion, *Military Intervention Will Not Salvage the Nation – Councillor*, 9 February 2010, available at http: //allafrica. com/stories/201002090053.html (9 September 2011) and Financial Times, *Nigeria Constitutional Crisis Looms*, 6 January 2010, available at http://www.ft.com/cms/s/0/c6a31dc2-fafd-11de-94d8-00144feab49a. html#axzz1XRZT4blg (accessed 9 September 2011).

Conclusions

1. BBC, *Nigerian Ex-Governor James Ibori Remanded in Custody*, 16 April 2011, available at http://www.bbc.co.uk/news/uk-13102655 (accessed 13 June 2011), p. 1.
2. Vanguard, *Ibori's Wife Gets 5yrs Jail*, 22 November 2010, available at http: //www.vanguardngr.com/2010/11/iboris-wife-gets-5yrs-jail/ (accessed 13 June 2011), p, 1.
3. Elombah, *Ibori's Lawyer, Bhadresh Gohil Sentenced to 7 years in Prison*, 9 March 2011, available at http://elombah.com/index.php/components /com_comment/joscomment/images/M_images/components/com_com-ment/joscomment/index.php?option=com_content&view=article&id=5 583:iboris-lawyer-bhadresh-gohil-sentenced-to-7-years-imprisonment&c atid=48:corruption-reports&Itemid=69 (accessed 13 June 2011), p. 1.
4. Next, *UK Court Declares Ibori's Associate Guilty*, 3 June 2010, available at http://234next.com/csp/cms/sites/Next/News/Metro/Crime/5575623–146/uk_court_declares_iboris_associate_guilty.csp (accessed 13 June 2011), p. 1.
5. Senior member of the British High Commission Abuja, interview by author, Oxford, 9 November 2010.
6. Daily Telegraph, *Nigeria: President Yar'Adua's 'Useful' London Visit, July 16–17*, 4 February 2011, available at http://www.telegraph.co.uk/news /wikileaks-files/london-wikileaks/8304685/NIGERIA-PRESIDENT-YARAD UAS-USEFUL-LONDON-VISIT-JULY-16–17.html (accessed 17 June 2011), p. 1, and senior member of the British High Commission Abuja, interview by author, Oxford, 9 November 2010.

150   *Notes*

7. The EFCC was set up by President Obasanjo in 2003 to investigate and prosecute senior public figures who engaged in corruption. The commission conducted some high-profile cases which won it, and the government, considerable international praise. Yet its conviction rate was poor and it remained dogged by allegations of political manipulation, of only going after individuals who had fallen out with the president. Daniel Jordan Smith, *A Culture of Corruption: Everyday Deception and Popular Discontent in Nigeria* (Princeton and Oxford: Princeton University Press, 2007), p. 116.

8. Aondoakaa was succeeded as Attorney-General by Abetokunbo Kayode on 10 February 2010.

9. BBC, *Supporters of Nigeria Ex-Governor Ibori Attack Police*, 21 April 2010, available at http://news.bbc.co.uk/1/hi/world/africa/8634835.stm (accessed 14 June 2011), p. 1.

10. Nigerian Tribune, *Security Agencies Reinforce to Arrest Ibori: SSS Officers Deployed in Delta: EFCC has no Evidence against Me – Ibori*, 23 April 2010, available at http://www.tribune.com.ng/index.php/front-page-news/4453 – security-agencies-reinforce-to-arrest-ibori-sss-officers-deployed-in-delta-efcc-has-no-evidence-against-me-ibori (accessed 14 June 2011), p. 1.

11. Punch, *Ibori Seeks Political Asylum in Dubai*, 27 May 2010, available at http://punchng.com/Articl.aspx?theartic=Art201005272304760 (accessed 14 June 2011), p. 1.

12. BBC, *Nigeria Ex-Governor James Ibori 'Freed on Bail,'* 14 May 2010, available at http://news.bbc.co.uk/1/hi/world/africa/8682020.stm (accessed 14 June 2011), p. 1.

13. Punch, *Ibori Loses Bail in Dubai, Remanded on Police Custody*, 11 June 2010, available at http://www.punchng.com/Articl.aspx?theartic=Art20100611226918 (accessed 14 June 2011), p. 1.

14. Punch, *Regarding Ibori Seeking UAE Asylum*, 13 June 2010, available at http://www.punchng.com/Articl.aspx?theartic=Art20100613304696 (accessed 14 June 2011), p. 1.

15. Pointblanknews, *James Ibori Down with Hypertension in Dubai*, 16 August 2010, available at http://www.pointblanknews.com/News/os3770.html (accessed 14 June 2011), p. 1.

16. Ibori pled guilty to all charges on 27 February 2012. BBC, *Nigeria Ex-Delta State Governor James Ibori Guilty Plea*, 27 February 2012, available at http://www.bbc.co.uk/news/world-africa-17181056 (accessed 28 March 2012).

17. BBC, *Former Nigeria Governor James Ibori Jailed for 13 Years*, 17 April 2012, available at http://www.bbc.co.uk/news/world-africa-17739388 (accessed 18 April 2012).

18. The Guardian, *Boko Haram Vows to Fight until Nigeria Establishes Sharia Law*, 27 January 2012, available at http://www.guardian.co.uk/world/2012/jan/27/boko-haram-nigeria-sharia-law (accessed 18 March 2012).

19. Ricardo Soares de Oliveira, *Oil and Politics in the Gulf of Guinea* (London: Hurst and Company, 2007), pp. 49–62.

Select Bibliography

Olayiwola Abegunrin, *Nigerian Foreign Policy under Military Rule, 1966–1999* (Westport, Connecticut and London: Praeger, 2003).

Chinua Achebe, *Things Fall Apart* (London: Heinemann, 1958).

Chinua Achebe, *The Trouble with Nigeria* (London: Heinemann, 1983).

Chinua Achebe, *Anthills of the Savannah* (London: Heinemann, 1987).

Adekeye Adebajo and Abdul Raufu Mustapha, *Gulliver's Troubles: Nigeria's Foreign Policy after the Cold War* (Cape Town: University of KwaZulu-Natal Press, 2008).

A. Adepoju, 'Military Rule and Population Issues in Nigeria,' *African Affairs*, January 1981, Vol. 80, No. 318, pp. 29–47.

R.A. Adeshina, *The Reversed Victory: Story of Nigerian Military Intervention in Sierra Leone* (Ibadan: Heinemann Educational Books, 2002).

Abimbola Adesoji, 'The Boko Haram Uprising and Islamic Revivalism in Nigeria,' *Africa Spectrum*, 2010, Vol. 45, No. 2, pp. 95–108.

Agence France Presse, *Nigerian Forces Executed over 90 in Riot-Hit City: HRW*, 20 December 2008, available at http://www.google.com/hostednews/afp/article/ALeqM5jykb6YuRihPbvGCvNovQkvWtzIFA (accessed 23 June 2011).

Adegboyega Issac Ajayi, *The Military and the Nigerian State, 1966–1993* (Trenton, New Jersey: Africa World Press, 2007).

Anthony A. Akinola, 'A Critique of Nigeria's Two-Party System,' *Journal of Modern African Studies*, March 1989, Vol. 27, No. 1, pp. 109–123.

Amnesty International, *Nigeria: Armed Groups Targeting Civilians in Latest Bombings*, 27 June 2011, available at http://www.amnesty.org/en/for-media/press-releases/nigeria-armed-groups-targeting-civilians-latest-bombings-2011–06–27 (accessed 28 April 2012).

Amnesty International, *Tens of Thousands Caught in Crossfire in Niger Delta Fighting*, 21 May 2009, available at http://www.amnesty.org/en/news-and-updates/news/tens-thousands-caught-crossfire-niger-delta-fighting-20090521 (accessed 6 July 2011).

Amnesty International, *Annual Report 2011: Nigeria*, 2011, available at http://www.amnesty.org/en/region/nigeria/report-2011 (accessed 6 July 2011).

Benedict Anderson, *Imagined Communities* (2nd ed.) (London and New York: Verso, 1991).

Okoi Arikpo, *The Development of Modern Nigeria* (London: Penguin, 1967).

Guy Arnold, *Modern Nigeria* (London: Longman, 1977).

Obefemi Awolowo, *Path to Nigerian Freedom* (London: Faber and Faber, 1948).

John A. A. Ayoade, 'States without Citizens: An Emerging African Phenomenon,' in Donald Rothchild and Naomi Chazan (eds.), *The Precarious Balance: State and Society in Africa* (Boulder, Colorado: Westview Press, 1988).

152 *Select Bibliography*

Mohammed Ayoob, *The Third World Security Predicament: State Making, Regional Conflict and the International System* (Boulder, Colorado: Lynne Rienner Publishers, 1995).

Nnamdi Azikiwe, 'Essentials for Nigerian Survival,' *Foreign Affairs*, April 1965, Vol. 43, No. 3, pp. 447–461.

J.A. Ballard, 'Administrative Origins of Nigerian Federalism,' *African Affairs*, 1971, Vol. 70, No. 281, pp. 333–348.

Karin Barber, 'Popular Reactions to the Petro-naira,' *Journal of Modern African Studies*, September 1982, Vol. 20, No. 3, pp. 431–450.

Celestine Oyom Bassey and Charles Quarker Dukobo, *Defence Policy of Nigeria: Capability and Context: A Reader* (Bloomington, Indiana: AuthorHouse, 2011).

Robert H. Bates, *When Things Fell Apart: State Failure in Late Century Africa* (Cambridge: Cambridge University Press, 2008).

Jean-François Bayart, Stephen Ellie and Béatrice Hibou, *The Criminalization of the State in Africa* (Oxford: James Currey, 1999).

Jean-François Bayart, *The State in Africa: The Politics of the Belly* (2nd ed.) (Cambridge: Polity Press, 2009).

BBC, *Deadly Attack on Nigeria's Bayero University in Kano*, 30 April 2012, available at http://www.bbc.co.uk/news/world-africa-17886143 (accessed 6 May 2012).

BBC, *Nigeria Rescue Bid: Kidnapped Briton and Italian Killed*, 8 March 2012, available at http://www.bbc.co.uk/news/uk-17305707 (accessed 6 May 2012).

BBC, *Nigeria Ex-Delta State Governor James Ibori Guilty Plea*, 27 February 2012, available at http://www.bbc.co.uk/news/world-africa-17181056 (accessed 28 March 2012).

BBC, *Nigeria Jailbreak: Boko Haram Claims Kogi Prison Attack*, 16 February 2012, available at http://www.bbc.co.uk/news/world-africa-17059895 (accessed 29 April 2012).

BBC, *Nigerians Living in Poverty Rises to Nearly 61%*, 13 February 2012, available at http://www.bbc.co.uk/news/world-africa-17015873 (accessed 18 February 2012).

BBC, *Nigeria Unrest: 'Suicide Attack' on Kaduna Barracks*, 7 February 2012, available at http://www.bbc.co.uk/news/world-africa-16931981 (accessed 6 May 2012).

BBC, *German Engineer Kidnapped in Kano Nigeria*, 26 January 2012, available at http://www.bbc.co.uk/news/world-africa-16745509 (accessed 6 May 2012).

BBC, *Nigeria Violence: Scores Dead after Kano Blasts*, 21 January 2012, available at http://www.bbc.co.uk/news/world-africa-16663693 (accessed 6 May 2012).

BBC, *Nigerian Christians Hit by Fresh Islamist Attacks*, 7 January 2012, available at http://www.bbc.co.uk/news/world-africa-16442960 (accessed 6 May 2012).

BBC, *Nigeria Church Hit by Deadly Gun Attack in Gombe*, 5 January 2012, available at http://www.bbc.co.uk/news/world-africa-16436112 (accessed 6 May 2012).

Select Bibliography   153

BBC, *Nigerians Protest at Removal of Fuel Subsidy*, 3 January 2012, available at http://www.bbc.co.uk/news/world-africa-16390183 (accessed 7 May 2012).

BBC, *Nigeria Boko Haram Islamists 'Bomb Maiduguri Drinkers'*, 27 June 2011, available at http://www.bbc.co.uk/news/world-africa-13920980 (accessed 28 April 2012).

BBC, *'Boko Haram' Gunmen Kill Nigerian Muslim Cleric Birkuti*, 7 June 2011, available at http://www.bbc.co.uk/news/world-africa-13679234 (accessed 8 June 2011).

BBC, *Maiduguri: 'Boko Haram' Attacks Nigeria Police Stations*, 7 June 2011, available at http://www.bbc.co.uk/news/world-africa-13688814 (accessed 8 June 2011).

BBC, *Nigeria Ex-Governor James Ibori 'Freed on Bail,'* 14 May 2010, available at http://news.bbc.co.uk/1/hi/world/africa/8682020.stm (accessed 14 June 2011).

BBC, *Nigerian Ex-Governor James Ibori Remanded in Custody*, 16 April 2011, available at http://www.bbc.co.uk/news/uk-13102655 (accessed 13 June 2011).

BBC, *Supporters of Nigeria Ex-Governor Ibori Attack Police*, 21 April 2010, available at http://news.bbc.co.uk/1/hi/world/africa/8634835.stm (accessed 14 June 2011).

BBC, *Nigeria Nearing a 'Failed State,'* 18 August 2009, available at http://news.bbc.co.uk/go/pr/fr/-/1/hi/world/africa/8207736.stm (accessed 15 February 2011).

BBC, *Nigeria Sect Head Dies in Custody*, 31 July 2009, available at http://news.bbc.co.uk/1/hi/8177451.stm (accessed 3 December 2010).

BBC, *Nigeria Needs $85 Billion to Fix Power*, 26 June 2008, available at http://news.bbc.co.uk/1/hi/7475284.stm (accessed 16 March 2012).

BBC, *Nigeria Power Shortage to Persist*, 30 May 2008, available at http://news.bbc.co.uk/1/hi/world/7426593.stm (accessed 16 March 2012).

Hazem Beblawi, 'The Rentier State in the Arab World,' in Giacomo Luciani (ed.), *The Arab State*, (Berkeley and Los Angeles: University of California Press, 1990), pp. 85–98.

Hazem Beblawi and Giacomo Luciani (eds.), *The Rentier State* (London: Croom Helm, 1997).

E. Morberly Bell, *Flora Shaw (D.B.E.)* (London: Constable, 1947).

Hilary Benn, *A Shared Challenge: Promoting Development and Human Security in Weak States*, 23 June 2004, available at http://www.cgdev.org/doc/weakstates/WeakStates_Benn.pdf (accessed 21 July 2011).

David L. Bevan, Paul Collier and J.W. Gunning, *The Political Economy of Poverty, Equity and Growth: Nigeria and Indonesia* (Oxford: Oxford University Press, 1999).

Henry Bienen, *Political Conflict and Economic Change in Nigeria* (London: Frank Cass, 1985).

Henry Bienen, 'Nigeria: From Windfall Gains to Welfare Losses?' in Alan Gelb and Associates (eds.), *Oil Windfalls: Blessing or Curse?* (New York: World Bank, 1988), pp. 227–261.

154 *Select Bibliography*

Pinar Bilgin and Adam David Morton, 'Historicising Representations of "Failed States": Beyond the Cold War Annexation of the Social Sciences?' *Third World Quarterly*, 2002, Vol. 23, No. 1, pp. 55–80.

Catherine Boone, *Political Topographies of the African State: Territorial Authority and Institutional Choice* (Cambridge: Cambridge University Press, 2003).

Charles T. Call, 'The Fallacy of the "Failed State,"' *Third World Quarterly*, 2008, Vol. 29, No. 8, pp. 1491–1507.

John Campbell, 'Nigeria on the Brink: What Happens if the 2011 Elections Fail?' *Foreign Affairs*, 9 September 2010, available at http://www.foreignaffairs.com/articles/66746/john-campbell/nigeria-on-the-brink?page=show (accessed 15 July 2011).

John Campbell, *Nigeria: Dancing on the Brink* (New York: Rowman and Littlefield, 2011).

David Carment, 'Assessing State Failure: Implications for Theory and Practice,' *Third World Quarterly*, 2003, Vol. 24, No. 3, pp. 407–427.

Patrick Chabal and Jean-Pascal Daloz, *Africa Works: Disorder as Political Instrument* (Bloomington, Indiana: Indiana University Press, 1999).

Christopher Clapham, 'Degrees of Statehood,' *Review of International Studies*, April 1998, Vol. 24, No. 2, pp. 143–157.

Matthew J. Connelly, *A Diplomatic Revolution: Algeria's Fight for Independence and the Origins of the Post-Cold War Era* (Oxford: Oxford University Press, 2002).

Peter Cunliffe-Jones, *My Nigeria: Five Decade of Independence* (New York: Palgrave Macmillan, 2010).

Daily Telegraph, *Nigeria: President Yar'Adua's 'Useful' London Visit, July 16–17*, 4 February 2011, available at http://www.telegraph.co.uk/news/wikileaks-files/london-wikileaks/8304685/NIGERIA-PRESIDENT-YARADUAS-USEFUL-LONDON-VISIT-JULY-16–17.html (accessed 17 June 2011).

Daily Telegraph, *Car Bomb Attacks on Nigeria's Independence Day Kill 10*, 1 October 2010, available at http://www.telegraph.co.uk/news/worldnews/africaandindianocean/nigeria/8037584/Car-bomb-attacks-on-Nigerias-independence-day-kill-10.html (accessed 12 October 2010).

Daily Telegraph, *Nigerian Politician Faces Extradition to Britain on Money Laundering Charges*, 14 May 2010, available at http://www.telegraph.co.uk/news/worldnews/africaandindianocean/nigeria/7720634/Nigerian-politician-faces-extradition-to-Britain-on-money-laundering-charges.html (accessed 15 June 2011).

Daily Telegraph, *British Oil Contractor Kidnapped by Gunmen in Nigeria*, 20 February 2006, available at http://www.telegraph.co.uk/news/worldnews/africaandindianocean/nigeria/1510983/British-oil-contractor-kidnapped-by-gunmen-in-Nigeria.html (accessed 3 May 2012).

Daily Trust, *Boko Haram – Why We Executed Them*, 22 September 2009, available at http://allafrica.com/stories/200909221140.html (accessed 3 December 2010).

Thomas Dempsey, *Counter-Terrorism in African Failed States: Challenges and Potential Solutions* (Carlisle, Pennsylvania: U.S. Army War College Strategic Studies Institute, 2006).

Select Bibliography   155

Department for International Development, *Nigeria*, June 2008, available at www.dfid.gov.uk/countries/africa/Nigeria-facts.asp (accessed 11 February 2009).

Alan Detheridge and Noble Pepple, 'A Response to Frynas,' *Third World Quarterly*, September 1998, Vol. 19, No. 3, pp. 479–486.

Alan Detheridge and Noble Pepple, 'Shell in Nigeria: A Further Contribution,' *Third World Quarterly*, February 2000, Vol. 21, No. 1, pp. 157–164.

Larry Jay Diamond, 'Cleavage, Conflict and Anxiety in the Second Nigerian Republic,' *Journal of Modern African Studies*, December 1982, Vol. 20, No. 4, pp. 629–668.

Larry Jay Diamond, Anthony H.M. Kirk-Greene and Oyeleye Oyediran, *Transition without End: Nigerian Politics and Civil Society under Babangida* (Boulder, Colorado: Lynne Rienner Publishers, 1997).

B.J. Dudley, *Parties and Politics in Northern Nigeria* (London: Frank Cass, 1968).

The Economist, *Failed States: Where Talk Is Cheap and Talk Is Loose*, 17 May 2011, available at www.economist.com/node/18396240 (accessed 3 June 2011).

E.C. Ejiogu, *The Roots of Political Instability in Nigeria: Political Evolution and Development in the Niger Basin* (Farnham, Surrey: Ashgate, 2011).

John Boye Ejobowah, *Recognition in the Nigerian Public Sphere: A Liberal Argument about Justice in Plural Societies* (Lanham, Maryland: Lexington Books, 2001).

Elombah, *Ibori's Lawyer, Bhadresh Gohil Sentenced to 7 years in Prison*, 9 March 2011, available at http://elombah.com/index.php/components/com_comment/joscomment/images/M_images/components/com_comment/joscomment/index.php?option=com_content&view=article&id=5583:iboris-lawyer-bhadresh-gohil-sentenced-to-7-years-imprisonment&catid=48:corruption-reports&Itemid=69 (accessed 13 June 2011).

Environmental Resources Managers Ltd, *Niger Delta Environmental Survey Final Report Phase I; Volume I: Environmental and Socio-Economic Characteristics* (Lagos: Niger Delta Environmental Survey, 1997).

Thomas Hylland Eriksen, 'A Non-ethnic State for Africa? A Life-World Approach to the Imagining of Communities,' in Paris Yeros (ed.), *Ethnicity and Nationalism in Africa: Constructivist Reflections and Contemporary Politics* (Basingstoke, Hampshire: Palgrave Macmillan, 1999), pp. 45–65.

European Election Observation Mission, Nigeria Final Report: Gubernatorial and State Houses of Assembly Elections 14 April 2007 and Presidential and National Assembly Elections 21 April 2007, 23 August 2007, available at http://ec.europa.eu/external_relations/human_rights/eu_election_ass_observ/nigeria/report_final_annex_23–08–07_en.pdf (accessed 20 May 2009).

Kalu Ezera, *Constitutional Development in Nigeria* (Cambridge: Cambridge University Press, 1964).

Toyin Falola (ed.), *Britain and Nigeria: Exploitation or Development?* (London: Zed Books, 1987).

Toyin Falola, *Violence in Nigeria: The Crisis of Religious Politics and Secular Ideologies* (Rochester: Rochester University Press, 1998).

156 *Select Bibliography*

Toyin Falola, *Colonialism and Violence in Nigeria* (Bloomington, Indiana: University of Indiana Press, 2009).

Toyin Falola and Matthew M. Heaton, *A History of Nigeria* (Cambridge: Cambridge University Press, 2008).

Federal Republic of Nigeria, Constitution of the Federal Republic of Nigeria 1963 (1 October 1963).

Federal Republic of Nigeria, Constitution of the Federal Republic of Nigeria 1979 (1979).

Federal Republic of Nigeria, Constitution of the Federal Republic of Nigeria 1989 (1989).

Federal Republic of Nigeria, Constitution of the Federal Republic of Nigeria 1999 (5 May 1999).

Federation of Nigeria, Constitution of the Federation of Nigeria 1960 (1960).

Federal Republic of Nigeria, Mineral Oils (Safety) Regulations, 1963, available at http://www.lexadin.nl/wlg/legis/nofr/oeur/arch/nig/mineraloilsreg.pdf (accessed 7 August 2012).

Federal Republic of Nigeria, *Petroleum Act* (27 November 1969).

Tom Forrest, *Politics and Economic Development in Nigeria* (Boulder, Colorado: Westview Press, 1993).

Jedrezj George Frynas, 'Political Instability and Business: Focus on Shell in Nigeria,' *Third World Quarterly*, September 1998, Vol. 19, No. 3, pp. 547–478.

Fund for Peace, *Failed States Index Scores 2005*, 2005, available at http://www.fundforpeace.org/web/index.php?option=com_content&task=view&id=103&Itemid=325 (accessed 18 February 2011).

Fund for Peace, *Failed States Index Scores 2006*, 2006, available at http://www.fundforpeace.org/web/index.php?option=com_content&task=view&id=104&Itemid=324 (accessed 18 February 2011).

Fund for Peace, *Failed States Index Scores 2007*, 2007, available at http://www.fundforpeace.org/web/index.php?option=com_content&task=view&id=229&Itemid=366 (accessed 18 February 2011).

Fund for Peace, *Failed States Index Scores 2008*, 2008, available at http://www.fundforpeace.org/web/index.php?option=com_content&task=view&id=292&Itemid=452 (accessed 18 February 2011).

Fund for Peace, *Failed State Index Scores 2009*, 2009, available at http://www.fundforpeace.org/web/index.php?option=com_content&task=view&id=391&Itemid=549 (accessed 18 February 2011).

Fund for Peace, *Failed State Index Scores 2010*, 2010, available at http://www.fundforpeace.org/web/index.php?option=com_content&task=view&id=452&Itemid=900 (accessed 18 February 2011).

Fund for Peace, *Failed State Index Scores 2011*, 2011, available at http://www.fundforpeace.org/global/?q=fsi-grid2011 (accessed 17 February 2012) and Fund for Peace, *Failed State Index Scores 2010*, 2010, available at http://www.fundforpeace.org/web/index.php?option=com_content&task=view&id=452&Itemid=900 (accessed 18 February 2011).

John Ghazvinian, *Untapped: The Scramble for Africa Oil* (London: Harcourt, 2007).

Arthur A. Goldsmith, 'Sizing Up the African State,' *Journal of Modern African Studies*, March 2000, Vol. 38, No. 1, pp. 1–20.

Charles Gore and David Pratten, 'The Politics of Plunder: The Rhetorics of Order and Disorder in Southern Nigeria,' *Africa Affairs*, 2003, Vol. 102, No. 407, pp. 211–240.

William D. Graf, *The Nigerian State* (London: James Currey, 1988).

Jean-Germain Gros, 'Towards a Taxonomy of Failed States in the New World Order: Decaying Somalia, Liberia, Rwanda and Haiti,' *Third World Quarterly*, September 1996, Vol. 17, No. 3, pp. 455–471.

The Guardian, *Nigerian Prison Raid Frees 118 Inmates*, 16 February 2012, available at http://www.guardian.co.uk/world/2012/feb/16/attack-nigerian-prison-escape-118-inmates (accessed 6 May 2012).

The Guardian, *Pirates Attack Cargo Ship off Nigeria*, 13 February 2012, available at http://www.guardian.co.uk/world/2012/feb/13/pirates-attack-cargo-ship-nigeria (accessed 6 May 2012).

The Guardian, *Boko Haram Vows to Fight until Nigeria Establishes Sharia Law*, 27 January 2012, available at http://www.guardian.co.uk/world/2012/jan/27/boko-haram-nigeria-sharia-law (accessed 18 March 2012).

The Guardian, *Nigerian Churches Targeted by Christmas Day Bombs*, 25 December 2011, available at http://www.guardian.co.uk/world/2011/dec/25/nigerian-church-bombed-christmas-prayers (accessed 6 May 2012).

The Guardian, *Nigerian Militant Leader Charged over Car Bombs on Independence Day*, 4 October 2010, available at http://www.guardian.co.uk/world/2010/oct/04/nigeria-president-car-bombs (accessed 13 July 2011).

The Guardian, *Niger Delta Militants to Release British Hostage*, 19 April 2009, available http://www.guardian.co.uk/world/2009/apr/19/robin-hughes-hostage-nigeria-release (accessed 4 May 2012).

Johannes Harnischfeger, 'The Bakassi Boys: Fighting Crime in Nigeria,' *Journal of Modern African Studies*, 2003, Vol. 41, No. 1, pp. 23–49.

Johannes Harnischfeger, *Democratization and Islamic Law* (Frankfurt and New York: Campus Verlag, 2008).

Geoffrey Hawthorn, '"Waiting for a Text?" Comparing Third World Politics,' in James Manor (ed.), *Rethinking Third World Politics* (London and New York: Longman, 1991), pp. 24–50.

Jeffrey Herbst, 'Responding to State Failure in Africa,' *International Security*, Winter 1996, Vol. 21, No. 3, pp. 120–144.

J.N.C. Hill, 'Beyond the Other? A Postcolonial Critique of the Failed State Thesis,' *African Identities*, 2005, Vol. 3, No. 2, pp. 139–154.

J.N.C. Hill, 'Challenging the Failed State Thesis: IMF and World Bank Intervention and the Algerian Civil War,' *Civil Wars*, March 2009, Vol. 11, No. 1, pp. 39–56.

J.N.C Hill, 'Thoughts of Home: Civil–Military Relations and the Conduct of Nigeria's Peacekeeping Forces,' *Journal of Military Ethics*, November 2009, Vol. 8, No. 4, pp. 289–306.

J.N.C. Hill, *Sufism in Northern Nigeria: A Force for Counter Radicalisation?* (Carlisle, Pennsylvania: Strategic Studies Institute US Army War College, 2010).

158 *Select Bibliography*

J.N.C. Hill, 'Corruption in the Courts: The Achilles Heel of Nigeria's Regulatory Framework? *Third World Quarterly*, 2010, Vol. 31, No. 7, pp. 1161–1179.

Gerald B. Helman and Steven R. Ratner, 'Saving Failed States,' *Foreign Affairs*, Winter 1992–1993, No. 89, pp. 3–20.

A.G. Hopkins, 'Quasi-states, Weak States and the Partition of Africa,' *Review of International Studies*, April 2000, Vol. 26, No. 2, pp. 311–320.

Human Rights Watch, *The Price of Oil: Corporate Responsibility and Human Rights Violations in Nigeria's Oil Producing Communities* (New York: Human Rights Watch, 1999).

Human Rights Watch, *The Niger Delta: No Democratic Dividend* (New York: Human Rights Watch, 2002a).

Human Rights Watch, *Nigeria: Military Revenge in Benue – A Population under Attack* (New York: Human Rights Watch, 2002b).

Human Rights Watch, *The Bakassi Boys: The Legitimization of Murder and Torture* (New York: Human Rights Watch, 2002c).

Human Rights Watch, *The O'odua People's Congress: Fighting Violence with Violence* (New York: Human Rights Watch, 2003a).

Human Rights Watch, *The Warri Crisis: Fuelling Violence*, November 2003b, Vol. 15, No. 18, available at http://www.hrw.org/sites/default/files/reports/nigeria1103.pdf (accessed 5 September 2011).

Human Rights Watch, *Nigeria's 2003 Elections: The Unacknowledged Violence*, 1 June 2004, available at http://www.hrw.org/node/12130 (accessed 23 February 2011).

Human Rights Watch, *Rivers and Blood: Guns, Oil and Power in Nigeria's Rivers State*, 4 February 2005, available at http://www.hrw.org/en/reports/2005/02/04/rivers-and-blood (accessed 23 February 2011).

Human Rights Watch, *Nigeria: Presidential Election Marred by Fraud, Violence*, 25 April 2007, available at http://www.hrw.org/en/news/2007/04/24/nigeria-presidential-election-marred-fraud-violence (accessed 25 May 2009).

Human Rights Watch, *Nigeria: Arbitrary Killings by Security Forces in Jos*, 19 December 2008, available at http://www.unhcr.org/refworld/docid/49509c061a.html (accessed 6 July 2011).

Human Rights Watch, *Nigeria Prosecute Killings by Security Forces*, 26 November 2009, available at http://www.hrw.org/news/2009/11/26/nigeria-prosecute-killings-security-forces (accessed 11 August 2012).

Human Rights Watch, *World Report 2011: Nigeria*, January 2011, available at http: //www.hrw.org/en/world-report-2011/nigeria (accessed 21 February 2011).

Human Rights Watch, *Nigeria: New Wave of Violence Leaves 200 Dead*, 27 January 2011, available at http://www.hrw.org/en/news/2011/01/27/nigeria-new-wave-violence-leaves-200-dead (accessed 21 February 2011).

Human Rights Watch, *Nigeria: Post-Election Violence Killed 800*, 16 May 2011, available at http://www.hrw.org/en/news/2011/05/16/nigeria-post-election-violence-killed-800 (accessed 5 July 2011).

O. Okechukwu Ibeanu, 'Exiles in Their Own Home: Conflicts and Internal Population Displacement in Nigeria,' *Journal of Refugee Studies*, 1999, Vol. 12, No. 1, pp. 161–179.

Select Bibliography 159

Jibrin Ibrahim, 'The Politics of Religion in Nigeria: The Parameters of the 1987 Crisis in Kaduna State,' *Review of African Political Economy*, 1989, Vol. 16, No. 45/46, pp. 65–82.

Jibrin Ibrahim, 'Religion and Political Turbulence in Nigeria,' *Journal of Modern African Studies*, March 1991, Vol. 29, No. 1, pp. 115–136.

Julius O. Ihonvbere, 'A Critical Evaluation of the Failed 1990 Coup in Nigeria,' *Journal of Modern African Studies*, December 1991, Vol. 29, No. 4, pp. 601–626.

Immigration and Refugee Board of Canada, Nigeria: Treatment of Members of the Movement for the Actualisation of the Sovereign State of Biafra (MASSOB); availability of State Protection (August 2004–June 2005), 27 June 2005, available at http://www.unhcr.org/refworld/country,,IRBC,,NGA,,440 ed73221,0.html (accessed 7 May 2012).

The Independent, *Nigeria Is Falling Apart, Says Nobel Prize-Winning Author*, 16 March 2010, available at http://www.independent.co.uk/news/world /africa/nigeria-is-falling-apart-says-nobelprizewinning-author-1921835. html (accessed 15 February 2011).

International Commission on Intervention and State Sovereignty, *The Responsibility to Protect*, December 2001, available at http://www.iciss.ca /report2-en.asp (accessed 10 June 2011).

International Crisis Group, *Nigeria: Failed Elections, Failing State?* 30 May 2007, available at http://www.crisisgroup.org/~/media/Files/africa/west-africa /nigeria/Nigeria%20Failed%20Elections%20Failing%20State.ashx (accessed 15 February 2011).

Robert H. Jackson, *Quasi-states: Sovereignty, International Relations and the Third World* (Cambridge: Cambridge University Press, 1990).

Robert H. Jackson, 'Juridical Statehood in Sub-Saharan Africa,' *Journal of International Affairs*, 1992, Vol. 46, No. 1, pp. 1–16.

Robert H. Jackson, *The Global Covenant: Human Conduct in the World of States* (Oxford: Oxford University Press, 2000).

Robert H. Jackson and Carl G. Rosberg, 'Why Africa's Weak States Persist: The Empirical and the Juridical in Statehood,' *World Politics*, October 1982, Vol. 35, No. 1, pp. 1–24.

Robert H. Jackson and Carl G. Rosberg, 'Sovereignty and Underdevelopment: Juridical Statehood in the African Crisis,' *The Journal of Modern African Studies*, 1986, Vol. 24, No. 1, pp. 1–31.

Jane's, *The Movement for the Emancipation of the Niger Delta (MEND)*, 2009, available at http://articles.janes.com/articles/Janes-World-Insurgency-and-Terror ism/Movement-for-the-Emancipation-of-the-Niger-Delta-MEND-Nigeria. html (accessed 18 March 2012).

Richard Joseph, *Democracy and Prebendal Politics in Nigeria: The Rise and Fall of the Second Republic* (Cambridge: Cambridge University Press, 1987).

Richard Joseph (ed.), *State, Conflict and Democracy in Africa* (Boulder, Colorado: Lynne Rienner Publishers, 1999).

Mary Kaldor, Terry Lyn Karl and Yahia Said (eds.), *Oil Wars* (London: Pluto Press, 2007).

Kalu N. Kalu, *State Power, Autarchy, and Political Conquest in Nigerian Federalism* (New York: Lexington Books, 2008).

160   *Select Bibliography*

Terry Lynn Karl, *The Paradox of Wealth* (Berkeley, California: University of California Press, 1997).

Terry Lynn Karl, 'The Perils of the Petro-state: Reflections on the Paradox of Plenty,' *Journal of International Affairs*, 1999, Vol. 53, No. 1, pp. 31–48.

Jeremy Keenan, *The Dark Sahara: America's War on Terror in Africa* (London and New York: Pluto Press, 2009).

Robert O. Keohane, *After Hegemony: Cooperation and Discord in the World Political Economy* (Princeton, New Jersey: Princeton University Press, 1984).

Darren Kew and David L. Phillips, 'Seeking Peace in the Niger Delta: Oil, Natural Gas and Other Vital Resources,' *New England Journal of Public Policy*, 2007, Vol. 21, No. 2, pp. 154–170.

Sarah Ahmed Khan, *Nigeria: The Political Economy of Oil* (Oxford: Oxford University Press, 1994).

A.H.M. Kirk-Greene, *Crisis and Conflict in Nigeria 1967–70* (Oxford: Oxford University Press, 1971).

A.H.M. Kirk-Greene and D. Rimmer, *Nigeria since 1970: A Political and Economic Outline* (London: Hodder and Stoughton, 1981).

Peter Koehn, 'Competitive Transition to Civilian Rule: Nigeria's First and Second Experiments,' *Journal of Modern African Studies*, September 1989, Vol. 27, No. 3, pp. 401–430.

Kwasi Kwarteng, *Ghosts of Empire: Britain's Legacies in the Modern World* (London: Bloomsbury, 2011).

David D. Laitin, 'The Sharia Debate and the Origins of Nigeria's Second Republic,' *Journal of Modern African Studies*, September 1982, Vol. 20, No. 3, pp. 411–430.

Rene Lemarchand and Keith Legg, 'Political Clientelism and Development: A Preliminary Analysis,' *Comparative Politics*, January 1972, Vol. 4, No. 2, pp. 149–178.

Peter M. Lewis, 'Economic Statism, Private Capital, and the Dilemmas of Accumulation in Nigeria,' *World Development*, March 1994, Vol. 22, No. 3, pp. 437–451.

Peter M. Lewis, 'From Prebendalism to Predation: The Political Economy of Decline in Nigeria,' *Journal of Modern African Studies*, March 1996, Vol. 34, No. 1, pp. 79–103.

Peter M. Lewis, *Growing Apart – Oil, Politics and Economic Change in Indonesia and Nigeria* (Ann Arbor, Michigan: University of Michigan Press, 2007).

Robin Luckham, *The Nigerian Military: A Sociological Analysis of Authority and Revolt, 1960–67* (Cambridge: University of Cambridge Press, 1974).

Karl Maier, *This House Has Fallen: Nigeria in Crisis* (London: Penguin Books, 2000).

B.G. Martin, *Muslim Brotherhoods in 19th-Century Africa* (Cambridge: Cambridge University Press, 1976).

James Mayall, 'Oil and Nigerian Foreign Policy,' *African Affairs*, July 1976, Vol. 75, No. 300, pp. 317–330.

Jean-Francois Médard, 'The Underdeveloped State in Africa: Political Clientelism or Neo-Patrimonialism?' in Christopher Clapham (ed.), *Private Patronage and Public Power* (London: F. Pinter, 1982), pp. 172–192.

Select Bibliography 161

Ken Menkhaus, 'State Collapse in Somalia: Second Thoughts,' *Review of African Political Economy*, September 2003, Vol. 30, No. 97, pp. 405–422.

Joel S. Migdal, *Strong Societies and Weak States: State-Society Relations and State Capabilities in the Third World* (Princeton, New Jersey: Princeton University Press, 1988).

Paul D. Miller, The Case for Nation-Building: Why and How to Fix Failed States,' *Prism*, December 2012, Vol. 3, No. 1, pp. 63–74.

David Moffat and Olof Lindén, 'Perception and Reality: Assessing Priorities for Sustainable Development in the Niger River Delta,' *Ambio* (A Journal of the Human Environment), December 1995, Vol. 24, No. 7–8, pp. 527–538.

Martin Murphy, *Small Boats, Weak States, Dirty Money: Piracy and Maritime Terrorism in the Modern World* (London: Hurst and Company Publishers, 2010).

New York Times, *Suicide Bomber Attacks U.N. Building in Nigeria*, 26 August 2011, available at http://www.nytimes.com/2011/08/27/world/africa/27nigeria. html?pagewanted=all (accessed 27 April 2012).

Next, *UK Court Declares Ibori's Associate Guilty*, 3 June 2010, available at http://234next.com/csp/cms/sites/Next/News/Metro/Crime/5575623–146 /uk_court_declares_iboris_associate_guilty.csp (accessed 13 June 2011).

Tim Niblock, *Saudi Arabia: Power, Legitimacy and Survival* (Abingdon, Oxon: Routledge, 2006).

'Nigeria/Cameroon: Blundering into Battle,' *Africa Confidential*, 15 April 1994, Vol. 35, No. 8.

Nigeria National Bureau of Statistics, *2010 Review of the Economy* (2010), available at http://www.nigerianstat.gov.ng/ext/latest_release/2010_Review_of_the_Nigerian_Economy.pdf (accessed 15 March 2012).

Nigerian Guardian, *Gunmen Strike in N'Delta, Kill Three Naval Officers*, 4 February 2008, available at http://www.guardiannewsngr.com/news /article04//indexn3_html?pdate=040208&ptitle=Gunmen%20strike%20 in%20N'Delta,%20kill%20three%20naval%20officers&cpdate=040208 (accessed 2 April 2008).

Nigerian National Petroleum Corporation, *Oil Production*, 23 February 2012, available at http://www.nnpcgroup.com/NNPCBusiness/UpstreamVentures /OilProduction.aspx (accessed 23 February 2012).

Nigerian Tribune, *MEND Vows to Attack MTN, SACOIL, Others: Claims Responsibility for Agip Pipeline Attack*, 5 February 2012, available at http: //tribune.com.ng/index.php/front-page-news/35458-mend-vows-to-attack-mtn-sacoil-others-claims-responsibility-for-agip-pipeline-attack (accessed 18 March 2012).

Nigerian Tribune, *Suspected Boko Haram Members Ambush Police Patrol team in Damaturu*, 19 January 2012, available at http://www.tribune.com.ng/index. php/news/34589-suspected-boko-haram-members-ambush-police-patrol-team-in-damaturu – cp (accessed 29 April 2012).

Nigerian Tribune, *Security Agencies Reinforce to Arrest Ibori: SSS Officers Deployed in Delta: EFCC has no Evidence Against Me – Ibori*, 23 April 2010, available at http://www.tribune.com.ng/index.php/front-page-news/4453 – security-agencies-reinforce-to-arrest-ibori-sss-officers-deployed-in-delta-efcc-has-no-evidence-against-me-ibori (accessed 14 June 2011).

162 Select Bibliography

Cyril Obi and Siri Aas Rusta (eds.), *Oil and the Insurgency in the Niger Delta* (London and New York: Zed Books, 2011).

Andrew C. Okolie, 'Oil Rents, International Loans and Agrarian Policies in Nigeria, 1970–1992,' *Review of African Political Economy*, June 1995, Vol. 22, No. 64, pp. 199–212.

Ricardo Soares de Oliveira, *Oil and Politics in the Gulf of Guinea* (London: Hurst and Company, 2007).

Ayodeji Olukoju, 'Never Expect Power Always: Electricity Consumers' Response to Monopoly, Corruption and Inefficient Services in Nigeria,' *African Affairs*, 2004, Vol. 103, No. 410, pp. 51–71.

Adebayo Olukoshi and Tajudeen Abdulraheem, 'Nigeria Crisis Management under the Buhari Regime,' *Review of African Political Economy*, December 1985, Vol. 34, pp. 95–101.

Organisation of African Unity, *OAU Charter*, 25 May 1963, available at http://www.au.int/en/sites/default/files/OAU_Charter_1963_0.pdf (accessed 25 May 2011).

Organisation of Petroleum Exporting Countries, *Nigeria*, 2012, available at http://www.opec.org/opec_web/en/about_us/167.htm (accessed 23 February 2012).

Eghosa E. Osaghae, 'The Ogoni Uprising: Oil Politics, Minority Agitation and the Future of the Nigerian State,' *African Affairs*, Vol. 94, No. 376, pp. 325–344.

Eghosa E. Osaghae, *Nigeria since Independence: Crippled Giant* (London: Hurst, 1998).

Shehu Othman, 'Classes, Crises and Coup: The Demise of Shagari's Regime,' *African Affairs*, 1984, Vol. 83, No. 333, pp. 441–461.

Oyeleye Oyediran (ed.), *Nigerian Government and Politics under Military Rule, 1966–79* (Basingstoke, Hampshire: Palgrave Macmillan, 1979).

Oyeleye Oyediran and Adigun Agbaje, 'Two-Partyism and Democratic Transition in Nigeria,' *Journal of Modern African Studies*, June 1991, Vol. 29, No. 2, pp. 213–235.

John N. Paden, *Muslim Civic Cultures and Conflict Resolution: The Challenge of Democratic Federalism in Nigeria* (Washington D.C.: Brookings Institution Press, 2005).

John N. Paden, *Faith and Politics in Nigeria* (Washington D.C.: United States Institute of Peace Press, 2008).

John N. Paden, *Postelection Conflict Management in Nigeria: The Challenges of National Unity* (Arlington, Virginia: George Mason University, 2012).

Scott R. Pearson, *Petroleum and the Nigerian Economy* (Stanford, California: Stanford University Press, 1970).

J.D.Y. Peel, *Religious Encounter and the Making of the Yoruba* (Bloomington, Indiana: Indiana University Press, 2000).

Michael Peel, *A Swamp Full of Dollars: Pipelines and Paramilitaries at Nigeria's Oil Frontier* (London and New York: I.B. Tauris, 2009).

People's Democratic Party, *Constitution*, 28 July 1998, available at http://www.peoplesdemocraticparty.net/attachments/article/7/PDP%20constitution.pdf (accessed 7 August 2012).

Select Bibliography   163

Pointblanknews, *James Ibori Down with Hypertension in Dubai*, 16 August 2010, available at http://www.pointblanknews.com/News/os3770.html (accessed 14 June 2011).

Punch, *Kidnappings: Nigeria May become a Failed State – ASUU*, 1 February 2011, available at http://www.punchontheweb.com/Articl.aspx?theartic=Art2011 02013433382 (accessed 15 February 2011).

Punch, *Regarding Ibori Seeking UAE Asylum*, 13 June 2010, available at http://www.punchng.com/Articl.aspx?theartic=Art20100613304696 (accessed 14 June 2011).

Punch, *Ibori Loses Bail in Dubai, Remanded on Police Custody*, 11 June 2010, available at http://www.punchng.com/Articl.aspx?theartic=Art20100611226918 (accessed 14 June 2011).

Punch, *Ibori Seeks Political Asylum in Dubai*, 27 May 2010, available at http://punchng.com/Articl.aspx?theartic=Art201005272304760 (accessed 14 June 2011).

Punch, *Militants Abduct Lawmaker's Sister*, 8 January 2008, available at http://www.punchontheweb.com/Articl.aspx?theartic=Art200801081362242 (accessed 10 January 2008).

Terrence Ranger, 'The Invention of Tradition in Colonial Africa,' in Eric Hobsbawm and Terrence Ranger (eds.), *The Invention of Tradition* (Cambridge: Cambridge University Press, 1983), pp. 211–262.

Terrence Ranger, 'The Invention of Tradition Revisited: The Case of Colonial Africa,' in Terrence Ranger and Vaughn Olufen (eds.), *Legitimacy and the State in Twentieth-century Africa. Essays in Honour of A.H.M. Kirk-Greene* (Basingstoke, Hampshire: Palgrave Macmillan, 1993), pp. 62–111.

Willian Reno, *Warlord Politics and African States* (Boulder, Colorado: Lynne Rienner Publishers, 1998).

Reuters, *Suicide Car Bombs Hit Nigerian Newspaper Offices*, 26 April 2012, available at http://www.reuters.com/article/2012/04/26/us-nigeria-bomb-idUSBRE83P0NR20120426 (accessed 29 April 2012).

Reuters, *Islamists Kill Dozens in Nigeria Christmas Bombs*, 25 December 2011, available at http://www.reuters.com/article/2011/12/25/us-nigeria-blast-idUSTRE7BO03020111225 (accessed 29 April 2012).

Reuters, *Police Blame Islamist Sect for Deadly Nigeria Blast*, 16 June 2011, available at http://uk.reuters.com/article/2011/06/16/uk-nigeria-explosion-idUK-TRE75F27T20110616 (accessed 23 June 2011).

Reuters, *Bombs Rattle Independence Day in Nigeria*, 1 October 2010, available at http://af.reuters.com/article/worldNews/idAFTRE6902IJ20101001 (accessed 24 May 2011).

Michael Ross, 'What Do We Know about Natural Resources and Civil War?' *Journal of Peace Research*, 2004, Vol. 41, No. 3, pp. 337–356.

Robert I. Rotberg (ed.), *When States Fail* (Princeton, New Jersey: Princeton University Press, 2004).

Robert I. Rotberg, Nigeria: Elections and Continuing Challenges, CSR No. 27, April 2007 (New York: Council on Foreign Relations, 2007).

Guenther Roth, 'Personal Rulership, Patrimonialism, and Empire-Building in the New States,' *World Politics*, January 1968, Vol. 20, No. 2, pp. 194–206.

164   *Select Bibliography*

Andy Rowell, James Marriott and Lorne Stockman, *The Next Gulf* (London: Constable, 2005).

Lloyd I. Rudolph and Susan Hoeber Rudolph, 'Authority and Power in Bureaucratic and Patrimonial Administration: A Revisionist Interpretation of Weber on Bureaucracy,' *World Politics*, January 1979, Vol. 31, No. 2, pp. 195–227.

Walter Schwarz, *Nigeria* (New York: Praeger, 1968).

Timothy Shaw, 'Foreign Policy, Political Economy, and the Future: Reflections on Africa in the World System,' *African Affairs*, April 1980, Vol. 79, No. 315, pp. 260–268.

Timothy M. Shaw and Orobola Fasehun, 'Nigeria in the World System: Alternative Approaches, Explanations and Projections,' *Journal of Modern African Studies*, December 1980, Vol. 18, No. 4, pp. 551–573.

Nicholas Shaxson, *Poisoned Wells: The Dirty Politics of African Oil* (Basingstoke, Hampshire: Palgrave Macmillan, 2007).

Shell Petroleum Development Company, *Shell Nigeria Annual Report 2005: People and the Environment* (Nigeria: Shell Petroleum Development Company, August 2006).

Richard L. Sklar, *Nigerian Political Parties: Power in an Emergent African Nation* (Princeton: Princeton University Press, 1963).

Richard L. Sklar, 'Contradictions in the Nigerian Political System,' August 1965, *Journal of Modern African Studies*, Vol. 3, No. 2, pp. 201–213.

Daniel Jordan Smith, *A Culture of Corruption: Everyday Deception and Popular Discontent in Nigeria* (Princeton and Oxford: Princeton University Press, 2007).

Malinda S. Smith, *Securing Africa: Post-9/11 Discourses on Terrorism* (Farnham, Surrey: Ashgate, 2010).

Wole Soyinka, *The Open Sore of a Continent: A Personal Narrative of the Nigerian Crisis* (Oxford and New York: Oxford University Press, 1996).

Wole Soyinka, *You Must Set Forth at Dawn* (New York: Random House, 2007).

Jack Straw, *Failed and Failing States*, speech delivered 6 September 2002 at the European Research Institute, University of Birmingham.

Rotimi T. Suberu, 'The Struggle for New States in Nigeria, 1976–1990,' *African Affairs*, 1991, Vol. 90, No. 361, pp. 499–522.

Sunday Tribune, *Nigeria Is Showing Symptoms of a Failed State – Okei-Odumakin*, 31 July 2011, available at http://tribune.com.ng/sun/interview/4665-niger ia-is-showing-symptoms-of-a-failed-state-okei-odumakin (accessed 20 April 2012).

Tekena N. Tamuno, 'Separatist Agitation in Nigeria since 1914,' *Journal of Modern African Studies*, December 1970, Vol. 8, No. 4, pp. 563–584.

Time Magazine, *Iran: Another Crisis for the Shah*, 13 November 1978, available at http://www.time.com/time/magazine/article/0,9171,946149,00.html (accessed 1 March 2012).

The Times, *Nigeria*, 8 January 1897, Issue 35095.

This Day, *Nigeria: Borno ANPP Chairman Killed in Suspected Boko Haram Attack*, 7 October 2010, available at http://allafrica.com/stories/201010080326. html (accessed 27 April 2012).

Select Bibliography 165

This Day, *Boko Haram – Death Toll Now 700, Says Security Commander*, 2 August 2009, available at http://www.thisdayonline.info/nview.php?id=150423 (accessed 3 December 2010).

Terisa Turner, 'Multinational Corporations and the Instability of the Nigerian State,' *Review of African Political Economy*, January–April 1976, No. 5, pp. 63–79.

UK Cabinet Office, *The National Security Strategy of the United Kingdom: Update 2009: Security for the Next Generation*, June 2009, available at http://www.official-documents.gov.uk/document/cm75/7590/7590.pdf (accessed 21 July 2011).

UK Cabinet Office, *A Strong Britain in an Age of Uncertainty: The National Security Strategy*, October 2010, available at http://www.direct.gov.uk/prod_consum_dg/groups/dg_digitalassets/@dg/@en/documents/digitalasset/dg_191639.pdf?CID=PDF&PLA=furl&CRE=nationalsecuritystrategy (accessed 21 July 2011).

UK Home Office, *British Citizenship Statistics United Kingdom, 2008*, 20 May 2009, available at http://www.homeoffice.gov.uk/publications/about-us/non-personal-data/Passports-immigration/citizenship-statistics-1998–2008/british-citizenship-stats-2008?view=Binary (accessed 13 July 2011).

Ndaeyo Uko, *Romancing the Gun: The Press as a Promoter of Military Rule* (Trenton, New Jersey: Africa World Press, 2004).

United Nations, *Adult Literacy Rates both Sexes (% Aged 15 and Above)*, 2011, available at http://hdrstats.undp.org/en/indicators/101406.html (accessed 7 May 2012).

United Nations General Assembly, *1514 Declaration on the Granting of Independence to Colonial Countries and Peoples*, 14 December 1960, available at http://daccess-dds-ny.un.org/doc/RESOLUTION/GEN/NR0/152/88/IMG/NR015288.pdf?OpenElement (accessed 25 May 2011).

United Nations General Assembly, *1541 Principles Which Should Guide Members in Determining Whether or Not an Obligation Exists to Transmit the Information Called for Under Article 73e of the Charter*, 15 December 1960, available at http://daccess-dds-ny.un.org/doc/RESOLUTION/GEN/NR0/153/15/IMG/NR015315.pdf?OpenElement (accessed 25 May 2011).

United Nations General Assembly, *2005 World Summit Outcomes*, 15 September 2005, available at http://www.who.int/hiv/universalaccess2010/worldsummit.pdf (accessed 10 June 2011).

United Nations, *Country Profiles and Human Development Indicators*, 2010, available at http://hdr.undp.org/en/countries/ (accessed 23 May 2011).

United Nations Children' s Fund, *Nigeria*, 2 March 2010, available at http://www.unicef.org/infobycountry/nigeria_statistics.html#78 (accessed 6 July 2011).

United Nations, *Nigeria*, 2010, available at http://hdrstats.undp.org/en/countries/profiles/NGA.html (accessed 26 June 2011).

United Nations, *Nigeria*, 2011, available at http://data.un.org/CountryProfile.aspx?crName=NIGERIA#Social (accessed 26 June 2011).

U.S. Department of Energy, *Country Analysis Briefs: Nigeria*, July 2010, available at http://www.eia.doe.gov/emeu/cabs/Nigeria/pdf.pdf (23 February 2012).

166 *Select Bibliography*

U.S. Department of State, *Nigeria*, 6 March 2007, available at http://www.state.gov/g/drl/rls/hrrpt/2006/78751.htm (accessed 25 February 2011).

U.S. Department of State, *2010 Human Rights Report: Nigeria*, 8 April 2011, available at http://www.state.gov/g/drl/rls/hrrpt/2010/af/154363.htm (accessed 6 July 2011).

U.S. Department of State, *Background Note: Nigeria*, 20 October 2011, available at http://www.state.gov/r/pa/ei/bgn/2836.htm (accessed 23 February 2012).

U.S. House of Representatives Committee on Homeland Security Subcommittee on Counterterrorism and Intelligence, *Boko Haram: Emerging Threat to the U.S. Homeland*, 30 November 2011, available at http://homeland.house.gov/hearing/subcommittee-hearing-boko-haram-emerging-threat-us-homeland (accessed 22 May 2012).

U.S. Senate, *Congressional Record*, 20 January 1999, No. 9.

P. Chudi Uwazurike, 'Confronting Potential Breakdown: The Nigerian Redemocratization Process in Critical Perspective,' *Journal of Modern African Studies*, 1990, Vol. 28, No. 1, pp. 55–77.

Vanguard, *Nigeria: Army Court-Martials Two Colonels, 12 Others for Alleged Misconduct*, 28 May 2012, available at http://allafrica.com/stories/201205290252.html (accessed 11 August 2012).

Vanguard, *Boko Haram Bombs Kano Afresh*, 24 January 2012, available at http://www.vanguardngr.com/2012/01/boko-haram-bombs-kano-afresh / (accessed 29 April 2012).

Vanguard, *Fuel Subsidy Removal: A Nigerian Dilemma*, 9 January 2012, available at http://www.vanguardngr.com/2012/01/fuel-subsidy-removal-a-nigerian-dilemma/ (accessed 7 May 2012).

Vanguard, *Outrage in Delta Over JOINT TASK FORCE Invasion*, 9 December 2010, available at http://www.vanguardngr.com/2010/12/outrage-in-delta-over-Joint Task Force-invasion/ (accessed 15 July 2011).

Vanguard, *Ibori's Wife Gets 5yrs Jail*, 22 November 2010, available at http://www.vanguardngr.com/2010/11/iboris-wife-gets-5yrs-jail/ (accessed 13 June 2011).

Vanguard, *MEND Proposes 11-Point Agenda for Peace in the Niger Delta*, 18 February 2008, available at http://www.vanguardngr.com/index.php?option=com_content&task=view&id=2490&Itemid=43 (accessed 18 February 2008).

Vanguard, *Army Court-Martials 15 Officers over Missing Arms*, 14 January 2008, available at http://www.vanguardngr.com/index.php?option=com_content&task=view&id=4474&Itemid=0 (accessed 18 January 2008).

Olufemi Vaughan, *Nigerian Chiefs: Traditional Power in Modern Politics, 1890s–1990s* (Rochester, New York: University of Rochester Press, 2000).

WAC Global Services, *Peace and Security in the Niger Delta: Conflict Expert Group Baseline Report for Shell Petroleum Development Company*, December 2003, available at http://shellnews.net/2007/shell_wac_report_2004.pdf (accessed 6 September 2011).

Caroline M. Warner, 'The Political Economy of "Quasi-statehood" and the Demise of 19th Century African Politics,' *Review of International Studies*, April 1999, Vol. 25, No. 2, pp. 233–255.

Caroline M. Warner, 'A Reply to A.G. Hopkins,' *Review of International Studies*, April 200, Vol. 26, No. 2, pp. 321–325.

John Waterbury, 'Endemic and Planned Corruption in a Monarchical Regime,' *World Politics*, July 1973, Vol. 25, No. 4, pp. 533–555.

Michael Watts, 'Blood Oil: The Anatomy of a Petro-insurgency in the Niger Delta, Nigeria,' in Andrea Behrends, Stephen P. Reyna and Günther Schlee (eds.), *Crude Domination: An Anthropology of Oil* (Oxford: Berghahn Books, 2011), pp. 49–80.

Max Weber, *The Theory of Social and Economic Organization* (New York: The Free Press, 1947).

C. Whitaker, *The Politics of Tradition: Continuity and Change in Northern Nigeria, 1946–66* (Princeton: Princeton University Press, 1992).

Paul D. Williams, *State Failure in Africa: Causes, Consequences and Response*, 2007, available at http://elliott.gwu.edu/assets/docs/research/williams07.pdf (accessed 3 May 2011).

Paul D. Williams, *War and Conflict in Africa* (Cambridge: Polity Press, 2011).

P. Wilmot, *Nigeria's Southern Africa Policy, 1960–1988* (Uppsala: Nordiska Afikainstituet, 1989).

World Bank, *Education: Data and Statistics*, 2011, available at http://web.worldbank.org/WBSITE/EXTERNAL/TOPICS/EXTEDUCATION/0,,contentMDK:20573961~isCURL:Y~menuPK:282412~pagePK:148956~piPK:216618~theSitePK:282386,00.html (accessed 7 May 2012).

World Bank, *Nigeria*, 2011, available at http://web.worldbank.org/WBSITE/EXTERNAL/COUNTRIES/AFRICAEXT/NIGERIAEXTN/0,,contentMDK:22553025~pagePK:141137~piPK:141127~theSitePK:368896,00.html (accessed 6 July 2011).

World Bank, *Nigeria: Country Assistant Strategy*, 2011, available at http://web.worldbank.org/WBSITE/EXTERNAL/COUNTRIES/AFRICAEXT/NIGERIAEXTN/0,,menuPK:368909~pagePK:141132~piPK:141105~theSitePK:368896,00.html (accessed 23 February 2012).

World Health Organisation, *Nigeria: Health Profile*, 4 April 2011, available at http://www.who.int/gho/countries/nga.pdf (accessed 6 July 2011).

Crawford Young, *The Colonial State in Comparative Perspective* (New Haven, Connecticut: Yale University Press, 1994).

Crawford Young, 'The End of the Postcolonial State in Africa? Reflections on Changing Political Dynamics,' *African Affairs*, January 2004, Vol. 103, No. 410, pp. 23–49.

I. William Zartman (ed.), *The Political Economy of Nigeria* (New York: Praeger, 1983).

I. William Zartman (ed.), *Collapsed States: The Disintegration and Restoration of Legitimate Authority* (Boulder, Colorado: Lynne Rienner Publishers, 1995).

Index

Abacha, Sani, 33, 147n. 25
Aba declaration, 40
abduction, of Europeans, 37, 41,
  137n. 71
Abuja, 102–4
Academic Staff Union of
  Universities, 25
Action Group (AG), 48, 49–50
administrative divisions, 47–8
Africa
  decolonisation of, 12–14
  state failure in, 19–20
AG, *see* Action Group
Agbiti, Francis, trial of, 95–8
Agip, 86
Aguiyi-Ironsi, Johnson, 51, 52,
  147n. 25
Ajayi, Joseph, 95, 96
Akerdolu, Oluwarotimi, 25
Akpa, Patrick, 95
Alamieyeseigha, Diepreye, 30,
  134n. 23
Ali Ngala, Awana, 28
Anglo-Iranian Oil Company, 76,
  141n. 14–15
Aondoakaa, Michael, 122–3
armed forces, 119–21
  African Pride affair and, 98
  Federal Government's lack of
    control over, 22–3
  lack of exclusive authority over
    Nigeria's territory, 33–4
  nefarious activities of, 33
  Nigerian public and, 32–3
  Nigeria's failure and, 5, 99, 104–9
  Nigeria's integration and, 5–6,
    98–9, 100–3, 109–18
  under-resourced, 35
  use of violence, 23, 44
  see also police

assassinations
  by Boko Haram, 28
  by MEND, 30–1
Awolowo, Obafemi, 48, 50
Ayoade, John, on stages of weakness
  of states, 15
Aziegbemi, Anthony, 96, 97
Azikiwe, Nnamdi, 48, 50

Babangida, Ibrahim Badamasi, 33,
  102, 104, 116, 147n. 25
Balewa, Tafawa, 48, 49
Barder, Brian, assessment of
  Nigeria's problems, 66–7
Bello, Ahmadu, 48
Biafra, 110–13
Birkuti, Ibrahim, 28
Bob-Manuel, Antonio, 96–7
Boko Haram, 6, 22, 26–9, 88, 93
  and MEND compared, 126
  use of violence, 23, 27–8, 36–8
British Special Boat Service,
  involvement in hostage rescue
  attempt, Mar. 2012, 37, 41–2
Buhari, Muhammadu, 33, 101, 104,
  113, 147n. 25
  war against indiscipline, 113–15

census
  1962, 49
  1963, 49–50
Chevron, 86
collapsed states, 16
constitution
  1963, 53
  1999, 61
  1999, Article 133 and
    134, 64–5
  1999, Article 146, 58
  1999, Article 222 and 223, 65

170   *Index*

corruption, 134n. 23
  federalism and, 45, 59–62
  oil industry and, 71, 87–8, 93
  see also Ibori, James
coup d'état
  Jan. 1966, 51–2, 146n. 24
  July 1966, 52

decolonisation, 12–14
  democracy, damage to, 59,
    85–7, 93
Department of Petroleum Resources
    (DPR), 83, 84–5
Dikko, Umaru, 108
Dokubo-Asari, Mujahid, 29
DPR, *see* Department of Petroleum
    Resources
Dutch Disease, 73, 140n. 6

economy
  non-oil sectors of, 80–1, 92
  oil industry impact on, 71, 81–2
education, 24, 39
elections, 64–5, 86–7
environmental damage, and oil
    industry, 82–5
environmental regulations, 83–4
ethnic tensions, and federalism,
    55–6, 62–3
European imperial powers, 12–13

failed states, *see* state failure
failure of Nigeria, 1–7, 125
  concerns about, 25–6
  contributing factors, 26, 126
  international community's
    fears of, 42
  failure to control, 10, 20–1,
    32–4, 43
  failure to promote human
    flourishing, 10, 16–17, 20–1,
    34–9
  Federal Government's, 23, 93
  federalism's, 44–5
  oil industry's, 88–9
FCB, *see* Fourth Commando Brigade

Federal Environmental Protection
    Agency (FEPA), 84, 85
Federal Government
  disinterest in public
    taxation, 86
  failings of, 22–4
  failure to control, 32–4, 43
  failure to provide education and
    health care, 23–4, 38–9
  failure to provide security,
    34–8
  insurgencies and, 24–5
federalism
  functions of, 53–4
  Nigeria's failure and, 5, 44–5,
    54–62
  Nigeria's integration and, 5–6,
    45–6, 62–6
  post-independence background,
    46–53, 67–9
FEPA, *see* Federal Environmental
    Protection Agency
Foi, Buji, 26
Fourth Commando Brigade
    (FCB), 111
Fund for Peace, 19
  Failed State Index rankings, 3

Gohil, Bhadresh, 122
Gowon, Yakubu, 33, 52, 54
  social integration programme,
    116–17
  war on indiscipline, 110–13
Gros, John-Germain, on categories
    of weak states, 15

Hausa/Fulani, 47, 117
  health care provision, inadequate,
    23–4, 38
human rights abuse, by armed
    forces, 108–9
Human Rights Watch
  on 2007 presidential
    elections, 87
  on oil bunkering and its
    impact, 97–8

IBB, *see* Babangida, Ibrahim
Badamasi
Ibie-Ibori, Christine, 122
Ibori, James, 122–5
Ibori, Theresa, 122
ideal states, Weber's notion of,
130n. 11
Igbo, 47, 112–13, 117
army officers *coup d'état*, 51–2
insurgents and insurgencies, 4
Federal Government and,
24–5, 42–3
Federal Government's failure to
promote human flourishing
and, 88–9, 93
influencing factors, 5
in Niger Delta, 33, 105–7
oil industry and, 70, 90–1
at regional level, 107–8
use of violence, 23, 36–7
see also Boko Haram; Movement
for the Emancipation of the
Niger Delta
intelligence services, ineffectiveness
of, 35
Islamism, northern insurgent
groups and, 108

Joint Task Force (JTF), 34, 106, 107
composition of, 117
Jonathan, Goodluck, 58–9, 104,
123, 143n. 40
assumption of power, 118–20
JTF, *see* Joint Task Force

Kano, Amino, 48
Kolawole, Samuel, 96–7

Maduekwe, Ojo, 25
Maiduguri, 28
MASSOB, *see* Movement for the
Actualisation of the Sovereign
State of Biafra
MEND, *see* Movement for the
Emancipation of the Niger
Delta

Mineral Oils (Safety) Regulations, 83
Ministry of Justice, bombing of,
30–1
Mohammed, Murtala, 33, 101–2,
104, 113
MOPOL, 108
MOSOP, *see* Movement for the
Survival of the Ogoni People
Movement for the Actualisation of
the Sovereign State of Biafra
(MASSOB), 24, 40–1
Movement for the Emancipation of
the Niger Delta (MEND), 22, 26,
29–32, 70, 93, 106–7, 117
objectives of, 88–9
secession demands of, 72, 126
use of violence, 37, 107
Movement for the Survival of the
Ogoni People (MOSOP), 24, 29,
145n. 10
MT African Pride (ship), 95–8,
144n. 6

National Council of Nigerian
Citizens (NCNC), 48, 49–50,
138n. 3
National Council of State (NCS),
113–14
national unity
armed forces and, 98–9, 100–3
contributing factors, 6, 7, 126–7
damage to, 56–7
federalism and, 62–6
oil sector and, 72, 91–2, 93–4
National Youth Service Corps
(NYSC), 116–17
NCNC, *see* National Council of
Nigerian Citizens
NCS, *see* National Council of State
NDPVF, *see* Niger Delta Peoples
Volunteer Force
NDVF, *see* Niger Delta Vigilante
Force
negative sovereignty, 11–12
NEPU, *see* Northern Elements
Progressive Union

172 *Index*

Niger Delta, 75
  insurgencies and public-armed
    forces relationship in, 33
  local insurgents in, 106–7
  oil ownership and income
    derivation issues, 83, 90–1
  other states' dependence on, 91
  secessionism issue, 72
  violence in, 23
Niger Delta Peoples Volunteer Force
  (NDPVF), 4, 34, 70, 72, 106
Niger Delta Vigilante Force (NDVF),
  4, 34, 70, 72, 106
Nigeria, name coinage, 128n. 1–2
Nigerian Bar Association, 119
Nigerian National Alliance (NNA),
  50–1
Nigerian National Petroleum
  Corporation (NNPC), 74, 84–5
NNA, *see* Nigerian National Alliance
NNPC, *see* Nigerian National
  Petroleum Corporation
NNS *Beecroft* (ship), 95
Northern Elements Progressive
  Union (NEPU), 48, 49, 50
Northern People's Congress (NPC),
  48–51
NPC, *see* Northern People's
  Congress
NYSC, *see* National Youth Service
  Corps

Obasanjo, Olusegun, 58, 102, 104,
  113, 139n. 21, 150n. 7
Odesola, Samuel, 95
Odumegwu Ojukwu,
  Chukwuemeka, 52–3, 112, 117
  in Niger Delta, 33, 105–7
oil bunkering, 95–8, 144n. 3, 144n. 5
oil industry
  attacks on infrastructure, 31
  history of , 73–9
  Nigeria's failure and, 5, 70–2,
    80–91, 92–3
  Nigeria's integration and, 5–6, 72,
    91–2, 93–4

Okei-Odumakin, Joe, 26
Okoronkwo, Udoamaka, 122
Olufunlola, Adekeye, 95
Oni, Anthony, 95
OPEC, *see* Organisation of
  Petroleum Exporting Countries
Organisation of African Unity
  (OAU), 20
  on right to independent existence
    and self-government, 14
Organisation of Petroleum
  Exporting Countries (OPEC),
  74, 77, 78

party politics, 48–51
PDP, *see* People's Democratic Party
People's Democratic Party
  (PDP), 59
Petroleum Act, 83
police
  attacks on, 27
  ineffectiveness of, 35
  Oga mentality of, 35–6
  use of violence, 23, 44
  see also armed forces
political parties, obligations of, 65
political rights, federalism and,
  58–9
positive sovereignty, 11
president, 119
  election of, 64–5, 86–7
  regional rotation, 58–9
public participation, strengthening
  of, 112–15

Al Qaeda, 37, 41, 42
Qaqa, Abu, 27, 88, 126
  quality of life, oil industry and, 70

rentier state, 71, 85–6, 87, 93
responsibility to protect, 16–17
Rotberg, Robert, on categories of
  weak states, 15
Royal Dutch Shell, 75, 76, 86, 97
  opposition and criticism of,
    145n. 10

Index 173

Saraki, Bukola, 32
Saro-Wiwa, Ken, 108, 145n. 10
secessionism and secessionist
movements, 2, 4, 63–4, 126
Biafra, 110–12
dangers of, 39–41
of eastern region in 1967, 52–3
oil industry and, 72, 89–91
sectarianism
federalism and, 46, 55–6, 63–6
violence, 44, 63
security
lack of, 34–8
maintenance and preservation of,
110–12
see also insurgents and
insurgencies
Shagari, Shehu, 58
Shaw, Flora, 128n. 1–2
Shell-D'Arcy Petroleum
Development Company, 76,
141n. 14–15
social integration, armed forces
promotion of, 115–18
Somalia, secessionism in, 2
South Sudan, *de jure* statehood, 14
Soviet Union
African foreign policy, 12
military aid to Nigeria, 110–11
Soyinka, Wole, 25, 99–100
SSS, *see* State Security Service
state creation, 55–6, 62–3
as political tool, 112–13
state failure, 8–10, 20–1
in Africa, 19–20
associated terms of, 15–16
causes and consequences of, 10
identification of, 10–16
as places hosting threats to
Western countries, 18–19
spread of, 18–19

spread of the concept, 17–18
State Security Service (SSS), 36, 37
state weakness, stages and categories
of, 15
Steiner, Rolf, 111
successful states, 11, 14–15

telecommunications industry, 81

United Nations, 17
United Nations. General Assembly
Resolution 1514, 12–13, 14
responsibility to protect, 16–17
United Progressive Grand Alliance
(UPGA), 50, 51
United States, African foreign
policy, 12
United States. Department of
Energy, 74–5, 141n. 10
UPGA, *see* United Progressive Grand
Alliance
Uwazurike, Ralph, 40

violence
by Boko Haram, 27–8
by insurgents, 23, 36–8
by MEND, 30–2, 107
by security forces, 23, 44

weak states, *see* state weakness

Yakubu, Gowen, 82–3
Yakubu, Tanimu, 32
Yar'Adua, Shehu, 108
Yar'Adua, Tuari, 32, 58
Yar'Adua, Umaru Musa, 23,
32, 118
enforced withdrawal from public
life, 119–20
Yoruba, 47
Yusuf, Mohammed, 26, 27, 108

CPSIA information can be obtained
at www.ICGtesting.com
Printed in the USA
LVHW081712260520
656594LV00019B/1950